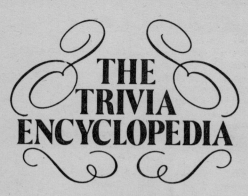

THE TRIVIA ENCYCLOPEDIA

Fred L. Worth

BERKLEY BOOKS, NEW YORK

THE TRIVIA ENCYCLOPEDIA

A Berkley Book / published by arrangement with
Brooke House Publishers

PRINTING HISTORY
Brooke House edition published 1974
Previously published by Ace Books
Berkley edition / May 1984
Second printing / November 1984

ISBN: 0-425-07581-8

A BERKLEY BOOK ® TM 757,375
Berkley Books are published by The Berkley Publishing Group,
200 Madison Avenue, New York, New York 10016.
The name "BERKLEY" and the stylized "B" with design
are trademarks belonging to Berkley Publishing Corporation.
PRINTED IN THE UNITED STATES OF AMERICA

To a girl named Sue

"Trifles make perfection and perfection is no trifle."
MICHAELANGELO

Mayor La Trivia: Character played by Gale Gordon on "Fibber McGee and Molly" radio show

The March of Trivia: Routine featured on radio's "The Fred Allen Show"

Introduction

A rather interesting observation can be made when you ask someone a trivial question. If the one you ask knows the answer, he will be more than happy to produce it. But if he doesn't know, he'll reply with "Who cares?" or "Who gives a damn?" The true trivia buff, on the other hand, does care about the correct answer. That is the enjoyable essence of trivia; no one need really give a damn to enjoy it. Trivia is the essence of life, the fine line in the drawing, the frosting on the cake. You don't need the frosting to enjoy the cake, but isn't it nice to have both?

Trivia is an interesting but unusual commodity in that it has several natures, never the same to any two people. It progresses from utter unimportance, to unimportant but interesting, important perhaps but uninteresting, doubtless important and fairly interesting, most interesting, to "Hell, that's not trivia!"

No two people will agree on what is trivia. Many believe it is limited to motion picture minutiae; others surely would include radio; but then how about the comic book fans? Sports fans quote statistics as trivia, while Civil War buffs cite unit commanders as trivial facts.

Trivia obviously means something different to each of us. So be it!

This book was written with a double purpose: one, to compile in one reference work a collection of interesting and trivial facts; and second, to collect interesting and perhaps not so trivial facts, facts that are difficult to find. If, therefore, tragic events are mentioned, no minimizing of the event is intended, for they are not meant to be considered trivial per se but fall under my second purpose.

The sources for a book like this are endless, which is as it should be. Trivia is everywhere.

I hope the book answers at least a few of the questions about some particular item or items. As new sources are tapped, and as time produces new trivial facts, more entries will surely be included within the scope of this work. Constant revision probably will be necessary. To this end, I welcome correspondence suggesting new areas, new concentrations. Likewise, any inaccuracies will be ironed out in subsequent printings, and I ask that such inadvertent errors be called to my attention: a note to me at my publishers'* will do the trick.

Until the next edition, "Think Trivia."

This personal statement would be incomplete without my giving thanks to those who kept the faith. My thanks go too to my editor, Jerry Fried, who brought some light into darkness and without whose help this book might better have been called an encyclopedia of chaos.

F.L.W.

*Brooke House Publishers, Inc., 9010 Reseda Blvd., Suite 226, Northridge, California 91324

A Note to the Reader

No attempt has been made to compile sports records; there are just too many, and there exist a sufficient number of books on most aspects of sport. A few key people, events, and feats are included, nevertheless.

No attempt has been made to compile the roles of actors in movies or on television—the list would be much too long and dull; the roles and personalities mentioned herein are those that are the most popular or unusual in nature.

Some seeming errors will have crept in, a result of differences of opinion of authors or sources on some point of fact. I have found in many cases that something appearing in a book or play version will have been changed in the movie or television adaptation, adding to confusion. An attempt has been made to make this work as valid as possible; therefore, movies or TV, having wider audiences, have been preferred over plays and books. The inference is not that one is "better" than the other, but rather that the "fact" is more widespread through the more popular of the media.

It should be noted, among other things, that couples mentioned as being married may no longer be together; that dates for movies given in sources are sometimes dates of completion and sometimes dates of release—there is great ambiguity in source material; that the arrangement of the book depends to a large extent on the compiler's own feeling, so far as under what name or letter of the alphabet information appears. Some cross-referencing has been done, but obviously the book would have gotten out of hand if everything had been sewed up tight and leakproof. Note also that numerical entries, for example "221B Baker Street," lead off in the letter of the alphabet in which the spelling of the number falls, i.e. "221B" is under "T" for "Two." These numerical entries are followed by capital letter combinations that do not form words ordinarily pronounced, for example "TBI" and "T.C." Then follow normal alphabetical entries for the given letter of the alphabet.

A

A

The Scarlet Letter, an "A" embroidered on Hester Prynne's dress, meaning "adultress" (*The Scarlet Letter* by Nathaniel Hawthorne)

A1ANA2

Lawrence Welk's California automobile license plate

A-1 Detective Agency

Jack, Doc, and Reggie's Agency (radio series "I Love a Mystery"). Motto: "No job too tough, no mystery too baffling"

A & M

Record company founded by recording artist Herb Alpert and Jerry Moss

A & W

(root beer stands) Barons are Allen and Wright

A. A. Fair

Pen name of Erle Stanley Gardner

ABC Powers

Argentina; Brazil; Chile

ABO Blood Groups

A; B; AB—universal recipient; O—universal donor

AU1

License plate number of Rolls Royce Phantom 337 owned by Auric Goldfinger (Gert Frobe) (1964 movie *Goldfinger*)

Abbott and Costello

Comedy team in radio, then (after 1940) movies. The team split in 1957.

Their "Meet" movies:

Meet Frankenstein, 1948

Meet the Killer, Boris Karloff, 1949

Meet the Invisible Man, 1951

Meet Captain Kidd, 1952

Meet Dr. Jekyll and Mr. Hyde, 1953

Meet the Keystone Kops, 1955

Meet the Mummy, 1955

Abel, Colonel Rudolf
Russian spy exchanged in 1962 for F. Gary Powers, U-2 pilot

Abraham Lincoln
Frigate on which Ned Land, Professor Pierre Aronnax, and Conseil were when it was rammed by the "Nautilus" (Jules Verne's *20,000 Leagues Under the Sea*)

Absolute Zero
$-273.16°$ C, which equals $-459.69°$ F

Academy Awards
Pictures:
The Sting, 1973
The Godfather, 1972
The French Connection, 1971
Patton, 1970
Midnight Cowboy, 1969
Oliver!, 1968
In the Heat of the Night, 1967
A Man for All Seasons, 1966
The Sound of Music, 1965
My Fair Lady, 1964
Tom Jones, 1963
Lawrence of Arabia, 1962
West Side Story, 1961
The Apartment, 1960
Ben-Hur, 1959
Gigi, 1958
The Bridge on the River Kwai, 1957
Around the World in 80 Days, 1956
Marty, 1955
On the Waterfront, 1954
From Here to Eternity, 1953
The Greatest Show on Earth, 1952
An American in Paris, 1951
All About Eve, 1950
All the King's Men, 1949
Hamlet, 1948
Gentleman's Agreement, 1947
The Best Years of Our Lives, 1946
The Lost Weekend, 1945
Going My Way, 1944
Casablanca, 1943
Mrs. Miniver, 1942
How Green Was My Valley, 1941
Rebecca, 1940

Gone with the Wind, 1939
You Can't Take It with You, 1938
The Life of Emile Zola, 1937
The Great Ziegfeld, 1936
Mutiny on the Bounty, 1935
It Happened One Night, 1934
Cavalcade, 1932/1933*
Grand Hotel, 1931/1932*
Cimarron, 1930/1931*
All Quiet on the Western Front, 1929/1930*
The Broadway Melody, 1928/1929*
Wings, 1927/1928*

Songs:

"The Way We Were," 1973
"The Morning After," 1972
"Theme from Shaft," 1971
"For All We Know," 1970
"Raindrops Keep Fallin' on My Head," 1969
"The Windmills of Your Mind," 1968
"Talk to the Animals," 1967
"Born Free," 1966
"The Shadow of Your Smile," 1965
"Chim Chim Cher-ee," 1964
"Call Me Irresponsible," 1963
"Days of Wine and Roses," 1962
"Moon River," 1961
"Never on Sunday," 1960
"High Hopes," 1959
"Gigi," 1958
"All the Way," 1957
"Whatever Will Be, Will Be," 1956
"Love Is a Many-Splendored Thing," 1955
"Three Coins in the Fountain," 1954
"Secret Love," 1953
"High Noon," 1952
"In the Cool, Cool, Cool of the Evening," 1951
"Mona Lisa," 1950
"Baby, It's Cold Outside," 1949
"Buttons and Bows," 1948
"Zip-A-Dee-Doo-Dah," 1947
"On the Atchison, Topeka and the Santa Fe," 1946
"It Might As Well Be Spring," 1945

---

* Award year: August 1 to July 31

"Swinging on a Star," 1944
"You'll Never Know," 1943
"White Christmas," 1942
"The Last Time I Saw Paris," 1941
"When You Wish upon a Star," 1940
"Over the Rainbow," 1939
"Thanks for the Memory," 1938
"Sweet Leilani," 1937
"The Way You Look Tonight," 1936
"Lullaby of Broadway," 1935
"The Continental," 1934

Academies

United States Air Force: Colorado Springs, Colorado
United States Army: West Point, New York
United States Coast Guard: New London, Connecticut
United States Merchant Marine: Kings Point, New York
United States Navy: Annapolis, Maryland

Acropolis

Hill in Athens, Greece, on which the Parthenon is located

Adam Troy, Captain

Captain of the "Tiki" (TV series "Adventures in Paradise")

Adams, John

President of the United States; father of President John Quincy Adams: only father-son presidential pair

Adjutant

Longest lived dog: 27 years old (1936-1963), a Labrador retriever, in England

Admiral Benbow

Inn owned by Jim Hawkins' widowed mother (Robert Louis Stevenson's *Treasure Island*)

Admiral Nelson

Commander of the nuclear submarine "Seaview" (TV series "Voyage to the Bottom of the Sea")

Adventure

Captain Lemuel Gulliver's merchantman ship in his later adventure in the land of the Houyhnhnms (rational, intelligent horses) (Jonathan Swift's *Gulliver's Travels*)

Adventure Galley

Captain Kidd's ship

Aerodrome

Samuel P. Langley's unsuccessful 1903 airplane, which twice crashed into the Potomac River

Ahab

Captain of the "Pequod" (Herman Melville's *Moby-Dick*)

Aircraft Carriers, United States*

CV-1: Langley (ex collier Jupiter), commissioned March 20, 1922

CV-2: Lexington (ex battle cruiser CC-1)

CV-3: Saratoga (ex CC-3)

CV-4: Ranger, first carrier built from keel up, commissioned Feb. 25, 1933

CV-5: Yorktown

CV-6: Enterprise

CV-7: Wasp

CV-8: Hornet

CV-9: Essex

CV-10: Yorktown (ex Bon Homme Richard)

CV-11: Intrepid

CV-12: Hornet (ex Kearsarge), recovered Apollo 11 capsule after Armstrong's first moon walk

CV-13: Franklin

CV-14: Ticonderoga (ex Hancock)

CV-15: Randolph

CV-16: Lexington (ex Cabot)

CV-17: Bunker Hill

CV-18: Wasp (ex Oriskany)

CV-19: Hancock (ex Ticonderoga)

CV-20: Bennington

CV-21: Boxer

CV-22: Independence (ex Amsterdam, light cruiser CL-59)

CV-23: Princeton (ex Tallahassee, CL-61)

CV-24: Belleau Wood (ex New Haven, CL-76)

CV-25: Cowpens (ex Huntington, CL-77)

CV-26: Monterey (ex Dayton, CL-78)

CVL-27: Langley (ex Fargo, CL-85; ex Crown Point)

CVL-28: Cabot (ex Wilmington, CL-79)

CVL-29: Bataan (ex Buffalo, CL-99)

CVL-30: San Jacinto (ex Newark, CL-100; ex Reprisal)

CV-31: Bon Homme Richard

CV-32: Leyte (ex Crown Point)

CV-33: Kearsarge

CV-34: Oriskany

CV-35: Reprisal

CV-36: Antietam

CV-37: Princeton

CV-38: Shangri-La

CV-39: Lake Champlain

---

* CV, aircraft carrier; CVA, attack aircraft carrier; CVB, large aircraft carrier; (N), nuclear-powered

CV-40: Tarawa
CV-41: Midway
CV-42: Franklin D. Roosevelt (ex Coral Sea)
CV-43: Coral Sea
CV-44: construction cancelled January 11, 1943
CV-45: Valley Forge
CV-46: Iwo Jima
CV-47: Philippine Sea (ex Wright)
CV-48: Saipan
CV-49: Wright
CV-50-55: construction cancelled March 27, 1945
CVB-56-57: construction cancelled March 28, 1945
CV-58: United States; construction cancelled April 23, 1949
CVA-59: Forrestal
CVA-60: Saratoga
CVA-61: Ranger
CVA-62: Independence
CVA-63: Kitty Hawk
CVA-64: Constellation
CVA(N)-65: Enterprise, largest mobile man-made structure ever
          built
CVA-66: America
CVA-67: John F. Kennedy
CVA(N)-68: Chester W. Nimitz
CVA(N)-69: Dwight D. Eisenhower
CVA(N)-70: Unnamed

Air Force One
The plane of the President of the United States

Airline Pilots' Creed
"In God we trust, everything else we check"

Airplane Crash
February 3, 1959
> Killed (in a Beech Bonanza) were rock 'n' roll singers
> Buddy Holly, J. P. Richardson (The Big Bopper), Richie
> Valens

March 5, 1963
> Killed were country-and-western singers Patsy Cline, Cow-
> boy Copas, Hawkshaw Hawkins

Airports, U.S.
Other than named after the city it serves:

Will Rogers, Oklahoma City	National, Washington, D.C.
General Mitchell, Milwaukee	O'Hare, Chicago
Lindbergh Field, San Diego	Logan Field, Boston
Friendship, Baltimore	John F. Kennedy, New York City
Dulles, Washington, D.C.	La Guardia, New York City

Hobby, Houston	Lambert Field, St. Louis
Jetero, Houston	Sky Harbor, Phoenix
Love Field, Dallas	McCarran, Las Vegas
Standiford Field, Louisville	Eppley Airfield, Omaha

Blue Grass Field, Lexington-Frankfort

Akron, Ohio

Location of annual All-American Soap Box Derby

Alamo

188 men died defending the Alamo against more than 4000 Mexicans under Antonio Lopez de Santa Anna; included among the dead Texans were William Barret "Buck" Travis, James "Jim" Bowie, Davy Crockett

Alan Brady Show

Television program for which Rob Petrie (Dick Van Dyke), Buddy (Morey Amsterdam), and Sally (Rose Marie) wrote (TV series "Dick Van Dyke Show"): Alan Brady played by Carl Reiner

Albert

Alligator who lives in the Okefenokee Swamp (comic strip "Pogo" by Walt Kelly)

Alcan Highway

Dawson Creek, British Columbia, to Fairbanks, Alaska: officially called the Alaska Highway

Alexander

Dagwood and Blondie's son

Alfred

Bruce Wayne's (Batman's) butler (one of the few persons who knows his secret identity)

Alfred E. Neuman

Mad magazine's "What Me Worry?" hero

Alice

George Gobel's wife (TV show)

Alice and Hank

Dennis the Menace's mother and father

Alice in Wonderland

Novel (*Alice's Adventures in Wonderland,* 1865) by Lewis Carroll (real name: Charles Lutwidge Dodgson)

Several times made into movies, especially in 1933 by Paramount and in 1951 as a cartoon feature by Disney

1933 movie starred Charlotte Henry as Alice, Gary Cooper as the White Knight, Edward Everett Horton as the Mad Hatter, W. C. Fields as Humpty Dumpty, Richard Arlen as the Cheshire Cat, Cary Grant as the Mock Turtle, Jack Oakie as Tweedledum, Edna Mae Oliver as the Red Queen, Louise Fazenda as the White Queen, Charles Ruggles as the March Hare, Sterling Hol-

loway, Roscoe Ates, Leon Erroll, and many other "name" actors
in miniature or "cameo" roles

Alice May

Derelict vessel used in cremating Sam McGee ("The Cremation
of Sam McGee" by Robert W. Service)

Alice's Restaurant

Established by Alice Brock

All that Money Can Buy

Movie version (1941, directed by William Dieterle) of Stephen
Vincent Benet's "The Devil and Daniel Webster." James Craig
played the farmer Jabez Stone; Walter Huston played the Devil,
Mr. Scratch, who bargained for his soul; Edward Arnold played
Daniel Webster, who pleaded successfully for Jabez' soul with a
jury of scoundrels and renegades from American folklore and
legend

Allen's Alley

Fred Allen's radio show featured its inhabitants: Senator Beaure-
gard Claghorn (Kenny Delmar); Titus Moody (Parker Fennelly);
Ajax Cassidy (Peter Donald); Mrs. Pansy Nussbaum (Minerva
Pious); Falstaff Openshaw (Alan Reed); Senator Bloat (Jack
Smart); Socrates Mulligan (Charles Cantor); Pierre Nussbaum
(never seen or heard)

Alley Oop

Caveman who fluctuates between modern and prehistoric times:
comic strip by Vince T. Hamlin. The prehistoric kingdom of
Moo is ruled by King Guz (or Guzzle), whose daughter Wootie
is enamored of Alley Oop, who in turn loves (and later marries)
Oola. Oop's pet is the dinosaur Dinny. Dr. Wonmug is the scientist who controls the time machine.

Alphabet, spoken

Words used to differentiate letters in voice transmission over
radio (also called phonetic alphabet)

Current usage			World War II usage		
Alpha	Lima	Whiskey	Able	Love	Whiskey
Bravo	Mike	X-Ray	Baker	Mike	X-Ray
Charlie	November	Yankee	Charlie	Nan	Yoke
Delta	Oscar	Zulu	Dog	Oboe	Zebra
Echo	Papa		Easy	Peter	
Foxtrot	Quebec		Fox	Queen	
Golf	Romeo		George	Roger	
Hotel	Sierra		How	Sugar	
India	Tango		Item	Tear	
Juliet	Uniform		Jig	Uncle	
Kilo	Victor		King	Victor	

Also Sprach Zarathustra
> Symphonic poem (1896) by Richard Strauss, part of which was used as thematic music in 1968 movie *2001: A Space Odyssey*

Altair IV
> The forbidden planet (1956 movie *The Forbidden Planet*)

Alvin
> David Seville's delinquent chipmunk

Amanda
> Mr. Spock's human mother (TV series "Star Trek"): played by Jane Wyatt

Amigiri
> Japanese destroyer that on August 2, 1943, rammed and sank PT-109, which was commanded by Lt. John F. Kennedy

Amazon Plane
> Wonder Woman's invisible robot jet airplane (comic book)

Amberjack II
> President Franklin D. Roosevelt's 45-foot sailboat

America
> National hymn ("My Country 'Tis of Thee") of the United States: words written in 1832 by Samuel Francis Smith; music same as "God Save the King (Queen)"

America
> Plane in which Admiral Richard Byrd crossed the Atlantic (1927)

America
> Winner of international yacht race, August 22, 1851, defeating the British yacht "Aurora" by eighteen minutes; hence America's Cup

America's Boy Friend
> Nickname of Charles "Buddy" Rogers, husband of Mary Pickford, "America's Sweetheart"

America's Sweetheart
> Nickname of Mary Pickford

American Baseball League
> Eastern Division:
>> Baltimore Orioles
>> Boston Red Sox
>> Cleveland Indians
>> Detroit Tigers
>> New York Yankees
>> Milwaukee Brewers
>
> Western Division:
>> California (Anaheim) Angels
>> Chicago White Sox
>> Texas (Arlington) Rangers

Minnesota (Bloomington) Twins
Kansas City Royals
Oakland Athletics (A's)

American Basketball Association

Eastern Division:

Carolina (Greensboro, N. C.) Cougars
Kentucky (Louisville) Colonels
Memphis Tams
New York (Carle Place) Nets
Virginia (Norfolk) Squires

Western Division:

Dallas Chaparrals
Denver Rockets
Indiana (Indianapolis) Pacers
San Diego Conquistadors
Utah (Salt Lake City) Stars

American universities

Order of establishment:

Harvard	Massachusetts	1636
William and Mary	Virginia	1693
Yale	Connecticut	1701
Pennsylvania	Pennsylvania	1740
Princeton	New Jersey	1746
Washington and Lee	Virginia	1749
Columbia	New York	1754

Ames Brothers

Ed (played Mingo in TV series "Daniel Boone"); Gene; Joe; Vic

Amigo

Bobby Benson's palomino

Amos 'n' Andy

On radio played by Freeman Gosden and Charles J. Correll (Amos Jones and Andrew H. Brown)

Amos Mouse

Mouse in cartoon "Ben and Me" (Walt Disney cartoon character): he helped Ben Franklin invent

An-An

Moscow zoo's giant panda

Ananias Club

Club of which all members are liars

Anastasia and Drizella

Cinderella's two step-sisters (Walt Disney cartoon feature movie)

Anatevka

Village in *Fiddler on the Roof*

Anchorman

Lowest man in Annapolis graduating class (low score in marks)

Andamo

Mr. Lucky's gambling partner (TV series "Mr. Lucky"): played by Ross Martin

Anderson

Name of family of which Robert Young and Jane Wyatt played father and mother (TV series "Father Knows Best")

Anderson quintuplets

Born April 26, 1973: Roger, Owen, Scott, Kay, Diane

Andersonville

Largest confederate military prison during the Civil War, in Georgia. More than 13,000 Union prisoners died there, mostly of neglect. Major Henry Wirz, commandant, was the only Civil War soldier executed for war crimes

Andrew John

Name of baby born to Rosemary (Mia Farrow) (1968 movie *Rosemary's Baby*)

Andrews

Fred and Mary, Archie's parents (Archie Andrews comic strip)

Andrews Sisters

Singing group: Maxene, LaVerne, Patty

Androcles

Removed the thorn from the lion's foot and was later spared by the same lion. The story is from Aesop's fables, with the moral: "One good deed deserves another"

Animals

Collective words ("an army of frogs" or "a bale of turtles")

Army—frogs	Clowder—cats
Bale—turtles	Cluster—cats
Band—gorillas, jays	Clutch—chicks
Barren—mules	Clutter—cats
Bed—clams, oysters	Colony—ants, gulls
Bevy—quail, swans	Congregation—plovers
Brace—ducks	Convocation—eagles
Brood—chicks	Covert—coots
Bury—conies	Covey—quail, partridge
Business—ferrets	Cry—hounds
Cast—hawks	Down—hares
Cavvy—extra cowboy mounts	Draught—fish
Cete—badgers	Dray—squirrels
Charm—goldfinches, hummingbirds	Drift—swine
	Drove—cattle, sheep, hares, oxen
Chattering—choughs	Exaltation—larks
Clamor—rooks	Field—racehorses
Cloud—gnats	Flight—birds

Flock—sheep, geese, bustards, camels
Gaggle—geese
Gam—whales
Gang—elks
Grist—bees
Herd—curlews, elephants, animals
Hive—bees
Horde—gnats
Host—sparrows
Hover—trout
Husk—hares
Kindle—kittens
Knot—toads
Leap—leopards
Leash—foxes, greyhounds
Litter—pigs, cats, dogs
Murder—crows
Muster—peacocks
Mustering—storks
Mute—hounds
Nest—vipers, pheasants
Nide—pheasants
Nye—pheasants
Pace—asses
Pack—hounds, wolves
Pair—horses
Plump—wildfowl

Pod—seals, whales, walruses
Pride—lions
Remuda—extra cowboy mounts
Run—poultry
School—fish
Sedge—cranes, bitterns
Siege—cranes, bitterns, herons
Shoal—fish, pilchards
Skein—geese
Skulk—foxes
Sleuth—bears
Sounder—boars, swine
String—racehorses
Span—mules
Spring—teals
Swarm—bees, eels
Team—ducks, horses
Tribe—goats, monkeys
Trip—goats, wildfowl
Troop—monkeys, kangaroos, lions
Volery—birds
Watch—nightingales
Wedge—swans
Wing—plovers
Yoke—oxen

Young

Ass—hinny, foal
Bear—cub
Beaver—kitten
Bird—nestling
Cat—kitten
Cattle—calf
Chicken—poult, chick
Codfish—codling
Cow—calf
Deer—fawn
Dog—pup
Duck—duckling
Eagle—eaglet
Eel—elver
Elephant—calf

Fish—fry, fingerling
Fox—cub, kit
Frog—tadpole
Goat—kid
Goose—gosling
Grouse—poult
Hare—leveret
Hawk—eyas
Hen—chick, pullet
Horse—colt, filt, filly, foal
Insect—nymph, pupa
Kangaroo—joey
Lion—cub
Monkey—baby
Moose—calf

Otter—whelp	Sheep—lamb
Oyster—spat	Swan—cygnet
Peafowl—peachick	Tiger—cub
Pig—shoat, piglet, farrow	Turkey—poult
Rabbit—bunny, leveret	Whale—calf
Rhinoceros—calf	Wolf—cub, whelp
Seal—pup	Zebra—colt

Ann Darrow
King Kong's *femme fatale* (in a one-sided romance) (1933 movie *King Kong*): played by Fay Wray

Anniversaries

1st—paper	13th—lace
2nd—cotton	14th—ivory
3rd—leather	15th—crystal
4th—fruit, flowers	20th—china
5th—wood	25th—silver
6th—sugar, candy	30th—pearl
7th—wool, copper	35th—coral
8th—bronze, pottery	40th—ruby
9th—pottery, willow	45th—sapphire
10th—tin	50th—gold
11th—steel	55th—emerald
12th—silk, linen	75th—diamond

Answer Man, The
Albert Mitchell (radio series)

Antelope
Ship, wrecked at sea, from which Lemuel Gulliver is washed ashore on Lilliput (Jonathan Swift's *Gulliver's Travels*)

Ape movies
Based on Pierre Boulle's novel *Planet of the Apes:*
> *Planet of the Apes* (1968)
> *Beneath the Planet of the Apes* (1970)
> *Escape from the Planet of the Apes* (1971)
> *Conquest of the Planet of the Apes* (1972)
> *Battle for the Planet of the Apes* (1973)

Roddy McDowall as Cornelius (later as the chimpanzee Caesar) starred in all but the second picture. Kim Hunter was the only actor to appear in all of the first three

Apollo 11 crew
First man-moon landing, July 20, 1969: Neil Armstrong and Edwin Aldrin walked on the moon's surface; Michael Collins remained with the command ship

Apple
The Beatles' record company

April Dancer
>The girl from U.N.C.L.E. (TV series starring Stefanie Powers)

Aqualad
>Aquaman's partner (comic book character)

Arbadella
>Amos's daughter (radio's "Amos 'n' Andy"): played by Terry Howard

Arcaro, Eddie
>Only jockey to win the Triple Crown twice: 1941, on Whirlaway; 1948, on Citation

Archangels
>In Christian belief: Michael, Chamuel, Raphael, Gabriel, Uriel, Zadkiel, Zophiel (Jophiel)

Archie
>Bartender (radio series "Duffy's Tavern"): played by Ed Gardner

Archie Goodwin
>Nero Wolfe's assistant

Archimedes
>Merlin's owl (Disney cartoon feature movie *Sword in the Stone*)

archy
>Cockroach who types by falling from height onto each key, thus no capitals (created by columnist-author Don Marquis: 1927 and after). His friend is the cat Mehitabel

Argo
>Ship on which Jason and the Argonauts sailed in quest of the Golden Fleece (Greek legend)

Argos
>Odysseus' dog (Homer's *The Odyssey*)

Argus
>Giant with 100 eyes (Greek mythology)

Argus, H.M.S.
>First aircraft carrier, Royal Navy, 1918

Arion
>Hercules' horse: given by him to Adrastus

Arizona, U.S.S.
>Only United States battleship still in commission (sunk at Pearl Harbor, 1941, now a memorial)

Ark Royal
>English Lord High Admiral Charles Howard's flagship in the battle against the Spanish Armada in 1588 (a later "Ark Royal," a British aircraft carrier, carried the planes credited with sinking the German "Bismarck" in May 1941 and was herself sunk in November 1941 by a German submarine in the Mediterranean)

Armistice Day

November 11, 1918, end of World War I: observance begun 1926; observed from 1954 to 1970 as Veterans' Day in late October

Armstrong, Neil A.

First man to walk on the moon (July 20, 1969). Apollo 11 LM (lunar module) landed 4:17:20 P.M. EDT. Armstrong's EVA (extravehicular activity) on surface 10:56 P.M. EDT; Aldrin on surface 11:14 P.M. EDT

Army rank

Generals

General of the Army—	5 stars
General—	4 stars
Lieutenant General—	3 stars
Major General—	2 stars
Brigadier General—	1 star

Arnold

Pet pig (TV series "Green Acres")

Arrangement in Grey and Black

Original name of the painting "Whistler's Mother" or "The Artist's Mother" by James McNeill Whistler: in the Louvre, Paris

Arrow, The

Al Capone's 32-foot cabin cruiser, kept at his Florida villa

Ars Gratia Artis

"Art for Art's Sake": motto of MGM films, appears in the circle above the lion's head

Arsène Lupin

French detective in novels by Maurice Leblanc: played in movies, among others, by John Barrymore (1932) and Melvyn Douglas (1938)

Artemus Gordon

Jim West's partner (TV series "The Wild, Wild West"): played by Ross Martin

Arthur Godfrey and His Friends

(TV series)

Announcer:

Tony Marvin

His Friends:

Janette Davis, Bill Lawrence, Julius La Rosa (fired on the air), Marion Marlowe, The Mariners, Lu Ann Simms, Carmel Quinn, McGuire Sisters, Chordettes, Haleloke

Arthur Hastings, Captain

Hercule Poirot's assistant

Artistry in Rhythm
> Stan Kenton's theme song

Ashenden
> British spy created (1928) by W. Somerset Maugham in novel *Ashenden; or, The British Agent*

Ashford, Emmett Littleton
> First black umpire (after 1966) in major league baseball (American League)

Asp, The
> Henchman of Daddy Warbucks

Assassinations, U.S.

Assassin	*Assassinated*
John Wilkes Booth	Abraham Lincoln (1865)
Charles J. Guiteau	James Garfield (1881)
Leon Czolgosz	William McKinley (1901)
Dr. Carl A. Weiss	Huey Long (1935)
Lee Harvey Oswald	John F. Kennedy (1963)
James Earl Ray	Martin Luther King, Jr. (1968)
Sirhan Sirhan	Robert Kennedy (1968)

Aston Martin DB-5
> James Bond's customized automobile (1964 movie *Goldfinger*): in the novel by Ian Fleming it is a DB-3

Astro
> The Jetsons' family dog (TV cartoon series "The Jetsons")

Astrodome
> Roofed athletic stadium in Houston, Texas (location of Lyndon B. Johnson Spacecraft Center of NASA, hence the Astro- prefix) available for football (Houston Oilers of NFL), baseball (Houston Astros of National League), basketball (Houston Rockets of NBA), tennis (Billie Jean King defeated Bobby Riggs here), etc.

Atlantic City, New Jersey
> Location of all the streets mentioned in the game of Monopoly (American version). Site also of the Miss America Pageant (since 1921)

Atlantis
> Legendary island in the Atlantic Ocean west of Gibraltar believed by Plato to have sunk into the ocean

Atlantis
> World's largest yacht, built (1974) by Aristotle Onassis' brother-in-law Stavros Niarchos: Onassis' yacht "Christina" had been the largest

Atomic Annie
> First atomic cannon, United States, 1953

Attucks, Crispus
>   Negro-Indian leader killed in the Boston Massacre (March 5, 1770)

AuH₂O
>   "Goldwater," Senator Barry Goldwater's 1964 election slogan

Auld Lang Syne
>   Guy Lombardo's theme song

Aunt Em
>   Dorothy's aunt (L. Frank Baum's *The Wizard of Oz*): played by Clara Blandick in 1939 movie

Aunt Harriet
>   Bruce Wayne's aunt and housekeeper, ignorant of his secret identity, Batman

Aunt Polly
>   Tom Sawyer's aunt (Mark Twain's novels *Tom Sawyer* and *Huckleberry Finn*)

Aurora Australis
>   The Southern Lights

Aurora Borealis
>   The Northern Lights

Australia
>   Capital: Canberra

State	Capital
New South Wales	Sydney
Queensland	Brisbane
South Australia	Adelaide
Tasmania	Hobart
Victoria	Melbourne
Western Australia	Perth
(Northern Territory	Darwin)

Avalon
>   Isle of the blest, or dead, where King Arthur went after his death

Avenger, The
>   Leader of Justice, Inc.; real identity: Richard Henry Benson (adventure series by Kenneth Robeson)

Avengers, The
>   John Steed (Patrick Macnee); Mrs. Emma Peel (Diana Rigg); Tara King (Linda Thorson) (TV series made in Great Britain). Honor Blackman was Macnee's first partner, then Elizabeth Sheppard, then Diana Rigg, and finally Linda Thorson

Aviation Hall of Fame
>   At Dayton, Ohio
>   Orville and Wilbur Wright were first two elected (1962)

Awards
> First place: blue ribbon; gold medal
> Second place: red ribbon; silver medal
> Third place: white ribbon; bronze medal

Axis Countries
> World War II; Japan; Germany (includes Austria); Italy; Thailand; Bulgaria; Hungary; Romania; Finland

Axis Sally
> Rita Louise Zucca (Italy); Mildred E. Gillars (Germany). The Japanese propaganda equivalent was Tokyo Rose

B

B Bar B
> Bobby Benson's ranch (H Bar O ranch while Hecker's H-O cereal was the sponsor)

BAR
> Browning Automatic Rifle

b.v.d.'s
> Men's underwear: name from initials of the firm of Bradley, Voorhees, and Day

Babe
> Paul Bunyan's blue ox

Babe, The
> Nickname of George Herman Ruth (1893-1948). Babe was the nickname of other ballplayers and athletes, too, like Babe Pinelli, National League infielder and later umpire

Babieca
> El Cid's horse

Babs
> Chester Riley's daughter (radio/TV series "The Life of Riley")

Babs Gordon
> Daughter of Commissioner Gordon and real identity of Batgirl (comic book series)

Baby Dumpling
> Alexander's nickname as an infant (Dagwood and Blondie's son)

Baby Snooks
> Character played on radio by Fannie Brice

Back in the Saddle Again
> Gene Autry's theme song

Backus, Jim
> Voice of Mr. Magoo; the rich Herbert Updike of the Alan Young

radio show; Joan Davis' husband on TV's "I Married Joan"; and many other roles in movies and other media

Bader, Douglas

World War II British ace who had lost both legs before the war

Badge 714

Sergeant Joe Friday's badge number (TV series "Dragnet," called "Badge 714" on reruns)

Badge 744

Officer Pete Malloy's badge number (TV series "Adam-12")

Badge 2430

Officer Jim Reed's badge number (TV series "Adam-12")

Baer brothers

Heavyweight boxers: Max (Maximilian), champion 1934; Buddy

Baer quintuplets

Born January 5, 1973: Douglas, Elizabeth, Leslie, Thomas, Vickie

Balkan states

Present: Yugoslavia, Albania, Greece, Romania, Bulgaria, European Turkey

Balto

Dog that led a sled team through a blizzard to Nome, Alaska, in the winter of 1925, to bring serum to halt an epidemic among the Eskimos (sled driver was Gunnar Kaasen). A statue of Balto by F. G. Roth stands near the zoo in Central Park, New York

Bambino, The

Babe Ruth

Banana Nose

Nickname of jockey Eddie Arcaro

Banana Splits

Bingo, a gorilla
Drooper, a lion
Fleagle, a dog
Snorky, a baby elephant

Bandari

Native tribe living in Bengali jungle with the Phantom (comic strip and books)

Banjo Eyes

Nickname of comedian Eddie Cantor

Bank of Italy

Name of Bank of America before the founder, Amadeo P. Giannini, changed it

Bannister, Roger

First person to break 4 minutes for the mile: 3:59.4, May 6, 1954, Oxford, England, in a meet between British AAA and Oxford University. Race paced by Chris Brasher and Chris Chataway

Barbarossa
> Frederick I, Holy Roman Emperor (The Red Beard): reigned 1155-1190; died during 3rd Crusade

Barbours
> Family who lived in San Francisco (radio series "One Man's Family")

Bard of Avon, The
> Nickname of William Shakespeare

Bard of Ayrshire, The
> Nickname of Robert Burns

Barkley
> Family (TV series "The Big Valley")

Barnard, Dr. Christiaan
> Performed first successful heart transplant, Capetown, South Africa, December 3, 1967, on Louis Washkansky, who lived for 18 days

Barnum, P. T.
> Phineas Taylor Barnum (1810-1891), American showman
> His most famous exhibits and clients: Jenny Lind, General Tom Thumb, Jumbo the Elephant, the Siamese Twins (Chang and Eng), the Bearded Lady (Josephine Clofullia), Commodore Nutt, Wild Man of Borneo, The Feejee Mermaid, Joyce Heth

Barrymore
> Family name (original name: Blythe) of actors Lionel (1878-1954), Ethel (1879-1959), John (1882-1942). Father: Maurice (1845-1905)

Barton, Clara
> Founder (1881) of the American Red Cross Society

Bar-20 Ranch
> Hopalong Cassidy's ranch

Baseball Hall of Fame
> Cooperstown, New York
> First 5 members elected (1936): Ty Cobb, Babe Ruth, Honus Wagner, Christy Mathewson, Walter Johnson

Baseball stadiums, major leagues

City	Team	Stadium
Atlanta	Braves	Atlanta Stadium
Baltimore	Orioles	Memorial Stadium
Boston	Red Sox	Fenway Park
California	Angels	Anaheim Stadium
Chicago	Cubs	Wrigley Field
Chicago	White Sox	White Sox Park
Cincinnati	Reds	Riverfront Stadium
Cleveland	Indians	Municipal Stadium

Detroit	Tigers	Tiger Stadium
Houston	Astros	Astrodome
Kansas City	Royals	Royals Stadium
Los Angeles	Dodgers	Dodger Stadium
Milwaukee	Brewers	Milwaukee County Stadium
Minnesota	Twins	Metropolitan Stadium
Montreal	Expos	Jarry Park
New York	Mets	Shea Stadium
New York	Yankees	Yankee Stadium
Oakland	Athletics	Oakland-Alameda County Coliseum
Philadelphia	Phillies	Veterans Stadium
Pittsburgh	Pirates	Three Rivers Stadium
St. Louis	Cardinals	Busch Memorial Stadium
San Diego	Padres	San Diego Stadium
San Francisco	Giants	Candlestick Park
Texas	Rangers	Arlington Stadium, Arlington (near Dallas-Fort Worth

Bastille Day

July 14: France's national holiday. The Bastille, a Paris prison, was stormed and taken this day in 1789

Bates Motel

Motel where Marion Crane (Janet Leigh) is stabbed to death in the shower (movie *Psycho*)

Batgirl

Secret identity of Babs Gordon, daughter of Commissioner Gordon (comic book series)

Batman

Secret identity of Bruce Wayne (played in TV series by Adam West; on radio by Stacy Harris, Gary Merrill, and Matt Crowley; in 1950s movie serial played by Robert Lowery). Debut: Detective Comics #27, May 1939; Batman Comics, 1940 (created by Bob Kane). His sidekick is Robin

Batman's enemies

In TV series "Batman":

Foe	Played by
The Joker	Julie Newmar (also Eartha Kitt)
Catwoman	Julie Newmar (also Eartha Kitt)
The Joker	Cesar Romero
The Penguin	Burgess Meredith
The Riddler	Frank Gorshin

Battle Hymn of the Republic, The

Words written by Julia Ward Howe in 1862 to the tune of "John Brown's Body"

Battle of Bunker Hill

Actually took place (June 17, 1775) on Breed's Hill, where the Bunker Hill monument is located, across the Charles River from Boston: "Don't shoot until you see the whites of their eyes"

Battle of the Coral Sea

First modern naval engagement (first carrier battle) in which surface ships did not exchange a single shot or sight each other visually (May 7-8, 1942)

Battle of New Orleans

January 8, 1815: fought two weeks after the Treaty of Ghent had been signed ending the War of 1812. U.S. forces under Andrew Jackson defeated British under Edward Pakenham

Battle of the Sexes

Tennis match, Houston Astrodome, Sept. 20, 1973, in which Billie Jean King defeated Bobby Riggs 6-4, 6-3, 6-3 before over 30,000 spectators (largest live audience for tennis) and television viewers in 37 countries: Riggs had swept the Wimbledon championships in 1939, 4 years before Mrs. King's birth

Baxter

Name of family for whom Hazel is housekeeper and maid (cartoon/TV series "Hazel")

Bay City

City where TV serial "Another World" takes place

Be Prepared

Boy Scouts' motto

Beach Boys, The

Rock 'n' Roll group: Brian Wilson, Carl Wilson, Al Jardine, Bruce Johnston, Mike Love, Dennis Wilson (Glen Campbell was a substitute for a short time)

Beagle, H.M.S.

Ship on which Charles Darwin made his scientific voyage (1831-1836) to Patagonia and the Pacific and thence around the world back to England

Beagle Boys, The

Foes of Scrooge McDuck (Walt Disney character). Uniform numbers: 671-176, 617-716, 176-671

Bean, Judge Roy

"The Law West of the Pecos"

Beany

Boy puppet (TV show "Time for Beany"). Other puppets: Cecil the Seasick Sea Serpent, Caboose Goose

Bear Band Jamboree

> Walt Disney characters:
>> *Five Bear Rugs Band:* Zeke, Zeb, Ted, Fred, Tennessee (Sammy sits with his teddy bear)
>> *Entertainers:* Henry, the M. C.; Wendall, Big Al, Trixie, Liverlips, Terrance, Gomer, Teddi Barra
>> *Sun Bonnets:* Bunny, Bubbles, Beulah

Beatles

> George Harrison
> John Lennon
> Paul McCartney
> Ringo Starr (Richard Starkey)
> Previous members: Pete Best, Stu Sutcliffe

Beatles' movies

> *A Hard Day's Night* (1964), *Help* (1965), *Yellow Submarine* (1968), *Let It Be* (1970)

Beau James

> Nickname of New York City Mayor Jimmie Walker: title of his biography (1949) by Gene Fowler

Beauregard

> Pappy of Bret and Bart Maverick (TV series "Maverick")

Beaurigard

> Dog (TV series "Hee Haw")

Becky Sharp

> Heroine of William Makepeace Thackeray's *Vanity Fair*

Becky Thatcher

> Tom Sawyer's girlfriend

Bedrock

> Home of the Flintstones (TV cartoon)

Beer that Made Milwaukee Famous

> Schlitz beer, but originally the slogan was Miller Beer's

Beery brothers

> Actors: Noah (1884-1946) and Wallace (1889-1949). Noah Beery, Jr., was prominent in movies and TV. Wallace won an Oscar in 1932 for *The Champ*

Bell X-1

> First airplane (officially) to exceed the speed of sound, flown October 14, 1947, by Major Charles E. Yeager

Belle

> Lorenzo Jones' wife: played by Betty Garde and Lucille Wall

Bellerophon, H.M.S.

> Ship on which Napoleon made his formal surrender, July 15, 1815, after Waterloo, Captain Maitland commanding, off the port of Rochefort

Belts, Judo

White belt (lowest), Brown belt (3 grades), Black belt (10 degrees)*

Ben

Willard's pet rat (movie *Willard*)

Ben Casey

Neurosurgeon (TV series): played by Vincent Edwards

Ben Gunn

Pirate marooned on Treasure Island (not by Captain Flint, but by another unnamed pirate). The first thing he wanted when he saw Jim Hawkins was a piece of cheese (Robert Louis Stevenson's *Treasure Island*)

Ben Romero

Sergeant Friday's partner on "Dragnet" (radio series): played by Barton Yarborough

Ben-Hur

Novel by General Lew Wallace published 1880 while he was governor of New Mexico territory. (The movie of 1959 has won the most Oscars with 11)

Bennett

Family name of actresses Constance, Joan, and Barbara. Father: Richard (1873-1944)

Bennett, Floyd

Pilot who flew Admiral Richard Evelyn Bird over the North Pole (1926)

Beppo

Superman's super monkey (comic book)

Beretta .25

Automatic pistol carried by James Bond

Bergen, Edgar

His dummies: Charlie McCarthy, Mortimer Snerd, Effie Klinker

Bertha Cool

Woman detective in novels by A. A. Fair (Erle Stanley Gardner)

Bessie, the Yaller Cow

Paul Bunyan's blue ox Babe's mate

Best Selling Novels

1973: *Jonathan Livingston Seagull* by Richard Bach

1972: *Jonathan Livingston Seagull* by Richard Bach

1971: *Wheels* by Arthur Hailey

1970: *Love Story* by Erich Segal

1969: *Portnoy's Complaint* by Philip Roth

1968: *Airport* by Arthur Hailey

---

* 6th thru 8th degree may wear Red and White belt; 9th and 10th degree may wear a solid Red belt

1967: *The Arrang,ment* by Elia Kazan
1966: *Valley of the Dolls* by Jacqueline Susann
1965: *The Source* by James A. Michener
1964: *The Spy Who Came in from the Cold* by John Le Carré
1963: *The Shoes of the Fisherman* by Morris L. West
1962: *Ship of Fools* by Katherine Anne Porter
1961: *The Agony and the Ecstasy* by Irving Stone
1960: *Advise and Consent* by Allen Drury
1959: *Exodus* by Leon Uris
1958: *Doctor Zhivago* by Boris Pasternak
1957: *By Love Possessed* by James Gould Cozzens
1956: *Don't Go Near the Water* by William Brinkley
1955: *Marjorie Morningstar* by Herman Wouk
1954: *Not As a Stranger* by Morton Thompson
1953: *Battle Cry* by Leon Uris
1952: *The Silver Chalice* by Thomas B. Costain
1951: *From Here to Eternity* by James Jones
1950: *The Cardinal* by Henry Morton Robinson
1949: *The Egyptian* by Mika Waltari
1948: *The Big Fisherman* by Lloyd C. Douglas
1947: *The Miracle of the Bells* by Russell Janney
1946: *The King's General* by Daphne du Maurier
1945: *Forever Amber* by Kathleen Winsor
1944: *Strange Fruit* by Lillian Smith
1943: *The Robe* by Lloyd C. Douglas
1942: *The Song of Bernadette* by Franz Werfel
1941: *The Keys of the Kingdom* by A. J. Cronin
1940: *How Green Was My Valley* by Richard Llewellyn
1939: *The Grapes of Wrath* by John Steinbeck
1938: *The Yearling* by Marjorie Kinnan Rawlings
1937: *Northwest Passage* by Kenneth Roberts
1936: *Gone With the Wind* by Margaret Mitchell
1935: *Green Light* by Lloyd C. Douglas
1934: *So Red the Rose* by Stark Young
1933: *Anthony Adverse* by Hervey Allen
1932: *The Fountain* by Charles Morgan
1931: *The Good Earth* by Pearl S. Buck
1930: *Cimarron* by Edna Ferber
1929: *All Quiet on the Western Front* by Erich Maria Remarque
1928: *The Bridge of San Luis Rey* by Thornton Wilder
1927: *Elmer Gantry* by Sinclair Lewis
1926: *The Private Life of Helen of Troy* by John Erskine
1925: *Soundings* by A. Hamilton Gibbs
1924: *So Big* by Edna Ferber
1923: *Black Oxen* by Gertrude Atherton

1922: *If Winter Comes* by A. S. M. Hutchinson
1921: *Main Street* by Sinclair Lewis
1920: *The Man of the Forest* by Zane Grey
1919: *The Four Horsemen of the Apocalypse* by V. Blasco Ibañez
1918: *The U. P. Trail* by Zane Grey
1917: *Mr. Britling Sees It Through* by H. G. Wells
1916: *Seventeen* by Booth Tarkington
1915: *The Turmoil* by Booth Tarkington
1914: *The Eyes of the World* by Harold Bell Wright
1913: *Pollyanna* by Eleanor H. Porter
1912: *The Harvester* by Gene Stratton Porter
1911: *The Broad Highway* by Jeffrey Farnol
1910: *The Rosary* by Florence Barclay
1909: *The Inner Shrine* by Basil King (published anonymously)
1908: *Mr. Crewe's Career* by Winston Churchill
1907: *The Lady of the Decoration* by Frances Little
1906: *Coniston* by Winston Churchill
1905: *The Marriage of William Ashe* by Mrs. Humphry Ward
1904: *The Crossing* by Winston Churchill
1903: *Lady Rose's Daughter* by Mrs. Humphry Ward
1902: *The Virginian* by Owen Wister
1901: *Graustark* by George Barr McCutcheon
1900: *To Have and To Hold* by Mary Johnston
1899: *David Harum* by Edward Noyes Westcott
1898: *When Knighthood Was in Flower* by Charles Major
1897: *Quo Vadis* by Henryk Sienkiewicz
1896: *Tom Grogan* by F. Hopkinson Smith
1895: *Beside the Bonnie Brier Bush* by Ian Maclaren

Betty Boop
Doll-like cartoon character created by Max Fleischer in 1915. In movie cartoons her voice was Helen Kane's

Betty Lou
Teen Angel's girlfriend (7-Up commercials)

Beulah, the maid
First played on radio program "Fibber McGee and Molly" by Marlin Hurt, a white male. It later became a radio show as "The Marlin Hurt and Beulah Show" and finally "Beulah"

Big Ben
The bell in the clock tower of the Houses of Parliament in London (the name is often incorrectly applied to the clock itself)

Big Bertha
Traditionally, a very large cannon used by the Germans to bombard Paris at a distance of over 60 miles in World War I (named for Bertha Krupp). The name is properly applied to the 42 cm

howitzers used in Belgium in 1914. The Paris gun was a railroad-mounted 38/21 cm gun (1918) fired by navy, not army

Big Bopper, The

Stage name of rock 'n' roll singer J. P. Richardson, killed in air crash with Buddy Holly and Richie Valens: biggest hit "Chantilly Lace"

Big Bunny

Hugh Hefner's super-jet (DC-9): N950PB

Big Lucy

Nickname of the passenger ship "Lusitania"

Big Red

Nickname of Man O' War (grandfather of racehorse Seabiscuit)

Big Red Cheese, The

Name given to Captain Marvel by Dr. Sivana (comic books)

Big Three, The

Colleges: Harvard, Princeton, Yale

Big Town

Radio and TV series about a newspaperman, Steve Wilson: also titled *Headline, Heart of the City, City Assignment*

Bill

Sgt. Preston's first name ("Challenge of the Yukon" on radio)

Billy Joe McAllister

Boy who jumped off the Tallahatchee Bridge ("Ode to Billy Joe" sung by Bobbie Gentry)

Billy the Kid

Pseudonym of William H. Bonney (1859-1881), Brooklyn-born gunman
Played in movies by:

> Johnny Mack Brown, *Billy the Kid,* 1930
> Roy Rogers, *Billy the Kid Returns,* 1939
> Robert Taylor, *Billy the Kid,* 1941
> Jack Beutel, *The Outlaw,* 1943
> Audie Murphy, *The Kid From Texas,* 1949
> Don "Red" Barry, *I Shot Billy the Kid,* 1950
> Scott Brady, *The Law Versus Billy the Kid,* 1954
> Anthony Dexter, *The Parson and the Outlaw,* 1955
> Paul Newman, *The Left Handed Gun,* 1958
> (Others were Buster Crabbe and Bob Steele)

Bingo

Dog on box of Cracker Jacks

Bird Woman

Sacajawea, Lewis and Clark's guide

Birdie

Airboy's airplane (comic book series "Airboy"): it resembles a P-39 Airacobra

Birdman of Alcatraz

Nickname of convict Robert Stroud: played by Burt Lancaster in the movie of that name (1962)

Birmingham, U.S.S.

U. S. Navy cruiser from which the first airplane took off, November 14, 1910, piloted by Eugene Ely, a civilian

Birmingham Brown

Charlie Chan's assistant (movies): played by Mantan Moreland

Birthdates

Living:

Gene Autry, Tioga, Texas, 1907 -

Lauren Bacall, New York, N. Y., 1924 -

Lucille Ball, Jamestown, N. Y., 1911 -

Jack Benny, Waukegan, Ill., 1894 -

Red Buttons, New York, N. Y., 1919 -

Johnny Carson, Corning, Iowa, 1925 -

Charles Chaplin, London, England, 1889 -

Ray Charles, Albany, Ga., 1930 -

Dick Clark, Mt. Vernon, N. Y., 1929 -

Sean Connery, Edinburgh, Scotland, 1930 -

Harry Lillis "Bing" Crosby, Tacoma, Wa., 1904 -

Tony Curtis, New York, N. Y., 1925 -

Sammy Davis, Jr., New York, N. Y., 1925 -

Doris Day, Cincinnati, Ohio, 1924 -

Redd Foxx, St. Louis, Mo., 1922 -

Benny Goodman, Chicago, Ill., 1909 -

Alfred Hitchcock, London, England, 1899 -

Bob Hope, London, England, 1903 -

Rock Hudson, Winnetka, Ill., 1925 -

Howard Hughes, Houston, Texas, 1905 -

Tom Jones, Pontypridd, Wales, 1940 -

Jerry Lewis, Newark, N. J., 1926 -

Ann-Margret, Stockholm, Sweden, 1941 -

Dean Martin, Steubenville, Ohio, 1917 -

Steve McQueen, Indianapolis, Indiana, 1930 -

Paul Newman, Cleveland, Ohio, 1925 -

Elvis Presley, Tupelo, Miss., 1935 -

Mickey Rooney, Brooklyn, N. Y., 1922 -

Frank Sinatra, Hoboken, N. J., 1917 -

John Wayne, Winterset, Iowa, 1907 -

Natalie Wood, San Francisco, Calif., 1938 -

No longer living:

Bud Abbott, 1898-1974

Fred Allen, 1894-1956

Gracie Allen, 1906-1964

Louis Armstrong, 1900-1971
Dan Blocker, 1928-1972
Humphrey Bogart, 1899-1957
Nat "King" Cole, 1919-1965
Lou Costello, 1906-1959
Walt Disney, 1901-1966
W. C. Fields, 1879-1946
Clark Gable, 1901-1960
Oliver Hardy, 1892-1957
Jean Harlow, 1911-1937
Gabby Hayes, 1885-1969
Jimi Hendrix, 1943-1970
Janis Joplin, 1943-1970
Boris Karloff, 1887-1969
Alan Ladd, 1913-1964
Stan Laurel, 1890-1965
Jayne Mansfield, 1933-1967
Glenn Miller, 1909-1944
Tom Mix, 1880-1940
Marilyn Monroe, 1926-1962
Audie Murphy, 1924-1971
Spencer Tracy, 1900-1967
Hank Williams, 1923-1953

Birthdays

Monday's child is fair of face;
Tuesday's child is full of grace;
Wednesday's child is full of woe
Thursday's child has far to go;
Friday's child is loving and giving;
Saturday's child works hard for a living;
But the child that is born on the Sabbath day
Is blithe and bonny, good and gay

Births

Twins	2 babies
Triplets	•3 babies
Quadruplets	4 babies
Quintuplets	5 babies
Sextuplets	6 babies
Septuplets	7 babies
Octuplets	8 babies

Birthstones and Flowers

January	Garnet
	Carnation or Snowdrop
February	Amethyst
	Violet or Primrose

March	Bloodstone or Aquamarine
	Jonquil or Daisy
April	Diamond
	Sweet Pea or Daisy
May	Emerald
	Lily of the Valley or Hawthorn
June	Pearl, Alexandrite, or Moonstone
	Rose or Honeysuckle
July	Ruby
	Larkspur or Waterlily
August	Sardonyx or Peridot
	Gladiolus or Poppy
September	Sapphire
	Aster or Morning Glory
October	Opal or Tourmaline
	Calendula or Cosmos
November	Topaz
	Chrysanthemum
December	Zircon or Turquoise
	Narcissus or Holly

Bismarck
Germany's largest battleship in World War II: sunk May 27, 1941, off Brest, France

Black
Only color worn by country-western singer Johnny Cash during a performance: reasons stated in his song "The Man in Black"

Black Arrow
Sky King's jet airplane (radio series)

Black Beauty
Green Hornet's car

Black Betsy
Babe Ruth's baseball bat

Black Condor, The
Tom Wright, member of the Justice League of America (comics)

Black Eagle
Nickname of Hubert Fauntleroy Julian (Negro soldier of fortune)

Blackbeard
Nickname of Edward Teach (died 1718), West Indies pirate

Blackhawks
Comic book characters: Blackhawk, Andre, Chuck, Hendrickson, Olaf, Stanislaus, Chop Chop (Chinese cook)

Blackie
The Blackhawks' pet hawk (comic book series "Blackhawks")

Black Jack

Nickname of General John Joseph Pershing (1860-1948)

Black Knights

U. S. Army's precision parachute team

Black Pete

Mickey Mouse's foe (early cartoon features)

Black Rebels

Motorcycle gang led by Johnny (Marlon Brando) who invade the town of Wrightsville (1954 movie *The Wild One*). The rival gang is led by Chino (Lee Marvin). Johnny rides a Triumph motorcycle

Black Sox scandal

1919 World Series—Chicago White Sox lost to Cincinnati Reds, 5 games to 3.

Eight (White Sox) players did not play major league baseball again: Eddie Cicotte, pitcher; Happy Felsch, center field; Chick Gandil, first baseman; Joe Jackson, left field; Fred McMullin, utility player; Swede Risberg, shortshop; Buck Weaver, third base; Claude Williams, pitcher

Black Tooth

The kindest dog in the country (Soupy Sales TV show)

Blair General Hospital

Where Dr. Kildare worked

Blanc, Mel

Voice of Bugs Bunny, Sylvester, Tweetee Pie, Jack Benny's Maxwell, and other radio and cartoon characters

Blefuscu

Nation at war with Lilliput (Swift's *Gulliver's Travels*)

Blondi

Adolf Hitler's dog

Blondie

Mrs. Dagwood Bumstead of Chic Young's cartoon strip "Blondie." In the movie and radio series Blondie is played by Penny Singleton, Dagwood by Arthur Lake

Bloopy

Gold statuette presented by Kermit Schafer (Mr. Blooper) for the best bloopers (verbal errors on radio and TV)

Blossom

Tumbleweeds' horse (comic strip "Tumbleweeds" by Tom K. Ryan)

Blossom

Gabby Hayes' mule (movies)

Blue Angels

United States Navy's aerobatic team

Blue Bird Special
>Boy pilot Jimmie Allen's airplane (radio's "Air Adventures of Jimmy Allen")

Bluebird
>Donald Campbell's land speed vehicle

Bluebird Special
>Malcolm Campbell's land speed vehicle (301.13 mph in 1935)

Blue Boy
>Painting (1779) by Sir Thomas Gainsborough (which he painted to prove that a blue painting need not be dull): now in Huntington Library and Art Gallery, San Marino, California

Blue Boy
>Prize-winning pig (movie *State Fair*)

Blue Eagle
>Symbol of NRA (National Recovery Administration), 1933-1936

Blue Flame
>Theme song of Woody Herman's orchestra

Blue Meanies
>The bad guys in the Beatles' 1968 movie *Yellow Submarine*

Blue Moon
>Theme song of radio series "Hollywood Hotel"

Llue Parrot Cafe
>Cafe of Signor Ferrari (Sydney Greenstreet) (movie *Casablanca*)

Bluto
>Popeye's foe (also called Brutus)

Boatswain
>Lord Byron's dog

Boatswain
>Dog upon the whaler ship "Dolly" (Herman Melville's *Typee*)

Bob
>Sheena Queen of the Jungle's mate (movie serial)

Bob and Ray
>Radio and television comedians Bob Elliot and Ray Goulding

Bobby
>Bull in Schlitz Malt Liquor TV commercials

Bobby Benson
>Played by Billy Halop in radio and movie serials, but originally on radio by Richard Wanamaker
>Tex Mason, the ranch foreman, played by Al Hodge or Tex Ritter on radio
>Harka, Indian ranchhand, played by Craig McDonnell
>Windy Wales, cowboy, played by Don Knotts on radio
>Diogenes Dodwaddle, played by Tex Ritter

Bobcats
>Bob Crosby's band

Bobbsey Twins

Two series: Nan and Bert, 8 years old; Flossie and Freddie, 4 years old

Bock's Car

B-29 that dropped the atomic bomb on Nagasaki, piloted by Major Charles Sweeney (August 9, 1945)

Bodega Bay

Sonoma County, Calif., seaside town, north of San Francisco, where the attack of the birds occurs (Alfred Hitchcock 1963 movie *The Birds*)

Bogart, Humphrey

Marriages: Helen Mencken, 1926-1928; Mary Phillips, 1928-1938; Mayo Methot, 1938-1945; Lauren Bacall, 1945-1957

His movies and roles:

1930—*Broadway's Like That*, no name (10-minute feature)
1930—*A Devil with Women*, Tom Standish
1930—*Up the River*, Steve
1931—*Body and Soul*, Jim Watson
1931—*Bad Sister*, Valentine Corliss
1931—*Women of All Nations*, Stone
1931—*A Holy Terror*, Steve Nash
1932—*Love Affair*, Jim Leonard
1932—*Big City Blues*, Adkins
1932—*Three on a Match*, The Mug
1934—*Midnight*, Garboni
1936—*The Petrified Forest*, Duke Mantee
1936—*Bullets or Ballots*, Nick "Bugs" Fenner
1936—*Two Against the World*, Sherry Scott
1936—*China Clipper*, Hap Stuart
1936—*Isle of Fury*, Val Stevens
1937—*Black Legion*, Frank Taylor
1937—*The Great O'Malley*, John Phillips
1937—*Marked Woman*, David Graham
1937—*Kid Galahad*, Turkey Morgan
1937—*San Quentin*, Joe "Red" Kennedy
1937—*Dead End*, Baby Face Martin
1937—*Stand-In*, Douglas Quintain
1938—*Swing Your Lady*, Ed Hatch
1938—*Crime School*, Mark Braden
1938—*Men Are Such Fools*, Harry Galleon
1938—*The Amazing Dr. Clitterhouse*, Rocks Valentine
1938—*Racket Busters*, Pete Martin
1938—*Angels with Dirty Faces*, James Frazier
1939—*King of the Underworld*, Joe Gurney
1939—*The Oklahoma Kid*, Whip McCord

1939—*Dark Victory*, Michael O'Leary
1939—*You Can't Get Away with Murder*, Frank Wilson
1939—*The Roaring Twenties*, George Hally
1939—*The Return of Doctor X*, Marshall Quesne
1939—*Invisible Stripes*, Chuck Martin
1940—*Virginia City*, John Murrell
1940—*It All Came True*, Grasselli (Chips Maguire)
1940—*Brother Orchid*, Jack Buck
1940—*They Drive by Night*, Paul Fabrini
1941—*High Sierra*, Roy Earle
1941—*The Wagons Roll at Night*, Nick Coster
1941—*The Maltese Falcon*, Sam Spade
1942—*All Through the Night*, Gloves Donahue
1942—*The Big Shot*, Duke Berne
1942—*Across the Pacific*, Rick Leland
1943—*Casablanca*, Rick Blaine
1943—*Action in the North Atlantic*, Joe Rossi
1943—*Thank Your Lucky Stars*, Humphrey Bogart (as himself
1943—*Sahara*, Sergeant Joe Gunn
1944—*Passage to Marseille*, Matrac
1944—*To Have and Have Not*, Harry Morgan
1945—*Conflict*, Richard Mason
1946—*Two Guys from Milwaukee*, Humphrey Bogart (as himself)
1946—*The Big Sleep*, Philip Marlowe
1947—*Dead Reckoning*, Rip Murdock
1947—*The Two Mrs. Carrolls*, Geoffrey Carroll
1947—*Dark Passage*, Vincent Parry
1948—*The Treasure of the Sierra Madre*, Fred C. Dobbs
1948—*Key Largo*, Frank McCloud
1949—*Knock on Any Door*, Andrew Morton
1949—*Tokyo Joe*, Joe Barrett
1950—*Chain Lightning*, Matt Brennan
1950—*In a Lonely Place*, Dixon Steele
1950—*Deadline U. S. A.*, Ed Hutchinson
1951—*The Enforcer*, Martin Ferguson
1951—*Sirocco*, Harry Smith
1951—*The African Queen*, Charlie Allnut
1953—*Battle Circus*, Major Jed Webbe
1954—*Beat the Devil*, Billy Dannreuther
1954—*The Caine Mutiny*, Captain Queeg
1954—*Sabrina*, Linus Larrabee
1954—*The Barefoot Contessa*, Harry Dawes

1955—*We're No Angels,* Joseph
1955—*The Left Hand of God,* Jim Carmody
1955—*The Desperate Hours,* Glenn Griffin
1956—*The Harder They Fall,* Eddie Willis

Bomba

The Jungle Boy (movie series "Bomba"): played by Johnny Sheffield

Bonanza

TV series. Original cast: Ben Cartwright (Lorne Greene); Joe Cartwright (Michael Landon); Hoss (Eric) Cartwright (Dan Blocker); Adam Cartwright (Pernell Roberts)

Bones

Nickname (probably short for "Sawbones," traditional appellation for a surgeon) used by Captain Kirk for Dr. McCoy (TV series "Star Trek")

Bongo

Unicycling bear (cartoon)

Bonhomme Richard

Captain John Paul Jones' ship, a French Indiaman 14 years old, the "Duras," renamed in honor of Benjamin Franklin, who wrote Poor Richard's almanacs

Bonnie and Clyde

Bank robbers Bonnie Parker and Clyde Barrow: played in Arthur Penn's movie by Warren Beatty and Faye Dunaway. The story had been filmed before, notably by Fritz Lang in 1951 and by William Witney in 1958 (with Dorothy Provine as Bonnie)

Bonzo

Chimpanzee that co-starred with Ronald Reagan (movie *Bedtime for Bonzo*)

Boo Boo

Yogi Bear's little bear sidekick (TV cartoon)

Booker T. and the M.G.'s

(M.G. stands for Memphis Group) Donald "Duck" Dunn, Steve Cropper, Al Jackson, Booker T. Jones

Booth, Edwin (Thomas)

John Wilkes Booth's actor brother (1833-1893). He has been elected to the Hall of Fame of Great Americans

Booth, William

Known as General Booth (1829-1912); founded the Salvation Army (1878, founded in 1865 as the Christian Revival Association or Christian Mission, and still earlier known as East London Revival Society)

Boots

Stationhouse dog (TV series "Emergency")

Borden, Lizzie

Alleged murderer (1892) of her mother and father in Fall River, Mass. Tried, she was acquitted.

"Lizzie Borden took an axe
And gave her mother forty whacks.
When she saw what she had done
She gave her father forty-one."

Borg-Warner Trophy

Award given for winning the Indianapolis 500-mile auto race

Boris and Natasha

Arch-enemies of Bullwinkle and Rocky (cartoon series)

Boroughs of the City of New York

Bronx (Bronx County)
Brooklyn (Kings County)
Manhattan (New York County)
Queens (Queens County)
Richmond (Richmond County; Staten Island)

Boston Blackie

Private eye created by Jack Boyle: on radio and in movies played by Chester Morris (in 1923 there were two movies starring William Russell). Replaced on radio by Richard Kollmar; on TV played by Kent Taylor. (His sidekick on radio was Shorty, in movies it was the Runt.) Mary was the helpful female on radio and TV.

His credo: "Enemy to those who make him an enemy, friend to those who have no friend"

Boston Strong Boy

Nickname of heavyweight boxing champion John L. Sullivan

Boston Tea Party

British ships raided (December 16, 1773) at Griffin's Wharf: "Beaver," "Dartmouth," "Eleanor"

Boswell Sisters

Singing group: Connee (originally Connie), Vet, Martha

Boulder Dam

Former name of Hoover Dam, on the Colorado River

Bounty, H.M.S.

British ship upon which Fletcher Christian led the famous mutiny against Lieutenant (later Captain) William Bligh, 1789

Bounty Hunter, The

Rerun title of TV series "Wanted—Dead or Alive"

Bounty trilogy

Novels based on fact, by Charles Nordhoff and James Norman Hall: *Mutiny on the Bounty* (1932); *Men Against the Sea* (1934); *Pitcairn's Island* (1934)

Bowery Boys

Acting group of teenagers originally belonging to the Dead End Kids who, led by Bobby Jordan and Leo Gorcey, joined Monogram Pictures for a series to be called "East Side Kids." Billy Benedict, Stanley Clements, Bennie Bartlett, and David Gorcey joined this group, and later Huntz Hall and Gabriel Dell left Universal to come in with them.

Leo Gorcey played Slip (or Terence Aloysius Mahoney), Huntz Hall was Satch (Horace Debussy Jones), Billy Benedict was Whitey, Bobby Jordan was Bobby, David Gorcey was Chuck, and Gabe Dell played the part of Gabe Moreno

The Bowery Boys pictures were made from 1940 to 1953

Bowl games, College football

Bowl	City	State
American Bowl	Tampa	Florida
Astro-Bluebonnet Bowl	Houston	Texas
Boardwalk Bowl	Atlantic City	New Jersey
Camellia Bowl	Sacramento	California
Cotton Bowl	Dallas	Texas
Fiesta Bowl	Tempe	Arizona
Gator Bowl	Jacksonville	Florida
Grantland Rice Bowl	Baton Rouge	Louisiana
Hula Bowl	Honolulu	Hawaii
Knute Rockne Bowl	Atlantic City	New Jersey
Liberty Bowl	Memphis	Tennessee
Lions American Bowl	Tampa	Florida
Ohio Shrine Bowl	Columbus	Ohio
Orange Bowl	Miami	Florida
Pasadena Bowl	Pasadena	California
Peach Bowl	Atlanta	Georgia
Rose Bowl	Pasadena	California
Senior Bowl	Mobile	Alabama
Shrine Classic (East/West)	San Francisco	California
Shrine Game (North/South)	Miami	Florida
Sugar Bowl	New Orleans	Louisiana
Sun Bowl	El Paso	Texas
Tangerine Bowl	Orlando	Florida

Boxer

The horse in George Orwell's *Animal Farm*

Boy Commandos
>   Young crimefighters (comic book series), overseen by Captain Rip Carter. They include Alfy Twidget (English), Andre (French), Jan (Dutch), Brooklyn (American)

Boys' Ranch
>   Comic book characters (Harvey comics): Angel, Clay Duncan, Dandy Dolan, Wabash, Wee Willie Weehawken

Boys Town
>   Founded, near Omaha, Nebraska, 1917, by Monsignor Edward J. Flanagan
>   Motto: "There is no such thing as a bad boy"

Boz
>   Pseudonym of Charles Dickens

B.P.O.E.
>   Benevolent and Protective Order of Elks

Braal
>   Home planet of Cosmic Boy (Rokk Krinn) (comic book series)

Brian's song
>   Movie for TV about former Chicago Bears running back Gale Sayers (played by Billy Dee Williams) and his teammate Brian Piccolo (played by James Caan) who died of cancer in 1970

Braun, Eva
>   Adolf Hitler's mistress

Breadfruit trees
>   Cargo of H.M.S. "Bounty" at time of mutiny, 1789

Brer Fox
>   Slung Brer Rabbit right in de brier-patch

Bridge of San Luis Rey, The
>   Novel (1927; Pulitzer Prize 1928) by Thornton Wilder.
>   The five killed when the bridge fell were Esteban, Uncle Pio, Marquesa de Montemayor, Pepita, Jaime. Brother Juniper, a Franciscan, investigated why these particular five were chosen to die in this way

Brigadoon
>   Mythical Scottish town that appears for a single day every one hundred years (musical play, 1947, and movie, 1954, by Alan Jay Lerner and Frederick Loewe)

Brigham
>   William Cody's (Buffalo Bill's) horse

Britt Reid
>   Name of the Green Hornet

Broadway Joe
>   Nickname of New York Jets quarterback Joe Namath

Brobdingnag
>   The land of the giants (Jonathan Swift's *Gulliver's Travels*)

Brock, Alice

> Founder of Alice's Restaurant

Brockton Bomber

> Nickname of heavyweight champion Rocky Marciano (Rocco Francis Marchegiano)

Brodie, Steve

> Claimed to have jumped off the Brooklyn Bridge on a bet, and lived: July 23, 1886. He re-enacted the scene in a play, *On the Bowery*, opening in 1894.
>
> His reply, when asked to jump again: "I done it oncet."

Brom Bones

> Nickname of Abraham Van Brunt, Ichabod Crane's rival for the hand of Katrina (Irving's "The Legend of Sleepy Hollow")

Broncho Billy

> Early western film hero, played by Gilbert M. Anderson (Max Aronson) (1882-1971) who starred in the first western, *The Great Train Robbery* (1903, 11 minutes long). Anderson and George K. Spoor founded Essanay Studios, named from their initials.

Brontë sisters

	Pen Name	*Principal Novel*
Charlotte	Currer Bell	*Jane Eyre*
Emily	Ellis Bell	*Wuthering Heights*
Anne	Acton Bell	*Agnes Grey*

Brookfield

> The school at which Mr. Chips taught (James Hilton's novel *Goodbye, Mr. Chips*)

Brothers Karamazov

> Dmitri, Ivan, Alyosha, Smerdyakov (illegitimate): novel by Feodor Dostoevsky (1880)

Brown, Roy

> Canadian pilot who claimed the victory over the Red Baron, Manfred von Richthofen, April 21, 1918

Brown Beauty

> Reputed name of borrowed horse Paul Revere rode when he warned the countryside of the approach of the British

Browns, The

> Country and Western singing group: Bonnie, Jim Ed, Maxine

Bruno

> Bear who played Gentle Ben (TV series "Gentle Ben")

Bruno

> Cinderella's dog (Walt Disney cartoon feature movie)

Brutus

> The ugly dachshund: Great Dane who thinks he is a dachshund (Disney feature movie *The Ugly Dachshund*): the other dachshunds are Tokey, Norma, Pesky, and Heidi

Brutus
    Another name for Popeye's antagonist Bluto

Bryant, Jimmy
    Sang for Richard Beymer (Tony) in movie *West Side Story*

Bryant's Gap
    Where the Lone Ranger, his brother Captain Daniel Reid, and four other Texas Rangers were ambushed by Butch Cavendish and the Hole-in-the-Wall gang. Only John Reid, thus "the lone Ranger," survived. He was nursed back to health by Tonto

Bucephalus
    Horse of Alexander the Great: given to him by his father, Philip II, and died in India at the age of 30

Buchanan, James
    Only bachelor United States president

Bucher, Lloyd
    Commander of the U.S.S. "Pueblo," captured by North Koreans, January 1968

Buck
    Horse of Ben Cartwright (Lorne Green) (TV series "Bonanza")

Buck
    Hero dog (Jack London's *The Call of the Wild*)

Buckshot
    Horse of Wild Bill Hickok (TV series "Wild Bill Hickok")

Buckwheat, Stymie, and Farina
    Three Negro boys in the "Our Gang" movie series. Buckwheat Thomas appeared in 89 of the 132 talkies made, Stymie Beard in 33, and Farina Hoskins, the first of the group, in 20. Sunshine Sammy Morrison, who appeared in the earliest "Our Gang" films in the mid-twenties, did not appear in talkies.

Bucky Barnes
    Captain America's partner (comic books)

Bucky Beaver
    Animal character in Ipana toothpaste commercials and ads

Budd
    Colonel Lemuel Q. Stoopnagle's sidekick: Budd was Wilbur Budd Hulick

Buddha
    Sacred name of Siddhartha Gautama

Buddy
    First Seeing Eye dog in America (1928), brought to the U. S. from Switzerland by owner Morris Frank

Buffalo Bill
    Nickname of William Frederick Cody, given to him by E. Z. C. Judson

Buffalo nickel
> U.S. 5 cent piece from 1913 through 1938: designed by James Earle Fraser, sculptor of Indian statue "End of the Trail"
> The buffalo is modeled after Black Diamond, a bison in the Bronx Park Zoo, New York; it appears on the reverse of the coin
> The Indian head (on the obverse) is a combination made from photographs of 3 visitors to President Theodore Roosevelt: Iron Tail, a Sioux; Big Tree, a Kiowa; Two Moons, a Cheyenne

Bull Martin
> One of G8's Battle Aces (comic book series)

Bulldog Drummond
> Detective created (1920) by Herman Cyril McNeile ("Sapper")

Bullet
> Roy Rogers' wonder dog

Bulletgirl
> Secret identity of Susan Kent, Bulletman's partner

Bulletman
> Secret identity of Jim Barr, crimefighter (comic book series "Bulletman")

Bullitt
> Movie starring Steve McQueen: San Francisco automobile chase scene involved a Ford Mustang (Bullitt's) and Dodge Charger (bad guys)

Bunin, Hope and Morey
> Puppeteers on "Lucky Pup" show and many other features (TV)

Buntline Special
> Long-barreled pistol used by Wyatt Earp

Burma-Shave
> Roadside advertisements appearing on small boards spaced so they could be read sequentially by motorists driving by:
> A peach / looks good / with lots of fuzz / but man's no peach / and never was / Burma-Shave
> Does your husband / misbehave / grunt and grumble / rant and rave? / shoot the brute some / Burma-Shave
> Don't take a curve / at 60 per / we hate to lose / a customer / Burma-Shave
> Every shaver / now can snore / six more minutes / than before / by using / Burma-Shave
> He played / a sax / had no B. O. / but his whiskers scratched / so she let him go / Burma-Shave
> Henry the Eighth / Prince of Friskers / lost five wives / but kept / his whiskers / Burma-Shave
> Listen, birds / those signs cost / money / so roost a while but / don't get funny / Burma-Shave

My man / won't shave / sez Hazel Huz / but I should worry / Dora's does / Burma-Shave

Past schoolhouses / take it slow / let the little / shavers / grow / Burma-Shave

Rip a fender / off your car / send it in / for a half-pound jar / Burma-Shave

Burnette, Smiley

Gene Autry's sidekick. Played also in "Petticoat Junction" (TV series)

Burr, Raymond

Canadian actor (born 1917) noted for two successful TV series: "Perry Mason" (1957-1966), "Ironside" (1967-   ). He was earlier familiar in the movies as a heavy or, for example, as the prosecuting attorney in *A Place in the Sun* (1951) or the narrator in *Godzilla* (1954)

Bush and Burritt Streets

San Francisco corner, above the Stockton Street tunnel, where Sam Spade's partner Miles Archer was shot and killed by Brigid O'Shaughnessy with a .38 eight shot Webley Fosbery automatic (Dashiell Hammett's *The Maltese Falcon*)

Bush, Guy

Pitcher off whom Babe Ruth hit home runs 713 and 714 on May 25, 1935, in Pittsburgh

Busted Flush

Private houseboat of detective Travis McGee, docked at Miami (John D. MacDonald novels)

Butch Cassidy

Nickname of western outlaw George Leroy Parker

Butch Cavendish

Leader of the Hole-in-the-Wall gang that ambushed the Rangers (Lone Ranger and Green Hornet radio series)

Butch's Bar

Favorite hangout (movie *The Best Years of Our Lives*). Proprietor: piano-player Butch Engle (played by Hoagy Carmichael)

Butterfly

Tom Swift's speedy monoplane

Buttermilk

Dale Evans' horse

Button

Thomas Paine's horse

Buttram, Pat

Gene Autry's sidekick on radio and in some movies of the late 40's and early 50's. He was also the Sage of Winston County, Alabama, on radio's "National Barn Dance"

Buz Murdock
> One of automobilists in TV's "Route 66" (replaced by Linc Case): played by George Maharis

Bwana Devil
> First full-length 3D movie, 1953

C

C. A. R. E.
> Cooperative for American Relief Everywhere (originally, Cooperative for American Remittances to Europe)

CQD
> International distress telegraph signal: come-quick-danger (used until 1911) before SOS

CX-4
> Hap Harrigan's airplane call sign (radio series)

Cabinet offices
> United States: Secretary of State; Secretary of the Treasury; Secretary of Defense (was War); Attorney General; (formerly, Postmaster General; Secretary of the Navy); Secretary of the Interior; Secretary of Agriculture; Secretary of Commerce; Secretary of Labor; Secretary of Health, Education and Welfare; Secretary of Housing and Urban Development; Secretary of Transportation

Cable car routes
> Current San Francisco routes:
> California Line (Route 61, between Market and Van Ness)
> Powell-Hyde Line (Route 60, between Market and Aquatic Park)
> Powell-Mason Line (Route 59, between Market and the Bay-Taylor turntable)

Cadets
> Football team of U. S. Military Academy at West Point (Army)

Caduceus
> Symbol of the medical profession: a snake (or two snakes) entwined on a rod

Caesar's wife
> Sid Caesar's, that is: on TV ("Your Show of Shows") played by Imogene Coca, Janet Blair, Nanette Fabray, Gisele MacKenzie

Calamity Jane
> Nickname of Martha Jane Canary Burke: said to have married 12 times

Caliburn
> Another name for Excalibur, King Arthur's sword

Calico
Gabby Hayes' horse (movies)

California Big Four
Built the Central Pacific Railroad: Charles Crocker, Sacramento drygoods merchant; Mark Hopkins, Sacramento hardware dealer, partner of Collis Potter Huntington; and Leland Stanford, Sacramento wholesale grocer

Calpurnia
Third wife of Julius Caesar.
First wife, Cornelia; second wife, Pompeia

Calvin Calaveras
Puppet frog (Bobby Goldsboro TV show)

Calypso
Jacques-Yves Cousteau's research ship

Camel
One hump: native to Africa and the Near East (dromedary)
Two humps: native to Central Asia

Camel Cigarettes
Times Square "Smoking Man" advertisement sign: blew smoke rings

Campuses
University of California: Berkeley, Davis,. Irvine, Los Angeles, Riverside, San Diego, San Francisco, Santa Barbara, Santa Cruz

Canada

Province or Territory	Capital
Alberta	Edmonton
British Columbia	Victoria
Manitoba	Winnipeg
New Brunswick	Fredericton
Newfoundland	St. John's
Northwest Territories	Yellowknife
Nova Scotia	Halifax
Ontario	Toronto
Prince Edward Island	Charlottetown
Quebec	Quebec
Saskatchewan	Regina
Yukon Territory	Whitehorse

Canadian Football League
Eastern Conference
Ottawa Rough Riders
Toronto Argonauts
Montreal Alouettes
Hamilton Tiger-Cats

Western Conference
    Edmonton Eskimos
    Saskatchewan Rough Riders
    British Columbia Lions
    Calgary Stampeders
    Winnipeg Blue Bombers

Candy
    One of the Marquis chimpanzees (TV series "The Hathaways")

Cannonball
    Train (TV series "Petticoat Junction")

Cannonball Express
    Casey Jones' regular train. He was killed April 30, 1900, as relief engineer on another train

Canton, Ohio
    Location of pro football's Hall of Fame; William McKinley, 25th president, is buried in Canton

Cape Canaveral
    Former name of Cape Kennedy. Cape Kennedy is also the former name of Cape Canaveral. (Cape Canaveral became Cape Kennedy in 1963, and in 1973 it was changed back to Cape Canaveral.)

Cape of Good Hope
    Often thought to be the tip of South Africa; actually Cape Agulhas is, 100 miles east and south of the Cape of Good Hope, 29 minutes of longitude further south

Cape Horn
    Tip of South America, southernmost continental point except for Antarctica, 55 degrees 59 minutes south latitude

Capitals, national

Country	Capital
Afghanistan	Kabul
Albania	Tirana
Algeria	Algiers
Andorra	Andorra la Vella
Angola	Luanda
Antigua	St. John's
Argentina	Buenos Aires
Australia	Canberra
Austria	Vienna
Bahamas	Nassau
Bahrain	Manama
Bangladesh	Dacca
Barbados	Bridgetown
Belgium	Brussels

Country	*Capital*
Bermuda	Hamilton
Bhutan	Thimphu
Bolivia	Sucre (La Paz: seat of government)
Botswana	Gaborone
Brazil	Brasilia
British Honduras	Belmopan
British Solomon Islands	Honiara
British Virgin Islands	Roadtown
Brunei	Bandar Seri Begawan
Bulgaria	Sofia
Burma	Rangoon
Burundi	Bujumbura
Cambodia	Phnom Penh
Cameroon	Yaoundé
Canada	Ottawa
Cape Verde Islands	Praia
Cayman Islands	Georgetown
Central African Republic	Bangui
Ceylon (now Sri Lanka)	Colombo
Chad	Fort-Lamy
Chile	Santiago
China, People's Republic of	Peking
China, Republic of (Taiwan)	Taipei
Colombia	Bogota
Comoro Islands	Moroni
Congo, Democratic Republic of (now Zaire)	Kinshasa
Congo, People's Republic of	Brazzaville
Costa Rica	San José
Cuba	Havana
Cyprus	Nicosia
Czechoslovakia	Prague
Dahomey	Porto-Novo, Cotonou
Denmark	Copenhagen
Dominica	Roseau
Dominican Republic	Santo Domingo
Dutch Guiana (now Surinam)	Paramaribo
Ecuador	Quito
Egypt	Cairo
El Salvador	San Salvador
Equatorial Guinea	Santa Isabel
Ethiopia	Addis Ababa
Faeroe Islands	Torshavn

Country	Capital
Falkland Islands	Stanley
Fiji	Suva
Finland	Helsinki
France	Paris
French Guiana	Cayenne
French Polynesia	Papeete
Gabon	Libreville
Gambia	Bathurst
Germany, West (BRD)	Bonn
Germany, East (DDR)	East Berlin
Ghana	Accra
Gilbert and Ellice Islands	Tarawa
Greece	Athens
Greenland	Godthaab
Grenada	St. George's
Guadeloupe	Basse Terre
Guatemala	Guatemala
Guernsey	St. Peter Port
Guinea	Conakry
Guyana	Georgetown
Haiti	Port-au-Prince
Honduras	Tegucigalpa
Hong Kong	Victoria
Hungary	Budapest
Iceland	Reykjavik
India	New Delhi
Indonesia	Jakarta
Iran	Tehran
Iraq	Baghdad
Ireland	Dublin
Isle of Man	Douglas
Israel	Jerusalem
Italy	Rome
Ivory Coast	Abidjan
Jamaica	Kingston
Japan	Tokyo
Jersey	St. Helier
Jordan	Amman
Kenya	Nairobi
Korea, North	Pyongyang
Korea, South	Seoul
Kuwait	Kuwait
Laos	Vientiane, Luang Prabang (royal capital)

Country	*Capital*
Lebanon	Beirut
Lesotho	Maseru
Liberia	Monrovia
Libya	Tripoli, Benghazi
Liechtenstein	Vaduz
Luxembourg	Luxembourg
Macao	Macao
Malagasy Republic	Tananarive
Malawi	Zomba
Malaysia	Kuala Lumpur
Maldives	Male
Mali	Bamako
Malta	Valletta
Martinique	Fort-de-France
Mauritania	Nouakchott
Mauritius	Port Louis
Mexico	Mexico City
Monaco	Monaco
Mongolia	Ulan Bator
Montserrat	Plymouth
Morocco	Rabat
Mozambique	Lourenco Marques
Namibia (South-West Africa)	Windhoek
Nauru	(No capital)
Nepal	Katmandu
Netherlands	Amsterdam
Netherlands Antilles	Willemstad
New Caledonia	Noumea
New Hebrides	Vila
New Zealand	Wellington
Nicaragua	Managua
Niger	Niamey
Nigeria	Lagos
Northern Ireland	Belfast
Norway	Oslo
Oman	Muscat
Orkney Islands	Kirkwall
Pakistan	Islamabad
Panama	Panama
Papua-New Guinea	Port Moresby
Paraguay	Asuncion
Peru	Lima
Philippines	Quezon City
Pitcairn Island	Adamstown

Country	Capital
Poland	Warsaw
Portugal	Lisbon
Portuguese Guinea	Bissau
Portuguese Timor	Dili
Qatar	Doha
Reunion	Saint-Denis
Rhodesia	Salisbury
Romania	Bucharest
Rwanda	Kigali
St. Helena	Jamestown
St. Kitts-Nevis	Basseterre
St. Lucia	Castries
St. Pierre et Miquelon	St. Pierre
St. Vincent	Kingstown
San Marino	San Marino
São Tomé e Principe	São Tomé
Saudi Arabia	Riyadh
Scotland	Edinburgh
Senegal	Dakar
Seychelles	Victoria
Siam (now Thailand)	Bangkok
Sierra Leone	Freetown
Sikkim	Gangtok
Singapore	Singapore
Somalia	Mogadishu
South Africa, Republic of	Pretoria (Administrative), Cape Town (Legislative)
Southern and Antarctic Lands	Port-aux-Francais
South-West Africa (now Namibia)	Windhoek
Spain	Madrid
Spanish Sahara	El Aaiún
Sri Lanka	Colombo
Sudan	Khartoum
Surinam (Dutch Guiana)	Paramaribo
Swaziland	Mbabane
Sweden	Stockholm
Switzerland	Bern
Syria	Damascus
Taiwan	Taipei
Tanzania	Dar es Salaam
Thailand	Bangkok
Tibet	Lhasa
Togo	Lomé

Country	Capital
Tonga	Nukualofa
Trinidad and Tobago	Port of Spain
Tunisia	Tunis
Turkey	Ankara
Turks and Caicos Islands	Grand Turk
Uganda	Kampala
Union of Soviet Socialist Republics	Moscow
United Arab Emirates	Abu Dhabi
United Kingdom	London
United States	Washington, D. C.
Upper Volta	Ouagadougou
Uruguay	Montevideo
Vatican City, State of	Vatican City
Venezuela	Caracas
Vietnam, North	Hanoi
Vietnam, South	Saigon
Wallis et Futuna Islands	Mata-Utu
Western Samoa	Apia
Yemen, People's Democratic Republic of	Aden, Medina as-Shaab
Yemen Arab Republic	Sana
Yugoslavia	Belgrade
Zaire	Kinshasa
Zambia	Lusaka

Capitals, U. S. states and possessions

Capital	State
Agana	Guam
Albany	New York
Annapolis	Maryland
Atlanta	Georgia
Augusta	Maine
Austin	Texas
Balboa Heights	Canal Zone
Baton Rouge	Louisiana
Bismarck	North Dakota
Boise	Idaho
Boston	Massachusetts
Carson City	Nevada
Charleston	West Virginia
Charlotte Amalie	Virgin Islands
Cheyenne	Wyoming
Columbia	South Carolina
Columbus	Ohio

Capital	*State*
Concord	New Hampshire
Denver	Colorado
Des Moines	Iowa
Dover	Delaware
Frankfort	Kentucky
Harrisburg	Pennsylvania
Hartford	Connecticut
Helena	Montana
Honolulu	Hawaii
Indianapolis	Indiana
Jackson	Mississippi
Jefferson City	Missouri
Juneau	Alaska
Lansing	Michigan
Lincoln	Nebraska
Little Rock	Arkansas
Madison	Wisconsin
Montgomery	Alabama
Montpelier	Vermont
Nashville	Tennessee
Oklahoma City	Oklahoma
Olympia	Washington
Pago Pago	American Samoa
Phoenix	Arizona
Pierre	South Dakota
Providence	Rhode Island
Raleigh	North Carolina
Richmond	Virginia
Sacramento	California
Salem	Oregon
Salt Lake City	Utah
San Juan	Puerto Rico
Santa Fe	New Mexico
Springfield	Illinois
St. Paul	Minnesota
Tallahassee	Florida
Topeka	Kansas
Trenton	New Jersey

Captain, The
    Horse (cartoon feature movie *101 Dalmatians*)
Captain Ahab
    Captain of the "Pequod" (Herman Melville's *Moby Dick*)
Captain America
    Nickname of Wyatt (Peter Fonda) (movie *Easy Rider*)

Captain America
Secret identity of Steve Rogers (comic book series)

Captain Andy (Hawks)
Captain and owner of the "Cotton Blossom" (Edna Ferber's *Show Boat*)

Captain (Roderick) Anthony
Captain of the "Ferndale" (Joseph Conrad's *Chance*)

Captain Binghamton
Captain (TV series "McHale's Navy"): played by Joe Flynn

Captain Braddock
Chief racket buster (TV series "Racket Squad"): played by Reed Hadley

Captain Crawford
Captain of H.M.S. "Defiant" (Frank Tilsley's *Mutiny*): played by Trevor Howard in movie *HMS Defiant (Damn the Defiant)*

Captain Crook
Bad guy in McDonald Land (McDonald's Hamburgers commercials)

Captain (C. G.) Culpeper
Police chief (movie *It's a Mad, Mad, Mad, Mad World*): played by Spencer Tracy

Captain (Roger) Dorn
Companion of detective Peter Quill (radio series "Peter Quill"): played by Ken Griffin

Captain Englehorn
Captain of the ship "Venture" which brought King Kong to New York: played in 1933 movie by Frank Reicher

Captain Flint
Pirate captain of the "Walrus" who buried the treasure on Treasure Island. His first mate was Billy Bones; his quartermaster was Long John Silver (Robert L. Stevenson's *Treasure Island*)

Captain Flint
Long John Silver's parrot, named for his old captain

Captain Freedom
Secret identity of Don Wright, newspaper publisher (comic book character)

Captain Greer
Police officer directly in charge of the Mod Squad (TV series "Mod Squad"): played by Tige Andrew

Captain Gregg
Ghost haunting (in a friendly way) Gull Cottage and Mrs. Muir (Hope Lange) (1947 movie and later TV series "The Ghost and Mrs. Muir"): played in movie by Rex Harrison and on TV by Edward Mulhare

Captain (Arthur) Hastings
> Hercule Poirot's assistant: Poirot calls him "mon ami"

Captain Henry
> Captain of the "Maxwell House Show Boat" (radio series): played by Charles Winninger and then Frank McIntire

Captain (Grey) Holden
> Skipper of riverboat "Enterprise" (TV series "Riverboat"): played by Darren McGavin

Captain Hook
> Villain, captain of pirate ship the "Jolly Roger" (James M. Barrie's *Peter Pan*): his first name is James

Captain Howdy
> Regan's imaginary playmate, who is actually the evil demon that possesses her (novel/movie *The Exorcist*)

Captain Jacobi
> Master of the ship "La Paloma" which brought the Maltese Falcon from Hong Kong to San Francisco (Dashiell Hammett's *The Maltese Falcon*): in 1941 movie played by Walter Huston

Captain Kinross
> Commander of H.M.S. "Torrin" (movie *In Which We Serve*): played by Noel Coward

Captain (James T.) Kirk
> Commander of the starship "Enterprise," serial number SC 937-0176 CEC (TV series "Star Trek"): played by William Shatner

Captain (Wolf) Larsen
> Captain of the schooner "Ghost" (Jack London's *The Sea Wolf*)

Captain Marlow
> Character in and narrator of Joseph Conrad's *Lord Jim, Youth, Chance, Heart of Darkness*

Captain Marvel
> Secret identity of Billy Batson. Debut: *Whiz Comics*, 1940; *Captain Marvel Adventures*, 1941 (see SHAZAM)

Captain Marvel, Jr.
> Secret identity of Freddie Freeman. "Captain Marvel" is the secret word that turns Freddy Freeman into Captain Marvel, Jr., and back again

Captain Midnight
> Secret identity of Captain Albright, chief of the Secret Squadron (radio series): played by Ed Prentiss (later by Bill Bouchey and Paul Barnes)

Captain Midnight's Secret Squadron
> SS-1, Captain Midnight; SS-2, Chuck Ramsey; SS-3, Joyce Ryan; SS-4, Ichabod "Ikky" Mudd, the mechanic. Senior officer, Major Steel

Captain Morton

Mr. Roberts' commanding officer (movie *Mr. Roberts*): played in 1955 movie by James Cagney

Captain Murphy

Commander of Sealab 2020 (TV cartoon series)

Captain Nazi

Captain Marvel's foe during World War II (comic books)

Captain Nemo

Captain of the submarine "Nautilus" (Jules Verne's *Twenty Thousand Leagues Under the Sea*). He also appears in *The Mysterious Island*

Captain Nice

Secret identity of Carter Nash (TV series "Captain Nice")

Captain (Christopher) Pike

First commander of the starship "Enterprise": played by Jeff Hunter. James T. Kirk, played by William Shatner, was the second (TV series "Star Trek")

Captain Queeg

Captain of U.S.S. "Caine" (Herman Wouk's *The Caine Mutiny*): played in 1954 movie by Humphrey Bogart

Captain Smollett

Captain of the "Hispanola" (Robert Louis Stevenson's *Treasure Island*)

Captain Sparks

Fighter pilot with whom Little Orphan Annie flew (radio serial)

Captain Herr Thiele

Captain of the "Vera" (Katherine Anne Porter's *Ship of Fools*)

Captain (Adam) Troy

Captain of the yacht "Tiki" (TV series "Adventures in Paradise"): played by Gardner McKay

Captain Van Straaten

Captain of the ship "The Flying Dutchman," condemned to wander forever on the oceans of the world

Captain (Edward Fairfax "Starry") Vere

Commanding officer of H.M.S. "Indomitable" upon which Billy Budd was foretopman (Herman Melville's *Billy Budd, Foretopman*)

Capulet

Juliet's family name (Shakespeare's *Romeo and Juliet*)

Car 54

Police officers Toody and Muldoon's police car (TV series "Car 54, Where Are You?")

Carabas, Marquis de

Puss in Boots' master

Carlisle
>   Government Indian college in Pennsylvania for which Jim
>   Thorpe played football on teams coached by Glenn "Pop"
>   Warner

Caroline
>   Air Force One's nickname under President John F. Kennedy

Caractacus Pott
>   Driver of "Chitty-Chitty-Bang-Bang"

Carousel Club
>   One of Jack Ruby's two Dallas night clubs

Carpathia
>   British ship that first answered the SOS of the "Titanic"

Carpenters, The
>   Singing team: Karen, Richard

Carry on
>   British movie series: *Carry on Sergeant*, 1958; *Carry on Nurse*,
>   1959; *Carry on Constable*, 1960; *Carry on Teacher*, 1961; *Carry
>   on Regardless*, 1961; *Carry on Admiral*, 1961; *Carry on Cruising*,
>   1962; *Carry on T. V.*, 1963; *Carry on Venus*, 1964; *Carry on Spy-
>   ing*, 1965; *Carry on Cleo*, 1965; *Carry on Cabby*, 1967; *Carry on
>   Jack; Carry on Cowboy; Carry on Screaming; Carry on Doctor;
>   Carry on Up the Khyber; Carry on Camping*, 1972; *Carry on
>   Again Doctor*

Carvel
>   Andy Hardy's hometown

Casa Loma Orchestra
>   Glen Gray's orchestra

Casey Jones
>   Folksong hero, based on accounts of John Luther Jones

Casper
>   The friendly ghost (TV/comic book series)

Catfish Row
>   Negro living quarters in Charleston, South Carolina (DuBose
>   Heyward's *Porgy* and *Porgy and Bess*)

Catwoman
>   One of Batman's foes (real name: Selina Kyle): on TV played by
>   Julie Newmar and Eartha Kitt

Cavern, The
>   Nightclub in Liverpool, England, where the Beatles were dis-
>   covered by Brian Epstein, 1961

Cavorite
>   Antigravity substance that allows Mr. Cavor's sphere to leave the
>   earth's surface and land on the moon (H. G. Wells' *The First
>   Men in the Moon*, 1901)

Caw-Caw

Jungle Jim's pet crow (movie series "Jungle Jim")

Cecil

The seasick sea serpent, Beanie's friend (hand puppets on TV)

Centillion

One followed by 600 zeros (British) or 300 zeros (American)

Centipede, H.M.S.

First British tank model built during World War I. The designation as a ship was meant to conceal what was essentially a new weapon, first used in 1916

Central City

American town where Barry Allen (The Flash) is a police scientist and super-crimefighter (comic book series). The Spirit also fights crime in Central City

Cerberus

Three-headed dog guarding the gates of Hell (Greek mythology). As one of his labors, Hercules had to bring Cerberus up from Hades

Cermak, Anton J.

Chicago mayor killed by assassin Giuseppe Zangara Feb. 15, 1933, in Miami, Fla. (Bay Front Park), in his attempt to shoot President-elect Franklin D. Roosevelt; Zangara's aim was deflected by Mrs. W. Cross, who yanked at his arm

Certainty, Security and Celerity

Motto of the United States Post Office

Challenger

Mickey Thompson's land speed dragster

Chamberlain, Wilt

Scored 100 points in a single basketball game the night of March 2, 1962, for the Philadelphia Warriors against New York Knicks at Hershey, Pa. Final score: Philadelphia 169; New York 147

Chambers, Marilyn

One-time Ivory soap-box girl who starred in X-rated movie *Behind the Green Door*

Chameleon Boy

Member of the Legion of Super Heroes (comic book character): born on the planet Durla, has the ability to alter his shape (true name: Reep Daggle)

Champion

Gene Autry's horse, star of "The Adventures of Champion" (TV series)

Chan Clan, The

Kids (TV cartoon series): Allen, Flip, Henry, Moon, Nancy, Scooter, Stanley, Susie, Tom

57

Chandu the Magician
>Secret identity of Frank Chandler (radio series)

Chaney, Lon
>"The man of a thousand faces"

Chang and Eng
>Original Siamese twins: born in Siam, May 11, 1811, died 1874 (in pictures of the brothers Eng is on the left, Chang is on the right)

Charlemane
>Lion puppet (TV series "The Morning Show")

Charles Atlas
>Pseudonym of Angelo Siciliano, "world's most perfectly developed man": once a "97-pound weakling"

Charleston Club
>Nightclub where Pinky Pinkham (Dorothy Provine) worked (TV series "The Roaring Twenties")

Charley
>Mr. Magoo's Chinese cook (cartoon)

Charley
>The cougar in Mercury TV advertising (Ford Motor Co.)

Charley
>John Steinbeck's dog (*Travels With Charley*)

Charlie
>Tuna in Star-Kist Tuna TV ads (as his little fish friend says, "But Charlie, they don't want tunas with good taste, they want tunas that taste good")

Charlie Chan
>Chinese detective created by Earl Derr Biggers, but never played in movies by a Chinese
>On radio played by Walter Connolly, Ed Begley, Santos Ortega
>In movies (46 feature pictures) played by George Kuwa (1926), Kamiyama Sojin (1928), E. L. Park (1929), Warner Oland (1931-1937), Sidney Toler (1938-1947), Roland Winters (1947-1952)
>On TV played by J. Carroll Naish (1957-1958)
>Sons played by Keye Luke, Victor Sen Yung, Benson Fong, Layne Tom, Jr., Edwin Luke

Charlie Chicken
>Andy Panda's friend (comic book)

Charlie Chicken's cousins
>He baby-sits for them (comic books): Herman, Sherman, Shiloh

Charlie McCarthy
>Edgar Bergen's principal dummy

Charlie O
>Charles O. Finley's mascot mule (Oakland A's baseball team)

Charlie Weaver
Character played by Cliff Arquette (radio)

Chastity
Daughter of Cher and Sonny Bono

Checkers
Richard M. Nixon's dog (during his 1952 campaign for the vice-presidency)

Cher Ami
World War I carrier pigeon that helped save the Lost Battalion (of the 77th Division), in the battle of the Argonne, October 1918 (she is enshrined in the Smithsonian Institution)

Cherokee
Theme song of Charlie Barnet's band

Chesapeake and Ohio
Railroad for which John Henry worked

Chessie
Cat used in Chesapeake and Ohio Railroad advertising

Chesty Pagett
The Marine Corps' mascot bulldog

Cheta
Tarzan's pet chimpanzee (movies): first appeared in first Weissmuller movie, *Tarzan the Ape Man*, 1931

Chevrolet brothers
Automobile makers: Gaston, Louis

Chicago 7, The
Found innocent of inciting riots during the 1968 Democratic National Convention: Rennie Davis, David Dellinger, John Froines, Tom Hayden, Abbie Hoffman, Jerry Rubin, Lee Weiner

Chi Chi
London Zoo's giant panda (see *An-An*)

Chick Carter
Boy detective, Nick Carter's adopted son (radio series)

Chief Brandon
Police chief (Dick Tracy comic strip)

Chief O'Hara
Mickey Mouse's hometown police chief

Chief O'Hara
Gotham City's police chief (comic book/TV series "Batman")

Chim
Pet chimpanzee of Sheena, Queen of the Jungle (TV series)

Chinese calendar, animal designations

Year of the . . .	Lunar	Gregorian
Tiger	4672	1974
Hare (Rabbit)	4673	1975
Dragon	4674	1976

Year of the . . .	Lunar	Gregorian
Snake (Serpent)	4675	1977
Horse	4676	1978
Sheep (Goat)	4677	1979
Monkey	4678	1980
Rooster	4679	1981
Dog	4680	1982
Pig (Boar)	4681	1983
Rat	4682	1984
Ox	4683	1985

Chingachgook

Hawkeye's companion, father of Uncas (James Fenimore Cooper's *The Last of the Mohicans*)

Chip 'n' Dale

Two cartoon chipmunks (Walt Disney cartoons)

Chipmunks

(Recording voices—speeded up—of David Seville records): Alvin; Simon; Theodore

Chips

First United States sentry dog sent overseas during World War II: awarded Silver Star and Purple Heart

Chisholm Trail

San Antonio, Texas, to Abilene, Kansas: sometimes spelled Chisum Trail

Choo Choo

The Chan Clan's dog (TV cartoon)

Chopper

Dog friend of Yakky Doodle (cartoon character)

Chopper One

Registration number on side of helicopter is N40MC; on the bottom of the helicopter it is N2098 (TV series "Chopper One")

Chopsticks

Theme music of radio series "Stoopnagle and Budd"

Christina

World's second largest yacht, belonging to Aristotle Onassis

Christopher Columbus

Theme song of Fletcher Henderson's orchestra

Christopher Pike, Captain

First commander of the starship "Enterprise" (TV series "Star Trek")

Christopher Robin

Winnie the Pooh's human friend: name of A. A. Milne's son, subject of some of the poems in *When We Were Very Young*

Chub

Horse of Hoss Cartwright (Dan Blocker) (TV series "Bonanza")

Chubby Checker
    Pseudonym of Ernest Evans ("Mr. Twist")

Chumly
    Walrus sidekick of the penguin Tennessee Tuxedo (TV cartoon series "Tennessee Tuxedo and His Tales")

Cicero
    Pseudonym of World War II spy Elyesa Bazna

Cincinnatus
    Ulysses S. Grant's horse

Cindy Bear
    Yogi Bear's girlfriend (cartoons)

Circus Hall of Fame
    Located at Sarasota, Florida

Ciribiribin
    Theme song of Harry James' orchestra

Cisco Kid, The
    Played by Warner Baxter, 1929, 1930, 1931, 1939; Cesar Romero, 1939-41; Gilbert Roland, 1946-47; Duncan Renaldo, 1945-50. Baxter won an Oscar for the part in 1929's *In Old Arizona*

Citation
    First thoroughbred racehorse to win a million dollars

Citizen Kane
    Charles Foster Kane, publisher of the newspaper *Enquirer* (movie *Citizen Kane*): played by Orson Welles

City Slickers, The
    Spike Jones' band

Clampetts
    Family name of the Beverly Hillbillies (TV series)

Clan, The
    Frank Sinatra; Sammy Davis, Jr.; Peter Lawford; Dean Martin; Joey Bishop

Clara Cluck
    Hen in Walt Disney cartoons

Clarabell
    Clown ("Howdy Doody" TV show): played by Bob Keeshan, who later was Captain Kangaroo

Clarabelle
    Cow in Walt Disney cartoons

Clarence
    Cross-eyed lion (TV series "Daktari")

Clark, Dick
    Host (TV series "American Bandstand")

Clark, Jim
    Scottish automobile racer (killed in 1968 crash) who won 7 Grand Prix races in 1963: Belgium, Netherlands, France, Great

Britain, Italy, Mexico, South Africa

Claw, The

Enemy of Mighty Mouse (comic book cartoon)

Cleaver

Family name of Beaver (TV series "Leave It To Beaver"): Beaver played by Jerry Mathers, Wally by Tony Dow, the father by Hugh Beaumont, the mother by Barbara Billingsley

Cleo

Goldfish (cartoon feature movie *Pinocchio*)

Cleo

Basset hound (TV series "The People's Choice," starring Jackie Cooper)

Cleo and Caesar

Early stage names of Cher and Sonny Bono

Clermont

Robert Fulton's steamboat, 1807

Clinton's Folly

The Erie Canal: so called for New York's Governor DeWitt Clinton

Clio

Statuette awarded annually for best TV commercial. In Greek mythology, Clio was the muse of history, or of playing the lyre

Clipper

Sky King's nephew

Clouseau

French police inspector (movies *The Pink Panther, A Shot in the Dark, Inspector Clouseau*): extremely inept

Clyde

Ahab the Arab's camel (novelty song by Ray Stevens)

Clyde Barrow Gang

Clyde Barrow, Bonnie Parker, Buck Barrow, Blanche Barrow, W. D. Jones (in movie *Bonnie and Clyde* he was named C. W. Moss)

Clydesdale

Breed of the horses that pull the St. Louis (Anheuser Busch) float in the Rose Tournament Parade and the Budweiser Beer Wagon in TV commercials

Coach Cleats

Archie Andrews' coach at Riverdale High (comic strip series "Archie")

Coca-Cola

Invented by Dr. John S. Pemberton of Atlanta, Georgia, in 1886

Cochise

Horse of Joe Cartwright (Michael Landon) (TV series "Bonanza")

Coconino County

 Arizona county in which Krazy Kat, Ignatz Mouse, and Offissa Pupp live

Cody, Iron-Eyes

 Cherokee Indian actor, notable for his "one tear" ecology spot on TV

Colada

 El Cid's sword

College Football

 Big Eight Conference
  Colorado Buffaloes
  Iowa State Cyclones
  Kansas Jayhawks
  Kansas State Wildcats
  Missouri Tigers
  Nebraska Cornhuskers
  Oklahoma Sooners
  Oklahoma State Cowboys
 Big Ten Conference
  Illinois Fighting Illini
  Indiana Fighting Hoosiers
  Iowa Hawkeyes
  Michigan Wolverines
  Michigan State Spartans
  Minnesota Gophers
  Northwest Wildcats
  Ohio State Buckeyes
  Purdue Boilermakers
  Wisconsin Badgers

 Pacific Eight
  California Golden Bears
  Oregon Ducks
  Oregon State Beavers
  Southern California Trojans
  Stanford Cardinals
  UCLA Bruins
  Washington Huskies
  Washington State Cougars
 Ivy League
  Brown Bruins
  Columbia Lions
  Cornell Big Red
  Dartmouth Big Green
  Harvard Crimson
  Pennsylvania Red and Blue
  Yale Bulldogs
  Princeton Tigers

College Football Hall of Fame

 Located at Rutgers University, New Brunswick, New Jersey

Collinwood

 Mansion (TV series "Dark Shadows")

Colonel J. T. Hall

 Post commander under whom Sergeant Ernie Bilko (Phil Silvers) served (TV series "You'll Never Get Rich"): played by Paul Ford

Colonel Lemuel Q. Stoopnagle

 Comic figure, Budd's partner: played by F. Chase Taylor

Colonel Sebastian Moran

 Professor Moriarty's partner: "The second most dangerous man in London" ("The Adventure of the Empty House" by A. Conan Doyle)

Colonel Steve Austin

 The "Six Million Dollar Man," a cyborg (TV series starring Lee Majors)

Colonies

Thirteen original (in order of adoption of Constitution):

Delaware, Dec. 7, 1787
Pennsylvania, Dec. 12, 1787
New Jersey, Dec. 18, 1787
Georgia, Jan. 2, 1788
Connecticut, Jan. 9, 1788
Massachusetts, Feb. 6, 1788
Maryland, April 28, 1788
South Carolina, May 23, 1788
New Hampshire, June 21, 1788
   (the 9th and ratifying state)
Virginia, June 25, 1788
New York, July 26, 1788
North Carolina, Nov. 21, 1789
Rhode Island, May 29, 1790

"Colored" Seas

Black (Europe), Red (Asia and Africa), White (Europe), Yellow (Asia)

Colossal Man

Colonel Glen Manning, after he was exposed to atomic radiation (1957 movie *The Amazing Colossal Man*)

Columbia

Apollo 11 command module; landing module was "Eagle"

Columbia

First United States ship to complete a trip around the world (1790). Full-sized replica of this ship sails on Frontierland River, Disneyland

Columbiad

Spaceship (Jules Verne's *From the Earth to the Moon*)

Comanche

Horse of Captain Miles W. Keogh, which was lone survivor of General George Custer's command at the battle of the Little Big Horn

Comet

Superman's super horse

Comet I

World's first commercial jet airliner, 1952

Comic strips and cartoon features

Creator or current artist follows the dash:
Abie the Agent—Harry Hershfield
Ain't It a Grand and Glorious Feelin'?—Clare Briggs
Alley Oop—V. T. Hamlin
Alphonse and Gaston—F. Opper
And Her Name Was Maud—F. Opper

Andy Capp—Smythe
Apartment 3G—Alex Kotzky
Archie—Bob Montana
Barnaby—Crockett Johnson
Barney Google—Billy de Beck
Barney Google and Snuffy Smith—Fred Lasswell
Beetle Bailey—Mort Walker
Believe It or Not?—Robert Ripley
Betty—Russ Westover
Big George—Virgil Partch
Blondie—Chic Young
Bobby Sox—Marty Links
Boner's Ark—Addison
Boob McNutt—Rube Goldberg
Bridge—Clare Briggs
Bringing Up Father—George McManus
Broom Hilda—Russ Myers
Buck Rogers—John Dille, Dick Calkins, and Phil Nowlan
Bungle Family—Harry Tuthill
Buster Brown—R. F. Outcault
Buz Sawyer—Roy Crane
Captain Easy—Roy Crane
Casper Milquetoast—Clare Briggs
Count Screwloose from Toulouse—Milt Gross
Crisis series—Gluyas Williams
Dagwood—Chic Young
Dave's Delicatessen—Milt Gross
Dennis the Menace—Hank Ketcham
Dick Tracy—Chester Gould
Donald Duck—Walt Disney
Doonesbury—G. B. Trudeau
Dowagers—Helen Hokinson
Ella Cinders—Charlie Plumb
Emmy Lou—Marty Links
Fatty Felix—Walt McDougall
Favorite Indoor Sports—T. A. Dorgan
Ferd'nand—Mik
Flappers—John Held, Jr.
Flash Gordon—Alex Raymond
Fliegende Blätter illustrations—Wilhelm Busch (called "father" of comic strip)
Foxy Grandpa—Bunny (Charles E. Schultze)
Fred Basset—Alex Graham
Fritzie Ritz—Ernie Bushmiller
Gasoline Alley—Frank King

Gordo—E. Goetz DePoynt (Gus Arriola)
Gumps, The—Sidney Smith
Hägar the Horrible—Dik Browne
Hairbreadth Harry—C. W. Kahles
Half Hitch—Hank Ketcham
Happy Hooligan—F. B. Opper
Harold Teen—Carl Ed
Hazel—Ted Key
Heart of Juliet Jones—Stan Drake
Henry—Carl Anderson
Hi and Lois—Mort Walker and Dik Browne
Inventions—Rube Goldberg
It Might Have Been Worse—T. E. Powers
It's a Great Life if You Don't Weaken—Gene Byrnes
Joe and Asbestos—Ken Kling
Joe Palooka—Ham Fisher
Katzenjammer Kids—Rudolph Dirks; also later H. H. Knerr
Keeping Up with the Joneses—Momand
Kelly—Jack Moore
Krazy Kat—George Herriman
Li'l Abner—Al Capp
Little Eve—Lolita
Little Iodine—Jimmy Hatlo
Little Jimmy—James Swinnerton
Little King—Otto Soglow
Little Lulu—Marge
Little Nemo—Winsor McCay
Little Orphan Annie—Harold Gray
Mandrake the Magician—Lee Falk and Phil Davis
Mark Trail—Ed Dodd
Mary Worth—Allen Saunders
Metropolitan Movies—Denys Wortman
Mickey Mouse—Walt Disney
Mighty Mouse—Paul Terry
Miss Peach—Mell Lazarus
Mister Magoo—U. P. A.
Mr. and Mrs.—Clare Briggs
Moon Mullins—Frank Willard
Mutt and Jeff—Bud Fisher
Nebbs—Sol Hess and W. A. Carlson
Nize Baby—Milt Gross
Our Boarding House—William Freyse
Out Our Way—J. R. Williams
Peanuts—Charles Schulz
Peter Rabbit—Harrison Cady

Phantom, The—Lee Falk
Pogo—Walt Kelly
Polly and Her Pals—Cliff Sterrett
Popeye—Elzie Segar
Prince Valiant—Hal Foster
Red Ryder—Fred Harman
Rex Morgan, M.D.—Bradley and Edgington
Sad Sack—George Baker
Skippy—Percy Crosby
Small Fry—William Steig
Smilin' Jack—Zack Mosley
Smitty—Walter Berndt
Smokey Stover—Bill Holman
Steve Canyon—Milton Caniff
Steve Roper—Saunders and Overgard
Strange As It Seems—Elsie Hix
Superman—Jerry Siegel and Joe Shuster
Sweetie Pie—Seltzer
Tarzan—Harold Foster
Terry & The Pirates—Milton Caniff
That's What They All Say—T. A. Dorgan
They'll Do It Every Time—Jimmy Hatlo
Thrill That Comes Once in a Lifetime—H. T. Webster
Tillie the Toiler—Russ Westover
Timid Soul—H. T. Webster
Toonerville Folks—Fontaine Fox
Toonerville Trolley—Fontaine Fox
Toots and Casper—Jimmy Murphy
Tumbleweeds—Lom K. Ryan
Us Moderns—Fred Neher
When a Feller Needs a Friend—Clare Briggs
Winnie Winkle—M. M. Branner
Wizard of Id—Parker and Hunt
Woody Woodpecker—Walter Lantz
Yellow Kid—R. F. Outcault

Commandant Klink

Commander of Stalag 13 (TV series "Hogan's Heroes"): played by Werner Klemperer

Commander Caractacus Pott

Driver of the car "Chitty-Chitty-Bang-Bang" (children's story by Ian Fleming): played by Dick Van Dyke in 1968 movie

Commando Cubs

Featured in the comic book series: Ace Browning, Horace Cosgrove II, Pokey Jones, Spud O'Shea, Whizzer Malarkey

Commissioner Cary
    Captain Video's boss (TV series "Captain Video")
Commissioner Gordon
    Police commissioner of Gotham City (TV series "Batman")
Commissioner Weston
    Police commissioner (radio series "The Shadow")
Commodore Nutt
    George W. Morrison, best man to General Tom Thumb (Charles
    Sherwood Stratton) at his wedding to Lavinia Warren (Mercy
    Lavinia Bump) in 1863. Tom Thumb was 36 inches tall, and
    Commodore Nutt 29 inches tall
Concorde
    England and France's joint supersonic airliner (SST)
Conelrad
    Control of Electromagnetic Radiation (640 and 1240 AM on
    radio dial): now obsolete civil defense measure
Confederate States

State	Date of Secession	Readmitted to Union
South Carolina	Dec. 20, 1860	June 25, 1868
Mississippi	Jan. 9, 1861	Feb. 23, 1870
Florida	Jan. 10, 1861	June 25, 1868
Alabama	Jan. 11, 1861	June 25, 1868
Georgia	Jan. 19, 1861	(1) June 25, 1868
		(2) July 15, 1870
Louisiana	Jan. 26, 1861	June 25, 1868
Texas	Feb. 1, 1861	March 30, 1870
Virginia	April 17, 1861	Jan. 26, 1870
Tennessee	May 6, 1861	July 24, 1866
Arkansas	May 7, 1861	June 22, 1868
North Carolina	May 20, 1861	June 25, 1868

Congressional Medal of Honor
    Authorized by joint resolution of Congress, July 12, 1862
    First awarded to the six Union soldiers who hijacked the Con-
    federate locomotive "The General"
    Awarded to both General Arthur MacArthur and General Doug-
    las MacArthur (father and son)
Connors, Chuck
    American actor (real name: Kevin Joseph Connor) in movies and
    TV (series: Branded, The Rifleman, Cowboy in Africa, Thrill
    Seekers). He played briefly for Brooklyn Dodgers (1949) and was
    first baseman for much of the 1951 season with the Chicago
    Cubs. He played basketball in the BAA 1946-1948.
Conquistador
    Pablito's horse (Walt Disney movie *The Littlest Outlaw*)

Conrad, William
> Played Marshal Matt Dillon (radio's "Gunsmoke")
> Played Cannon, private eye (TV series)

Conrad Birdie
> Rock 'n' roll star (movie *Bye Bye Birdie*)

Constantinople
> Former name for Istanbul (Turkey)

Contest
> On radio's "Truth or Consequences"

Clue	*Celebrity*
Miss Hush	Clara Bow
Mr. Hush	Jack Dempsey
The Walking Man	Jack Benny

Continents
> Africa, Antarctica, Asia, Australia, Europe, North America, South America

Control Agents
> Good guys (TV series "Get Smart"): Chief, Edward Platt; Agent 86 (Maxwell Smart), Don Adams; Agent 99, Barbara Feldon

Cookie
> Dagwood and Blondie's daughter

Cookie Bear
> Comedy bear (TV's "Andy Williams Show")

Copenhagen
> Duke of Wellington's horse

Copyright
> Good for 28 years with renewal for 28 years (U.S. statute). Foreign copyright usually runs for 50 years after the author's death

Cora
> Mr. Dithers' wife ("Blondie" series)

Corky
> Circus boy (TV series "Circus Boy"): played by Mickey Dolenz, later of the Monkees

Cornelius, Don
> Host of TV show "Soul Train"

Cornfield County (also **Kornfield Kounty**)
> Setting for TV series "Hee Haw"

Corvette
> Automobile in which Tod Stiles (Martin Milner) and Buz Murdock (George Maharis) or Linc Case (Glenn Corbett) tour the country (TV series "Route 66")

Cosby Kids, The
> Bill Cosby's cartoon gang: Fat Albert, Russell (Bill's brother), Dumb Donald, Rudy, Mushmouth, Weird Harold, Bucky

Cosmic Boy

    True name is Rokk Krinn, born on the planet Braal, member of the Legion of Super-Heroes (comic book character)

Cosmo Topper

    Central character of Thorne Smith's novel *Topper:* played in movies by Roland Young (3 pictures); played on TV by Leo G. Carroll

Cosmopolitan

    Magazine primarily for women, first to feature a nude male (Burt Reynolds) in a centerfold, under editorship of Helen Gurley Brown

Costello, Lou

    Chubby actor (1906-1959), member of the comedy team of Abbott and Costello: real name Louis Francis Cristillo. He made one picture without Abbott: *The 30-Foot Bride of Candy Rock*

Cotton Blossom

    Floating theater run by Captain Andy Hawks and his wife Parthenia (Edna Ferber's *Show Boat*)

Counterspy

    David Harding, head of fictional U.S. organization (radio): played by Don MacLaughlin

Country Music Hall of Fame

    First three members elected: Jimmy Rodgers, Hank Williams, Fred Rose

Country and western bands

Lead Artist	Group
Johnny Cash	Tennessee Three
Merle Haggard	Strangers
Tom T. Hall	Storytellers
Waylon Jennings	Waylors
Bill Monroe	Blue Grass Boys
Buck Owens	Buckaroos/Bakersfield Brass
Ray Price	Cherokee Cowboys
Jim Reeves	The Blue Boys
Hank Thompson	Brazos Valley Boys
Ernest Tubb	Texas Troubadours
Porter Wagoner	Wagonmasters
Hank Williams	Drifting Cowboys
Bob Wills	Texas Playboys

County General Hospital

    Hospital in which Ben Casey works (TV series "Ben Casey")

Courser

    Captain Stormalong's ship, biggest ship ever built (American folklore)

Coventry
   English town through which Lady Godiva made her famous ride

Cowboys, The
   TV series: Jimmy (Sean Kelly); Weedy Fimps (Clay O'Brien);
   Homer (Kerry MacLane); Hardy (Mitch Brown); Slim (Robert
   Carradine); Cimarron (A. Martinez); Steve (Clint Howard)

Crab Key
   Island retreat of Dr. No (James Bond adventure "Dr. No" by Ian
   Fleming)

Crabbe, Clarence Linden "Buster"
   American athlete, winner of 400-meter swim in 1932 Los Angeles
   Olympics (only U.S. victory in men's swimming)
   Played in movie serials: Buck Rogers, Captain Silver, Flash Gor-
   don, Mighty Phunda, Red Barry, Tarzan
   On TV he played Captain Gallant

Creedence Clearwater Revival
   Rock 'n' roll group: John Fogerty, Tom Fogerty, Doug Clifford,
   Stuart Cook

Crime Doctor
   Dr. Benjamin Ordway (radio series, 1940 and after, by Max Mar-
   cin): played by Ray Collins, House Jameson, Everett Sloane, and
   John McIntire.
   Dr. Robert Ordway (movie series, 1943-49): played by Warner
   Baxter

Croatoan
   Last message of the Lost Colony of Roanoke Island, Virginia,
   1587-91. It was carved on a doorpost but no trace was found of
   the 140 colonists

Crooper, Illinois
   Fictional town, 40 miles from Peoria, that was the locale of the
   radio serial "Vic and Sade"

Cuckoo Song
   Laurel and Hardy's theme song

Cumberland Road
   First federal highway

Curtiss
   Company producing Baby Ruth and Butterfinger candy bars

Cutty Sark
   19th-century American clipper ship that established a speed
   record on a run from China to England: last of the tea clippers

Cyclops
   One-eyed giants of Greek mythology and legend. Their king,
   Polyphemus, was blinded and fooled by Odysseus. In early myth,
   there are three: Arges, Brontes, Steropes

D

D. B. Cooper
Pseudonym of successful skyjacker who parachuted from airliner with $200,000 in 1971

D-Day Invasion beaches
Operation Overlord (June 6, 1944) in Normandy, France
American: Omaha, Utah
British/Canadian: Sword, Juno, Gold

Dafoe, Alan Roy
Doctor who delivered the Dionne quintuplets

Dagora
Space monster (Japanese movie, 1965)

Dagwood Bumstead
Blondie's husband: he works for Mr. Dithers

Daily Planet
Newspaper in the city of Metropolis for which Clark Kent (Superman), Jimmy Olsen, Lois Lane, and Perry White worked (originally it was called the *Daily Star*)

Daily Sentinel
Newspaper published by Britt Reid (The Green Hornet)

Daisy
Dagwood and Blondie's dog

Daisy
Trade name of popular air rifle, "the" BB gun

Daisy Duck
Donald Duck's girlfriend

Daisy Duck's nieces
April, May, and June

Daisy Mae
Li'l Abner's wife, maiden name, Scraggs: in stage musical played by Edie Adams

Dale Arden
Flash Gordon's girlfriend

Dan Briggs
Original chief agent (TV series "Mission Impossible"): played by Stephen Hill

Daniel
Caine's brother (TV series "Kung Fu"): Caine is in search of him in each episode

Danny Boy
Danny Thomas' theme song

Dapple
Sancho Panza's donkey (Cervantes' *Don Quixote*)

Dapsang

K2, mountain in Karakoram range

Dare, Virginia

First white child of English parents (William and Eleanor White Dare) born in the New World, Roanoke Island 1587

Darling

Family name of children who were Peter's friends (James M. Barrie's *Peter Pan*): John, Michael, Wendy

David St. John

A pseudonym of E. Howard Hunt_

Davis Cup

Trophy awarded since 1900 to the country whose team wins the International Lawn Tennis Championship

Dawes, William

Rode along with Paul Revere and Samuel Prescott in warning the colonists of the British advance on Concord (April 18, 1775)

Day

Family of Clarence Day, depicted by him in several books, including *Life with Father*, 1935: later popular on stage, in movies, on TV. Father was played, respectively, by Howard Lindsay, William Powell, and Leon Ames

Day of Infamy

December 7, 1941, when Pearl Harbor was attacked

De Marco Sisters

Singing group: Lily, Mary, Ann

De Salvo, Albert

Self-confessed "Boston Strangler"

Dead End Kids

Acting group originally appearing in *Dead End* on the stage (1935) and in the motion picture (1937): Billy Halop (Tommy); Huntz Hall (Dippy); Bobby Jordan (Angel); Leo Gorcey (Spit); Gabriel Dell (T.B.)

Bernard Punsley (Milty) joined the group in the movie

The Dead End Kids broke up in 1939, the Bowery Boys going to Monogram, the Little Tough Guys to Universal

Dead Man's hand

Aces and eights, poker hand held by Wild Bill Hickok when shot and killed by Jack McCall, Deadwood, Dakota Territory, August 2, 1876

Dean, James

American movie star (1931-1955): real name: James Byron. His movies: *Sailor Beware*, 1951; *Fixed Bayonets*, 1951; *Has Anybody Seen My Gal?*, 1952; *East of Eden*, 1955; *Rebel Without a Cause*, 1955; *Giant*, 1956

Biographical movie: *The James Dean Story* (1957) using Dean film clips

Dean Brothers

Baseball pitchers with St. Louis Cardinals: Paul (Daffy) and Jerome Herman or sometimes Jay Hanna (Dizzy)

Death Valley Days

Hosts on TV series: The Old Ranger (Stanley Andrews), Ronald Reagan, Dale Robertson, Robert Taylor

Decathlon

Olympic Event:

100-meter dash	110-meter dash
Long jump	Discus throw
16-pound shot put	Pole vault
High jump	Javelin throw
400-meter dash	1500-meter run

December 25, 1900

Birth date of Humphrey Bogart according to Warner Brothers publicists, with the implication that anyone born on Christmas Day can't be a real villain (Bogart's actual birth date was January 23, 1899)

Deep Forest

Theme song of Earl Hines' band

Deimos and Phobos

The two moons of Mars

Delaware

The first state of the United States (first state to ratify the Constitution, December 7, 1787)

Demara, Ferdinand Waldo, Jr.

Known as the Great Imposter because of his assuming a number of different identities

Denny

Bulldog Drummond's assistant

Derek

Flint's first name (1966 movie *Our Man Flint*)

Desert Fox, The

Nickname of German general Erwin Rommel (1891-1944)

Desire

Streetcar terminus in the city of New Orleans; hence *A Streetcar Named Desire*, play by Tennessee Williams

Desmond

Valet of detective Rip Kirby (comic book series "Rip Kirby")

Destroyer, The

Ex-cop Remo Williams who was framed for murder (novel series by Richard Sapir and Warren Murphy)

Detectives of fiction

Character	Author
Arsène Lupin	Maurice Leblanc
Bertha Cool	A. A. Fair (Erle Stanley Gardner)
Boston Blackie	Jack Boyle
Bulldog Drummond	Herman Cyril McNeile ("Sapper")
Charlie Chan	Earl Derr Biggers
Dick Tracy	Chester Gould
Doc Savage	Kenneth Robeson
Dr. Gideon Fell	John Dickson Carr
Ellery Queen	Ellery Queen (Frederic Dannay and Manfred Lee)
Hercule Poirot	Agatha Christie
Inspector Javert	Victor Hugo
Inspector Maigret	Georges Simenon (Georges Sim)
James Bond	Ian Fleming
Jane Marple	Agatha Christie
John J. Malone	Craig Rice
Lew Archer	Ross Macdonald
Mack Bolan	Don Pendleton
Martin Kane	Ted Hediger
Michael Lanyard (The Lone Wolf)	Louis Joseph Vance
Michael Shayne	Brett Halliday (Davis Dresser)
Mike Hammer	Mickey Spillane
Mike Waring (The Falcon)	Michael Arlen
Mr. Moto	John Phillips Marquand
Mr. & Mrs. North (Jerry and Pamela North)	Richard and Francis Lockridge
Nero Wolfe	Rex Stout
Nick Carter	John Russell Coryell
Nick Charles	Dashiell Hammett
Parker Pyne	Agatha Christie
Perry Mason	Erle Stanley Gardner
Pete Chambers	Henry Kane
Peter Gunn	Henry Kane
Peter Wimsey (Lord Peter Death Bredon Wimsey)	Dorothy Sayers
Philip Marlowe	Raymond Chandler
Philo Vance	S. S. Van Dine (Willard Huntington Wright)
Reggie Fortune	Henry Christopher Bailey

Remo Williams (The Destroyer)	Richard Sapir and Warren Murphy
Richard Henry Benson (The Avenger)	Kenneth Robeson
Sam Spade	Dashiell Hammett
Scott Jordan	Harold Q. Masur
Sergeant Cuff	Wilkie Collins
Shell Scott	Richard S. Prather
Sherlock Holmes	Arthur Conan Doyle
Simon Templar (The Saint)	Leslie Charteris
Sir Henry Merrivale	John Dickson Carr
Thatcher Colt	Anthony Abbott
Thinking Machine (Prof. S.F.X. Van Dusen)	Jacques Futrelle
Tommy Hambledon	Manning Coles
Travis McGee	John D. MacDonald

Devil

The Phantom's pet wolf (comic strip)

Devil and Daniel Webster, The

Stephen Vincent Benét story filmed (1941) as *All That Money Can Buy*

Dewey Defeats Truman

Election night headline of the Chicago *Tribune* 1948: actually Truman defeated Dewey

Diablo

Cisco Kid's horse

Diamond

Sir Isaac Newton's dog

Diamond Jim

Nickname of New York financier James Buchanan Brady (1856-1917)

Diamond Lil

Play (1928) by Mae West, adapted by her as the movie *She Done Him Wrong* (1933) in which she played Lady Lou

Dick Tracy

Comic strip detective created (1931) by Chester Gould, later on radio and TV and in movie serials

Dick West

The Range Rider's partner (TV series)

Dig 'Em

Cartoon frog advertising Kellogg's Sugar Smacks

Digger O'Dell

The Friendly Undertaker, a character in "The Life of Riley," played by John Brown on radio: "You're looking fine, Riley, very natural"

DiMaggio, Joe

Hit safely in 56 consecutive games for New York Yankees, beginning May 15 and ending July 17, 1941: stopped by Al Smith and Jim Bagby of Cleveland Indians

DiMaggio brothers

Baseball players: Vincent Paul (born 1912), Joseph Paul (born 1914), Dominic Paul (born 1918)

Ding-a-Ling

Hokey Wolf's small buddy (Hanna-Barbera cartoon)

Dingbat

Nickname used by Archie Bunker (Carroll O'Connor) for his wife Edith (Jean Stapleton) (TV series "All in the Family")

Dino

The Flintstones' dinosaur pet (TV cartoon series)

Dino's

Restaurant located at 77 Sunset Strip where "Kookie" (Edd Byrnes) parked cars (TV series "77 Sunset Strip")

Dionne Quintuplets

Born May 28, 1934, to Oliva and Elzire Dionne of Callander, Ontario: Annette, Cecile, Emilie, Marie, Yvonne. Doctor Alan Roy Dafoe delivered the babies

Dipsy Doodle

Theme song of Larry Clinton's orchestra

Dirty Dozen, The

Movie (1967) directed by Robert Aldrich. The dozen were: Victor Franko (John Cassavetes); Joseph Wladislaw (Charles Bronson); Robert Jefferson (Jim Brown); Archer Maggott (Telly Savalas); Vernon Pinkley (Donald Sutherland); Samson Posey (Clint Walker); Pedro Jiminez (Trini Lopez); Milo Vladek (Tom Busby); Glenn Gilpin (Ben Carruthers); Roscoe Lever (Stuart Cooper); Seth Sawyer (Colin Maitland); Tassos Bravos (Al Mancini)

Discovery

Spaceship (movie *2001: A Space Odyssey*)

Disney, Walt

Won 51 Oscars

Disneyland

Located in Anaheim, California: Adventureland; Fantasyland; Frontierland; Tomorrowland

Disneyworld

Located near Orlando, Florida

Dithers

Family name of Dagwood Bumstead's boss (Julius) and his wife (Cora)

Ditto
> Hi and Lois's son (comic strip)

Dixie
> Composed by Daniel Decatur Emmett 1859

Dixie Cup
> Contained ice cream; lid had pictures of Hollywood movie stars

Doby, Lawrence Eugene (Larry)
> First Negro player in American League (outfielder with Cleveland Indians, 1947)

Doc Gamble
> Visitor at 79 Wistful Vista (radio's "Fibber McGee and Molly"): played by Arthur Q. Bryan

Doc Holliday
> James Henry Holliday

Doc Savage
> Clark Savage, Jr., pulp magazine hero created by Kenneth Robeson, pen name of Lester Dent and others

Doc Savage's crew
> Brigadier General Theodore Morley Brooks (Ham); William Harper Littlejohn; Lieutenant Colonel Andrew Blodgett Mayfair (Monk); Colonel John Renwick (Renny); Major Thomas J. Roberts (Long Tom)

Doctor Ben Casey
> Neurosurgeon (TV series): played by Vincent Edwards. Dr. Zorba (Sam Jaffe) is his superior

Doctor Chegley
> Doctor for whom Julia (Diahann Carroll) works (TV series "Julia"): played by Lloyd Nolan

Doctor Christian
> Paul Christian, M.D., of Rivers End, Minn., played by Jean Hersholt (movies and radio)

Doctor Cobra
> Villain who supposedly killed Denny Colt by throwing chemicals on him (comic book series "The Spirit")

Doctor Fate
> Secret identity of Kent Nelson (comic books)

Doctor (Gideon) Fell
> Detective created by John Dickson Carr

Doctor (Victor) Frankenstein
> Creator of the monster that came to be known as "The Frankenstein Monster": from Mary Wollstonecraft Shelley's novel *Frankenstein* (1816). In the 1931 movie, directed by James Whale, Colin Clive played Dr. Henry Frankenstein and Boris Karloff, made up by Jack Pierce, was the Monster

Doctor Fu Manchu

Oriental villain created by Sax Rohmer (Arthur Sarsfield Ward) in 14 novels (1913-1957): played in movies by Warner Oland, Boris Karloff, Henry Brandon, and Christopher Lee. On radio the role was originated by Arthur Hughes

Doctor Gillespie

Mentor of Dr. Kildare, Leonard Gillespie, M.D., played by Lionel Barrymore (movies). After 1942, Dr. Gillespie was the central character of the series

On TV Raymond Massey and Gary Merrill played the part

Dr. Huer

Buck Roger's sidekick (radio and comic strip): played on radio by Edgar Stehli

Doctor I. Q.

Lew Valentine, Jimmy McClain, Stanley Vainrib (radio quizmaster): program sponsored by Mars candy bars

Doctor (Sean) Jamison

Children's doctor (TV series "The Little People"): played by Brian Keith. His daughter, played by Shelley Fabares, is also Dr. Jamison

Dr. Jekyll

Henry Jekyll, the "good" side (Robert Louis Stevenson's *Dr. Jekyll and Mr. Hyde*)

Doctor Joe Gannon

Played by Chad Everett (TV series "Medical Center")

Doctor Kildare

James Kildare, first played by Joel McCrea and then by Lew Ayres (movies) and Richard Chamberlain and Mark Jenkins (TV). Dr. Kildare worked at Blair General Hospital

Doctor (Steven) Kiley

Dr. Marcus Welby's assistant (TV series "Marcus Welby, M.D."): played by James Brolin

Doctor Konrad Styner

Medical doctor (TV series "Medic"): played by Richard Boone

Dr. No

Villainous opponent of James Bond (Ian Fleming's *Dr. No*): played in movie by Joseph Wiseman

Doctor Petrie

Companion of Scotland Yard's Sir Dennis Nayland Smith (Fu Manchu novel and movie series): first name in movies variously John, Jack, Walter

Doctor Richard Kimble

Fugitive (TV series "The Fugitive"): played by David Janssen. For five seasons he avoided Inspector Gerard, seeking him for supposedly killing his wife, Helen

Doctor Rossi
> Doctor (TV series "Peyton Place"): played by Ed Nelson

Dr. Seuss
> Pseudonym of children's author Theodor Seuss Geisel

Doctor Sivana
> World's maddest mad scientist, Captain Marvel's enemy (comic books)

Doctor Strangelove
> "Or, How I Learned To Stop Worrying and Love the Bomb" (subtitle of movie). The part of Dr. Strangelove, as well as President Muffley and Group Captain Mandrake, was played by Peter Sellers

Doctor Watson
> John Watson, Sherlock Holmes' assistant

Doctor (Marcus) Welby
> General practitioner (TV series "Marcus Welby, M.D."): played by Robert Young

Doctor (Hans) Zarkoff
> Flash Gordon's companion

Doctor Zorba
> Senior to Dr. Ben Casey (TV series "Ben Casey"): played by Sam Jaffe

Dodd, Jimmy
> Host of the Mickey Mouse Club (TV)

Dodge brothers
> Automobile makers: Horace, John

Dodge City
> Setting for TV series "Gunsmoke"

Dogpatch
> Li'l Abner's hometown, apparently somewhere in the Kentucky mountains

Doll Man
> Darrell Dane, member of the Justice League of America (comics)

Dolly
> Old whaling ship that brought the crew to the island of Nukuheva. The whaler "Julia" rescues Tommo (Melville) and Karakoee from the island (Herman Melville's *Typee*)

Dolly sisters
> Jeannie and June

Don Winslow's creed
> Winslow of the Navy (comic strip by Lt. Cdr. Frank V. Martinek, and then radio).
> On radio: "I consecrate my life to peace and to the protection of all my countrymen wherever they may be. My battle against Scorpia represents the battle between Good and Evil. Never will I

enter into any jingoistic proposition, but will devote my entire life to protecting my country. The whole purpose of my life is that of promoting peace—not war. I will work in the interests of peace and will promote the fulfillment of all things that are clean, wholesome, and upright. Join me not alone in observing this creed, but likewise be patriotic. Love your country, its flag, and all the things for which it stands. Follow the advice of your parents and superiors and help someone every day."

Donald Duck's
Nephews
Huey, Dewey, Louie
Voice
Clarence Nash

Doodyville
Home of Howdy Doody and his friends (TV)

Dopey
Only one of the seven dwarfs that does not have a beard (Walt Disney cartoon feature movie *Snow White and the Seven Dwarfs*)

Dow-Jones
Index of N.Y. Stock Exchange market level, comprising prices of 30 high-ranking industrial stocks, added and multiplied by a variable factor based on total shares

Downing Street
10—Home of British Prime Minister
11—Home of Chancellor of the Exchequer
12—Home of Government Chief Whip

Dracula movies
Nosferatu (German), 1923
Dracula, 1931
Dracula's Daughter, 1936
Son of Dracula, 1943
Return of the Vampire, 1944
House of Dracula, 1945
The House of Frankenstein, 1945
Abbott and Costello Meet Frankenstein, 1948
Blood of Dracula, 1957
The Return of Dracula, 1958
The Horror of Dracula, 1959
The Curse of Dracula, 1959
Brides of Dracula, 1960
Kiss of the Vampire, 1963
Billy the Kid Meets Dracula, 1965
Dracula Prince of Darkness, 1965
Dracula Has Risen from the Grave, 1968
Son of Dracula, 1974

Dragnet

Sergeant Joe Friday played by Jack Webb (radio and TV)

First TV series:

Frank Smith played by Ben Alexander

Second TV series:

Bill Gannon played by Harry Morgan

Theme music written by Walter Schumann

As part of wrap-up: "The story you have just heard is true. Only the names have been changed to protect the innocent."

Dragon Lady

Lai Choi San, Terry's foe ("Terry and the Pirates")

Dreadnought, H.M.S.

First heavy battleship in British Navy, launched 1906: 11-inch armor, ten 12-inch guns

Britain's first nuclear submarine

For a time, even until after World War I, "dreadnought" was a synonym for all heavily armed, heavily armored battleships

Dreyfus, Alfred

French military officer, convicted unjustly. Inmate of Devil's Island Penal Colony (1895)

Drifters, The

Rock 'n' roll singing group. Among the lead singers were: Clyde McPhatter, Bobby Hendricks, Ben E. King

Droodles

Simplified, abstract drawings: created by Roger Price

DRUNKY

Dean Martin's California automobile license plate

Duckburg

City where Donald Duck and his nephews, Scrooge McDuck, Daisy, etc., live

Dudley Do-right

Canadian Mounted Policeman who is like his name (comics). His commander is Inspector Fenwick

Dudley Nightshade

Crusader Rabbit's foe (TV cartoon series)

Duesenberg brothers

Automobile builders: August and Frederick S.

Duke

Tim Holt's horse

Duke

Kelly's dog (comic strip "Kelly")

Duke

Penrod's dog (Booth Tarkington's *Penrod*)

Duke and Turk

Dogs (Johann Rudolf Wyss's novel *Swiss Family Robinson*)

Duke of Wellington
  Arthur Wellesley (1769-1852), defeated Napoleon at Waterloo, Belgium, June 18, 1815

Dumbo
  Flying elephant (Disney cartoon feature picture)

Duncan, Lee
  Original owner and trainer of Rin-Tin-Tin

Durham, North Carolina
  Locale of the wartime 1942 Rose Bowl Game, between Oregon State (20) and Duke (16): only Rose Bowl game not played in Pasadena, California

Duchess, The
  Housemaid of Painted Valley Ranch, home of Red Ryder and Little Beaver

Dynamite
  Wild stallion that Spin and Marty try to capture (Mickey Mouse Club Spin and Marty episodes)

E

11
  Players on a cricket, soccer, or football team

18
  Football jersey worn by Sally (Mrs. McMillan) (TV series "McMillan and Wife"). The number is that of Gene Washington of the San Francisco 49'ers

80
  Victories credited to "The Red Baron," Manfred von Richtofen, World War I German ace: highest total of any flier in that war

87
  "Fourscore and seven," the number of years mentioned in the opening of Abraham Lincoln's Gettysburg Address: reference is to 1776

87th Precinct
  New York police precinct in which Detective Steve Carella works (novel/story series by Ed McBain)

88
  Keys (black and white) on a piano

88
  Number of consecutive basketball games won by UCLA Bruins, Jan. 24, 1971, to Jan. 29, 1974

802,701 A.D.
> Final year arrived at by the Time Traveler (H. G. Wells' *The Time Machine*)

E Pluribus Unum
> Motto ("Out of many, one") on Great Seal of the United States: adopted June 20, 1782. The national motto is "In God We Trust"

Eagle
> Apollo 11 lunar module: "The Eagle has landed"; command module was "Columbia"

Earp brothers
> Wyatt, Virgil, Morgan: Virgil was wounded at the O.K. Corral

East Side Kids
> A group formed from the original Dead End Kids to work at Monogram. See *Bowery Boys*

Eastwood, Clint
> His Italian western movies: *A Fistful of Dollars*, 1964; *For a Few Dollars More*, 1966; *The Good, The Bad and the Ugly*, 1967 (*Hang 'Em High* was made in the U.S.)

Easy Aces
> Radio series starring Goodman and Jane Ace

Easy Company
> Sergeant Rock's Army company (comic book series "Sgt. Rock")

Easy Rider
> Movie (1969) about two motorcycle travelers in search of America: Wyatt or Captain America (Peter Fonda), Billy (Dennis Hopper, who also directed)

Ebbets Field
> Home park, in Flatbush, of the Brooklyn Dodgers

Ebony Express
> Nickname for track star Jesse Owens

Echo 1
> First United States communications (TV) satellite (Telstar 1 was first United States communications satellite to amplify radio/TV signals)

Eddy, Mary Baker
> Founder of Christian Science; author of *Science and Health, with Key to the Scriptures* (1875); organized First Church of Christ, Scientist (Mother Church), Boston (1892)

Ederle, Gertrude
> First woman to swim the English Channel, Aug. 6, 1926

Edie Hart
> Peter Gunn's girlfriend (TV series "Peter Gunn")

Edmond Dantès

The Count of Monte Cristo (the elder Alexandre Dumas' *The Count of Monte Cristo*)

Edsel

Automobile named after Henry Ford's son Edsel Bryant Ford: produced 1957 to 1959 (the 1960 model was produced in 1959)

Edwards, Cliff

Known as Ukulele Ike: as Jiminy Cricket sang "When You Wish upon a Star" (cartoon movie *Pinocchio*)

Eeyore

Winnie the Pooh's donkey friend: likes to eat thistles

Effie Klinker

One of Edgar Bergen's dummies

Effie Perine

Sam Spade's secretary (on radio played by Lurene Tuttle; in 1941 movie *The Maltese Falcon* played by Lee Patrick)

Egypt

Ulysses S. Grant's saddle horse

Eighth Wonder of the World

Billing of Kong as theatrical act (movie *King Kong*)

El Goofo

A nickname of New York Yankees' pitcher Vernon Gomez

El Toro

Kit Carson's partner (TV series "The Adventures of Kit Carson")

Election Day

First Tuesday after the first Monday in November (national)

Elephants

African: large flapping ears; Asian: smaller ears, rounder head

Eliot, T. S.

Poet Thomas Stearns Eliot (1885-1965), born in St. Louis, Mo., lived in England

Elizabeth

Fred Sanford's deceased wife (TV series "Sanford and Son")

Ellery Queen

Pseudonym of Frederic Dannay and Manfred Bennington Lee who wrote the Ellery Queen detective novels

Elm Street

The main street in Peyton Place

Elmer

Original name of puppet Howdy Doody

Elmer

Borden's Milk's bull, who gave his name to Elmer's Glue (or vice versa)

Elmer the Moose
>   One of Paul Bunyan's three dogs (terrier)

Elmer Sneezeweed
>   Dummy of Max Terhune (cowboy ventriloquist in movies). Earlier, in vaudeville, Terhune had called the dummy Skully Null

Elmo
>   Elsie the cow's calf (Borden's Milk)

Elmwood
>   Town that is the locale of the radio serial "Pepper Young's Family"

Eloi
>   The people enslaved by the Morlocks (H. G. Wells' *The Time Machine*)

Elwood
>   The Old Pro's clumsy football player (Falstaff Beer TV cartoon commercial)

Emerald City
>   Home of the Wizard of Oz

Emmy
>   Statuette awarded annually for outstanding TV programs, actors, and technicians (personalization of Immy, for image orthicon, the television camera tube)

Emperor Ming
>   Ming, the Merciless, ruler of the planet Mongo (Flash Gordon's foe): played in movie serials by Charles Middleton

Emperor Norton
>   "Emperor of the United States and Protector of Mexico": self-proclaimed title of Joshua A. Norton (1819-1880), San Francisco rice merchant and local "character"

Endurance
>   Sir Ernest Shackleton's ship (1914-1916) on which he, with a crew of 27, survived for over five months in the Antarctic; the ship sank but the men survived

Engelbert Humperdinck
>   Pseudonym of singer Gerry Dorsey (the original Engelbert Humperdinck wrote the opera *Hansel and Gretel*)

Enola Gay
>   The B-29 that dropped the atomic bomb on Hiroshima, Aug. 6, 1945, piloted by Colonel Paul Tibbets, Jr.

Enquirer
>   Newspaper published by Charles Foster Kane (movie *Citizen Kane*)

Enterprise
>   Riverboat captained by Grey Holden (TV series "Riverboat")

Enterprise, U.S.S.

Federation's United Space Ship, on a five-year mission (TV series "Star Trek"): commanded by Captain James T. Kirk

Enterprise, U.S.S.

First atomic aircraft carrier, commissioned 1961

Epitaphs

Clark Gable: "Back to silents"

William Shakespeare: "Good friend, for Jesus' sake forbear, to dig the dust enclosed here! Blessed be the man that spares these stones, and cursed be he that moves my bones"

Reverend Martin Luther King, Jr.: "Free at last, free at last, thank God Almighty I'm free at last"

W. C. Fields: "On the whole I would rather be in Philadelphia"

George Bernard Shaw: "I knew if I stayed around long enough, something like this would happen"

Epstein, Brian

The Beatles' first manager until his death, August 27, 1967. Also was manager of Gerry and the Pacemakers; Billy J. Kramer and the DaKotas; Bee Gees; Foremosts; Cilla Black

Eric

Code name of Detective Matthew (Matt) Helm

Ericsson, Leif

Son of Eric the Red; discoverer of Vinland (America)

Erik (or Erique) Claudin

Name of the Phantom (movie *Phantom of the Opera*)

Eshlimar, Billie Jean

The wife of singer Hank Williams when he died, January 1953. She was also the wife of singer Johnny Horton when he died, November 1960

Esmeralda

Captain Nemo's pet seal (1954 movie *20,000 Leagues Under the Sea*)

Essanay

Early film company (1909), named from the initials of its founders, G. M. Anderson (Broncho Billy, or Max Aronson) and G. K. Spoor

Eton

James Bond's school (Ian Fleming's novel *You Only Live Twice*)

Euclid

Father of geometry

Eugene the Jeep

Swee' Pea's pet animal (Popeye cartoon)

Evel

Nickname of daredevil stunt rider Robert Craig Knievel

Everly Brothers
>   Singing duet: Don, Phil

Everybody Loves Somebody
>   Dean Martin's theme song

Excalibur
>   King Arthur's sword: obtained either by pulling it out of a stone
>   or from the Lady of the Lake. Arthur could not be wounded as
>   long as he wore the scabbard. The sword is also called Caliburn

Excursion boats
>   Canopied launches that take people through Adventureland
>   (Disneyland): named for the world's waterways—"Magdalena
>   Maiden," "Irrawaddy Maiden," "Congo Queen," "Suwannee
>   Lady," "Orinoco Adventuress," "Zambezi Miss," "Yangtze
>   Lotus," "Nile Princess," "Ucayali Una," "Mekong Maiden,"
>   "Hondo Hattie," "Ganges Gal," "Kissimmee Kate," "Amazon
>   Belle"

Executioner, The
>   Mack Bolan (novel series by Don Pendleton). He is out to destroy
>   the Mafia

Explorer 1
>   United States' first satellite, launched Jan. 31, 1958; it stayed up
>   until March 31, 1970

Extremities
>   50 states:
>>   North—Point Barrow, Alaska
>>   South—South Cape, Hawaii
>>   East—West Quoddy Head, Maine
>>   West—Cape Wrangell on Attu, Alaska
>>   Highest—Mount McKinley, Alaska
>>   Lowest—Death Valley, California
>>   Center—near Castle Rock, South Dakota
>   48 states:
>>   North—Northwesternmost point in Minnesota
>>   South—Key West, Florida
>>   East—West Quoddy Head, Maine
>>   West—Cape Alava, Washington
>>   Highest—Mount Whitney, California
>>   Lowest—Death Valley, California
>>   Center—near Lebanon, Kansas

Eyes and Ears of the World, The
>   Paramount News' motto

F

4

Players on a polo team

4 chaplains

Clergymen aboard the transport U.S.S. "Dorchester" who gave up their life jackets to other soldiers, February 3, 1943: Rabbi Alexander D. Goode, Father John P. Washington, Reverend George L. Fox, Reverend Clark V. Poling

4 Dimensions

Length; width; depth; time

4 Evangelists

Writers of the Gospels in the New Testament: Matthew, Mark, Luke, John

4 Freedoms

Incorporated in speech by Franklin D. Roosevelt in January 6, 1941, message to Congress: Freedom of speech and expression; Freedom of religion; Freedom from want; Freedom from fear

4 Horsemen of the Apocalypse

	Color of horse
Conquest (War)	White
Famine	Black
Pestilence (Slaughter)	Red
Death	Pale

4 Horsemen of Notre Dame

Football backfield from 1922 to Rose Bowl game of 1925: Harry Stuhldreher, quarterback; Don Miller, halfback; Jim Crowley, halfback; Elmer Layden, fullback

4 humors

Black bile, yellow bile, phlegm, blood

4H Club

Motto: "We learn to do by doing"
The four H's: Head, Heart, Hands, Health

5

Minimum number of victories over enemy aircraft to become an ace

5

Number of seconds in which tape will self-destruct (TV series "Mission Impossible")

Five Books of Moses

First five books of the Old Testament: Genesis, Exodus, Leviticus, Numbers, Deuteronomy. These constitute the Torah (Law) of Jewish religion

5 Civilized Tribes

Cherokees, Choctaws, Chickasaws, Creeks, Seminoles

Five Little Peppers and How They Grew

Novel (1881) by Margaret Sidney (pseudonym of Harriett Mulford Stone Lothrop)

The five Pepper children were Ben, Phronsie, Polly, Joel, Davie

5 Nations

Indian tribes also known as the Iroquois League: Seneca, Mohawk, Oneida, Onondaga, Cayuga

Five Pennies

Red Nichols' band

Five Points

Town, locale of radio series "The Guiding Light"

5 Rivers of Hades

In Greek mythology:

Acheron, river of woe

Cocytus, river of lamentation

Lethe, river of oblivion

Phlegethon, river of fire

Styx, river of hate

Five W's

Who . . . What . . . When . . . Where . . . Why

5 years

Length of mission of the U.S.S. "Enterprise": "To explore strange new worlds; to seek out new life and new civilizations; to boldly go where no man has gone before" (TV series "Star Trek")

15 Medals

Awarded to Audie Murphy, most decorated American soldier in World War II (Neville Brand the actor was the fourth most decorated)

40

In the Bible:

It rained for 40 days and 40 nights.

Moses was on the mount 40 days and 40 nights.

Israel spent 40 years in the wilderness.

Elijah spent 40 days and 40 nights in the wilderness.

Jonah gave Nineveh 40 days to repent.

Christ's sojourn in the wilderness was 40 days.

(Lent is also 40 days long)

40

Distance in feet between stakes in horseshoes

Fortymile Creek

Location of Alaskan gold discovery (1886)

41

Age of Delta Dawn, who lives in the town of Brownsville ("Delta Dawn," country and western song)

46

Height in inches of actor Michael Dunn (1935-1973), co-star of 1965 movie *Ship of Fools* (in which he played Glocken)

50

Eggs eaten by Cool Hand Luke in one hour (movie)

52-20 Club

Unemployed GI's after World War II, entitled to $20 a week for 52 weeks

53

Number painted on the side of Herbie the Volkswagen (movie *The Love Bug*)

53⅓

Width in yards of a football field (160 feet)

58

Consecutive shutout innings pitched by Don Drysdale, Los Angeles Dodgers (May 14-June 8, 1968)

59

Elapsed time of a 15-round boxing match:
3-minute rounds = 45 minutes
1 minute between = <u>14 minutes</u>
59 minutes

473FEM

License plate number of the Snoop Sisters' antique automobile (TV series "The Snoop Sisters")

500

Sheets of paper in a ream

500

Hats worn by Bartholomew Cubbins (book by Dr. Seuss, pen name of Theodor Geisel)

511

Games won as a pitcher by Cy Young, 1890-1911. Young pitched 751 complete games in the major leagues

558 DeKoven St.

Address of Mrs. O'Leary's barn. The October 8-9, 1871, Chicago fire began when her cow kicked over a kerosene lantern here: the Chicago Fire Academy is now located at this address

4004 B.C.

Sunday, October 23, the day of the Creation, calculated by Archbishop James Ussher of Armagh, Ireland, and contemporaries (about 1650)

4077th

Mobile Army Surgical Hospital unit (TV series "M*A*S*H")

4,280

Buffaloes killed by William Cody (Buffalo Bill)

4672

Chinese year as of January 23, 1974

$5,000,000

Price United States paid Spain for Florida, 1819

$5,368,709.12

One cent doubled every day for 30 days:

1st day - $.01

2nd day - $.02

3rd day - $.04

4th day - $.08

5th day - $.16, and so on to 30 days

$15,000,000

Price of Louisiana Territory, bought from Napoleon of France by President Jefferson (1803)

53310761

Elvis Presley's Army serial number

Fadda

White mule of Mohammed

Fahrenheit 451

"The temperature at which book paper catches fire, and burns"; novel (1953) by Ray Bradbury

Movie (1966) with Oskar Werner; directed by Francois Truffaut

Fala

President Franklin D. Roosevelt's Scottie dog (Medworth was his other dog)

Falcon, The

Nickname of Mike Waring (radio/TV series "The Falcon"): played by John Calvert

Movie serial detective played by George Sanders (Gay Lawrence) and Tom Conway (Tom Lawrence), who were brothers, and John Calvert

Falconhurst

Maxwell family plantation (Kyle Onstott's *Mandingo* novels)

Falcons

The Air Force's football team

Fang

Phyllis Diller's husband in her comedy routines

Fanny

Boat at Hampton Roads, Virginia, from which John LaMountain, Union aeronaut, ascended in a balloon, August 3, 1861: "Fanny" thus may be called the first aircraft carrier

Fantastic Four, The

Mr. Fantastic, Mr. Reed Richards; Human Torch, Johnny Storm; The Thing, Ben Grimm; Invisible Girl, Sue Masters (comic book series)

Fantasticar

The Fantastic Four's flying vehicle

Farmer in the Dell, The

(children's nursery rhyme)
Heigh-oh, the derry-oh
The Farmer takes a wife
The wife takes the child
The child takes the nurse
The nurse takes the dog
The dog takes the cat
The cat takes the rat
The rat takes the cheese
The cheese stands alone

Farrow, Mia

Actress, daughter of actress Maureen O'Sullivan and director/writer John Farrow (who won Oscar for script of *Around the World in 80 Days*)

Fat Albert

Nickname for the Boeing 737 jet airliner (from a character in "The Cosby Kids")

Fat Man

Name given A-bomb dropped on Nagasaki

Fat Man, The

Nickname of Brad Runyon (radio series "The Fat Man," created by Dashiell Hammett): played by J. Scott Smart (in movies as well). The character is based on Hammett's magazine detective The Continental Op

Fatima

Ahab the Arab's lover (novelty song by Ray Stevens, "Ahab the Arab")

Faust, Frederick Schiller

American writer (1892-1944), especially for pulp magazines and of Western novels under the pen name Max Brand: killed in Italy at age 52 serving as a war correspondent

Fay and Evey

Ma Perkins' daughters (radio show)

Federal Holidays

New Years Day (January 1)
Washington's Birthday (third Monday in February)
Memorial Day (last Monday in May)
Independence Day (July 4)

Labor Day (first Monday in September)
Columbus Day (second Monday in October)
Veterans Day (November 11 or fourth Monday in October)
Thanksgiving Day (fourth Thursday in November)
Christmas (December 25)

Federal penitentiaries

Atlanta, Georgia; Leavenworth, Kansas; Lewisburg, Pennsylvania; McNeil Island, Washington; Marion, Illinois; Terre Haute, Indiana

Federation Cup

Women's parallel to the Davis Cup: national-team championship

Felix the Cat

Newspaper syndicated cartoon character, drawn by Pat Sullivan

Felix Leiter

James Bond's American CIA contact (James Bond novels by Ian Fleming)

Fencing

Three weapons: foil, epee, saber

Ferdinand

Flower-smelling bull in Munro Leaf's book (1936) and later in movie cartoon

Ferdinand

Austrian archduke Francis Ferdinand (1863-1914), nephew of Emperor Francis Joseph of Austria-Hungary, and heir to the throne on the deaths of Rudolph, the crown prince (suicide with Marie Vetsera in 1889), and his father Charles Louis. On June 28, 1914, in Sarajevo, Bosnia, in Serbia, Ferdinand and his wife, Sophie Chotek, Duchess of Hohenberg, were assassinated by Gavrilo Prinzip (or Princip) as they rode in a 1912 Graf und Stift automobile. The unrelieved crisis that resulted ended in mobilization, ultimatum, and within weeks the outbreak of World War I

Ferndale

Captain Roderick Anthony's ship (Joseph Conrad's *Chance*)

Fibber McGee and Molly

Radio comedy starring Jim Jordan as Fibber and Marian Jordan as Molly. Fibber's closet at 79 Wistful Vista and such visitors as Mayor La Trivia, Throckmorton P. Gildersleeve, and Doc Gamble kept the show on the air from 1935 until 1952

Fields, W. C.

Actor and humorist (1879-1946): real name, William Claude Dukinfield

Fiery Furnace

Cast into the furnace (Daniel 3) were Daniel's brothers: Shadrach (Hananiah), Meshach (Mishael), Abednego (Azariah)

Figaro
>   The Barber of Seville (play by Beaumarchais; operas by Mozart, Rossini, Paisiello)

Figaro
>   Gepetto's cat (feature cartoon movie *Pinocchio*)

Fillmore
>   Name of rock 'n' roll auditoriums run by Bill Graham in late 1960's-early 1970's: Fillmore West in San Francisco, Fillmore East in New York City

Fire Chief, The
>   Nickname of Ed Wynn on the Texaco radio show

First Names

Last Name	First Name	Series	Starring
Banacek	Thomas	Banacek	George Peppard
Banyon	Miles	Banyon	Robert Forster
Bronson	Jim	Then Came Bronson	Michael Parks
Burke	Amos	Burke's Law	Gene Barry
Cade	Sam	Cade's County	Glenn Ford
Cain	Nicholas	Cain's Hundred	Mark Richman
Cannon	Frank	Cannon	William Conrad
Elliot	Ben	Doc Elliot	James Franciscus
Faraday	Steve (son)	Faraday and Co.	James Naughton (son)
	Frank (father)		Dan Dailey (father)
Hawk	John	Hawk	Burt Reynolds
Hawkins	Billy Jim	Hawkins	James Stewart
Ironside	Robert	Ironside	Raymond Burr
Judd	Clinton	Judd for the Defense	Carl Betz
Kojak	Theo	Kojak	Telly Savalas
McCloud	Sam	McCloud	Dennis Weaver
McMillan	Stuart	McMillan and Wife	Rock Hudson
	Sally		Susan St. James
Mannix	Joe	Mannix	Mike Connors
Petrocelli	Tony	Petrocelli	Barry Newman
Sanford	Fred (father)	Sanford and Son	Redd Foxx (father)
	Lamont (son)		Demond Wilson (son)
Shaft	John	Shaft	Richard Roundtree
Snoop	Ernesta	Snoop Sisters	Helen Hayes
	Gwen		Mildred Natwick
Tenafly	Harry	Tenafly	James McEachin
Toma	Dave	Toma	Tony Musante

First recorded message
>   "Mary had a little lamb": by Thomas Edison, 1877

First telegraph message
>   "What hath God wrought": Samuel F. B. Morse, May 1844

First telephone message

"Mr. Watson, come here, I need you": by Alexander Graham Bell (March 10, 1876) to his assistant Thomas Augustus Watson

First transoceanic cable message

"Europe and America are united by telegraph. Glory to God in the highest and on earth peace and good will towards men": August 16, 1858

Fischer Quintuplets

Born September 14, 1963, in Aberdeen, South Dakota: Jimmie, Cathy, Margie, Mary Ann, Maggie

Fisherman I and II

Zane Grey's private schooners

Fisherman's Ring, The

The Pope's ring

Fitzgerald, Barry

Irish character actor; winner of 1944 Oscar for supporting actor as Father Fitzgibbon in *Going My Way*: brother of actor Arthur Shields

Flag

Jody Baxter's tame fawn (Marjorie Kinnan Rawlings' *The Yearling*)

Flanagan, Father Edward Joseph

Founder of Boys Town, near Omaha, Nebraska

Flash, The

Original comic strip series: secret identity of Jay Garrick

Second comic strip series: secret identity of Barry Allen

Flash Gordon

Hero of comic strip by Alex Raymond, first appearing January 1934

Movie serials beginning in 1936, featured:

Flash Gordon—Buster Crabbe

Dr. Zarkov—Frank Shannon

Dale Arden—Jean Rogers

Princess Aura—Priscilla Lawson

Emperor Ming—Charles Middleton

Flatt and Scruggs

Earl Scruggs and Lester Flatt

Performed the theme song for the TV programs "Petticoat Junction" and "The Beverly Hillbillies." They also played "Foggy Mountain Breakdown," the sound-track theme song of the movie *Bonnie and Clyde*

Fleming, Ian

Creator of the James Bond adventure novels and author of *Chitty Chitty Bang Bang*

Flicka
> Ken's horse (TV series "My Friend Flicka")

Flight of the Bumblebee
> The Green Hornet's theme song

Flintstones
> Fred, Wilma, Pebbles, who live in town of Bedrock (TV cartoon series): created by Hanna-Barbera

Flo
> Andy Capp's wife (comic strip)

Flounder, The
> Ship on which Dr. Dolittle and his crew sailed

Flower
> Skunk (cartoon feature movie *Bambi*)

Floyd and Lloyd
> The two sons of Oswald the Rabbit (comic book cartoons)

Flush
> The Barretts' dog (Rudolph Besier's *The Barretts of Wimpole Street*)

Flyer
> Wright Brothers' 1903 airplane

Flying Crown Ranch
> Sky King's home, where he lives with his niece Penny and nephew Clipper

Flying Fish
> The A-1, first successful U. S. hydroplane, built by Glenn Curtiss, 1911

Flying Laboratory, The
> Amelia Earhart's Lockheed Electra in which she and navigator Fred Noonan disappeared in the Pacific, 1937

Flying Nun, The
> Sister Bertrille (TV series): played by Sally Field

Flying Red Horse
> Trademark of Mobil Gasoline

Foggy Mountain Breakdown
> Theme song (movie *Bonnie and Clyde*): written and played by Lester Flatt and Earl Scruggs

Fontaine, Joan
> Actress, 1941 Oscar winner for role of Lina in *Suspicion*: sister of actress Olivia de Havilland (real name Joan de Havilland)

Fontane Sisters
> Singing group: Geri, Bea, Marge

Foodini
> Puppet on "Lucky Pup" show (TV)

Football Hall of Fame
> Museum for professional football, located at Canton, Ohio

Forbes Field

Pittsburgh baseball stadium (1909-1970) where no one ever pitched a no-hit game. Since the Pirates moved to Three Rivers Stadium in 1970, the record seems secure

Forbidden Planet

Altair IV

Ford, Robert

"The dirty little coward" who shot and killed Jesse James, April 3, 1882, at St. Joseph, Mo.

Forester, C. S.

Cecil Scott Forester (1899-1966), English writer, author of Horatio Hornblower novels

Forsyte Saga, The

Novel, trilogy by John Galsworthy (1867-1933): *The Man of Property* (1906), *In Chancery* (1920), *To Let* (1921). The trilogy called *A Modern Comedy* (1924-1928) and several "interlude" novels complete the long family history

Fort Abraham Lincoln

The fort in Dakota Territory from which George Armstrong Custer departed May 17, 1876, with the Seventh Cavalry on his way to the Little Big Horn. The military band played "Garry Owen," the regimental march, while the troops were in the fort and "The Girl I Left Behind Me" as the troops were leaving

Fort Apache

Military post (TV series "Rin-Tin-Tin")

Fort Courage

Military post (TV series "F Troop")

Fort McHenry

Fort on Baltimore Harbor bombarded by the British, Sept. 13-14, 1814. Francis Scott Key was inspired to write a poem that later became "The Star Spangled Banner" as he watched from the British ship "The Minden"

Fort Sumter

Union fort located in Charleston Harbor, South Carolina, fired upon by Southern troops, April 12, 1861, to begin the Civil War

Fort Wilderness

Fort ("Adventureland" section of Disneyland)

Fortuna

Mr. Lucky's gambling yacht (TV series "Mr. Lucky")

Fourth Musketeer, The

Gascon nobleman, D'Artagnan (Alexandre Dumas' *The Three Musketeers*). He joins Athos, Porthos, and Aramis in many adventures, and is actually the hero

FOXXXX

Redd Foxx's California automobile license plate

Foxy Loxy
> Ate Chicken Little

Francis
> Talking mule (movie series). Voice: Chill Wills
> With Donald O'Connor:
>> *Francis*, 1949
>> *Francis Goes to the Races*, 1951
>> *Francis Goes to West Point*, 1952
>> *Francis Covers the Big Town*, 1953
>> *Francis Joins the WACS*, 1954
>> *Francis in the Navy*, 1955
> With Mickey Rooney:
>> *Francis in the Haunted House*, 1956

Frank Smith
> Sgt. Joe Friday's TV partner ("Dragnet"): played by Ben Alexander

Frankenstein
> Novel (1816) by Mary Wollstonecraft Shelley, the wife of Percy Bysshe Shelley. The full title is *Frankenstein; or, The Modern Prometheus*. Victor Frankenstein (in the 1931 movie his first name became Henry) is the scientist who revivifies the composite of corpses, NOT the monster

Frankenstein movies
> *Frankenstein* (produced by Thomas Edison), 1910
> *Frankenstein*, 1931 (K)
> *Bride of Frankenstein*, 1935 (K)
> *Son of Frankenstein*, 1939 (K)
> *Ghost of Frankenstein*, 1942
> *Frankenstein Meets the Wolf Man*, 1943
> *House of Frankenstein*, 1944
> *House of Dracula*, 1945
> *Abbott and Costello Meet Frankenstein*, 1948
> *The Curse of Frankenstein*, 1957
> *I Was a Teenage Frankenstein*, 1957
> *The Revenge of Frankenstein*, 1958
> *Frankenstein—1970*, 1958
> *Frankenstein's Daughter*, 1958
> *The Evil of Frankenstein*, 1964
> *Frankenstein Meets the Space Monster*, 1966
> *Jesse James Meets Frankenstein's Daughter*, 1966
> *Frankenstein Conquers the World* (Japanese), 1966
> *Frankenstein Created Woman*, 1967
> *Frankenstein Must Be Destroyed*, 1969
> *The Horror of Frankenstein*, 1970

Frankenstein's Bloody Terror, 1971

Dracula vs. Frankenstein, 1971

Boris Karloff as the Monster appeared only in those pictures with a (K) following the date, but played other roles in some of the subsequent pictures

Frankie and Johnny

Woman and her philandering man, respectively, in folk song

Frazier

19-year-old ex-circus lion who sired 35 cubs in less than two years

Fred

Super Chicken's lion partner

Freed, Alan

D. J. who coined phrase "Rock 'n' Roll"

Fresh Air Cab Company

Amos 'n' Andy's cab company

Friday

Robinson Crusoe's companion

Friendship 7

Capsule in which Colonel John Glenn became the first American to orbit the earth (February 20, 1962)

Fritz

Dr. Frankenstein's crippled assistant (1931 movie *Frankenstein*): played by Dwight Frye

Fritz

William S. Hart's horse (movies)

Fritz Brenner

Nero Wolfe's chef and housekeeper

Fritzie Ritz

Comic strip (1922) by Larry Whitington, later by Ernie Bushmiller: later the strip was titled "Fritzie Ritz and Nancy" and finally "Nancy," when Fritzie's little niece took over the general interest

Froggie the Gremlin

Wise-cracking frog (radio's "Buster Brown Show"): played by Ed McConnell (who was Buster Brown too)

Frosty

"The Snowman" (comic book character)

Fulton's Folly

Robert Fulton's double sidewheel steamboat "Clermont": first demonstrated 1807

Fu Manchu

Oriental villain in Sax Rohmer novels: always *Doctor* Fu Manchu

Fury

Straight Arrow's golden palomino horse

Fuzz

German shepherd dog (TV series "Chase")

Fuzzy

Lash LaRue's sidekick: played by Al St. John

G

G8 and His Battle Aces

Comic book series about a Spad-flying World War I pilot. His aces were Bull Martin and Nippy Weston

G. I. Jane

United States Army WAC

G. I. Joe

United States Army soldier: World War II

G. I. Joe

World War II carrier pigeon that saved the lives of over 1,000 British soldiers by delivering a message, enabling a rescue: Italy, October 18, 1943

G. O. P.

Grand Old Party (Republican)

Gabilan

Jody's pony (John Steinbeck's *The Red Pony*)

Gable, Clark

His wives: Josephine Dillon, 1924-1930; Rhea Langham, 1930-1939; Carole Lombard, 1939-1942; Silvia Hawkes, 1949-1952; Kay Spreckels, 1955-1960

Gabor sisters

Zsa Zsa; Magda; Eva (Mother: Jolie)

Gabor, Zsa Zsa

Her husbands: Burham Belge; Conrad Hilton; George Sanders; Herbert L. Huntner; Joshua Cosden, Jr.

Gaedel, Edward Carl

Midget (1925-1961) who pinch hit for the St. Louis Browns in a game against Detroit in 1951. He stood 43 inches tall, weighed 65 lb.; uniform number 1/8. Batting for Frank Saucier, he walked, was replaced by Jim Delsing, the regular outfielder, who ran for him; he never batted again in the major leagues. Ed Hurley, the plate umpire, permitted him to bat when Zack Taylor, Browns' manager, showed him a contract signed by Gaedel. The Detroit pitcher was Bob Cain

Gagarin, Yuri A.
   First man in space, on board Russian Vostok 1, April 12, 1961, for 1 hour 48 minutes

Galahad Glen
   Home of Crusader Rabbit (TV cartoon series)

Galaxie, The
   Captain Video's space ship (TV series)

Galileo
   U.S.S. "Enterprise's" shuttle craft, NCC-1701/7 (TV series "Star Trek")

Gallop, Frank
   Perry Como's deep-voiced TV announcer

Galloping Ghost
   Nickname for football player Harold "Red" Grange of University of Illinois

Gammera
   Giant prehistoric monster (Japanese movie)

Gangsters
   Nicknames:

   Arizona Barker—Ma   Alvin Karpis—Old Creepy
   Al Capone—Scarface   George Kelly—Machine Gun
   Vincent Coll—Mad Dog   George Nelson—Baby Face
   Jack Diamond—Legs   Arthur Flegenheimer—Dutch Schultz
   Charles Floyd—Pretty Boy   Earl Weiss—Hymie

Garco
   Robot that appeared in several 1950's TV programs, including Walt Disney's *Mars and Beyond*

Gardner, Ava
   Her real name: Lucy Johnson
   Her husbands: Mickey Rooney, 1942-1943; Artie Shaw, 1945-1947; Frank Sinatra, 1951-1957

Gargoyle
   Ex-Sing Sing convict and muscleman for The Bishop (radio series "The Bishop and the Gargoyle"): played by Milton Herman and Ken Lynch

Garland, Judy
   American actress and singer (1922-1969), real name Frances Gumm, famous as Dorothy in 1939 movie *The Wizard of Oz*. Married 4 times: David Rose (1941-1943), Vincente Minnelli (1945-1950), Sid Luft (1952-1955), Mark Herron (1955-1960); mother of Liza Minnelli

Garrett, Pat
   Sheriff who shot and killed Billy the Kid (July 14, 1881); later became a Texas Ranger. Killed in a dispute with a tenant

Gashouse Gang
St. Louis Cardinals of the early 1930's; Frank Frisch, manager
Outstanding players: Pepper Martin, third base; Ducky Medwick, outfield; Rip Collins, first base; Leo Durocher, short-stop; Bill Delancy, catcher; Tex Carleton, pitcher; Dizzy Dean, pitcher; Paul Dean, pitcher

Gehrig, Lou
Member, behind Babe Ruth, of Yankees' Murderers' Row
Hit the most grand-slam home runs in major league career: 23
Played in 2,130 consecutive baseball games (1925-1939): replaced Wally Pipp at first base (June 25, 1925) and was replaced by Babe Dahlgren (May 2, 1939)

Gehrig's Disease
Name applied (as in AMA *Journal*) to amyotrophic lateral sclerosis, the disease that killed Lou Gehrig

GEN II
Automobile license plate of Chitty Chitty Bang Bang, a magical Paragon Panther automobile (Ian Fleming's novel *Chitty-Chitty-Bang-Bang*). GEN II was supposed to mean Gentle, yet in the movie the license plate reads GEN 11

General, The
President John Tyler's horse

General, The
Confederate locomotive hijacked by 20 Union soldiers during the Civil War: see *Texas, The*

General Sherman
Sequoia, largest living thing in the world; it stands 272 feet, 4 inches tall (Sequoia National Park, California)

General Tom Thumb
Nickname of Charles S. Stratton. He stood 36 inches tall and worked for P. T. Barnum

Genoa City
Locale of TV daytime serial "The Young and the Restless"

Gentle Ben
650 lb. bear (TV movie series)

Gentle on My Mind
Glen Campbell's theme song

Gentleman Jim
Nickname of boxer James J. Corbett

Geoffrey
The Toys "Я" Us giraffe; Gi Gi, Mother; Baby Gee, Baby

George
(Lee) Liberace's brother

George and Marge
Union Oil Gasoline's husband and wife customers (TV ads)

George and Marion Kerby

Ghosts who are friends of Cosmo Topper (TV, radio, movies) from Thorne Smith's *Topper*. Their dog was named Neal (in novel the dog was called Oscar)

George Eliot

Pen name of Mary Ann Evans

Georgia Peach, The

Nickname of baseball player Ty Cobb

Gepetto

Pinocchio's creator and "father" (a woodcarver)

Gerald McBoing Boing

Cartoon boy (movie cartoon and TV show "The Boing Boing Show")

Geraldine Jones

Character in female costume played by Flip Wilson (TV show): "What you sees is what you get"

Gerber Baby, The

Said, in error, to be a portrait of Humphrey Bogart when he was a baby (Gerber Baby Foods). He actually was the Mellins Baby Food baby. The portrait was painted by his mother, Maude Humphrey Bogart

Gertie

Perry Mason's office receptionist (Erle Stanley Gardner's Perry Mason series)

Gertrude

Pocket Books' kangaroo trademark

Ghidrah

Three-headed monster that Godzilla, Rodan, and Mothra team up to stop (Japanese movie, 1965)

Ghosts

Spirits appearing to Ebenezer Scrooge (Charles Dickens' *A Christmas Carol*): Marley's ghost, The Ghost of Christmas Past, The Ghost of Christmas Present, The Ghost of Christmas to Come

Gideon Fell

Detective in John Dickson Carr novels

Gifts of the Magi

Gold, Frankincense, Myrrh (Luke 2:11)

Gigantis

Fire monster (Japanese movie, *Gigantis, the Fire Monster*, 1959)

Gilbert

Goofy's nephew (cartoon)

Girard, Joe

World's No. 1 car and truck salesman: award 1966-1973. In 1973 he sold 1,425 Chevrolet cars and trucks.

Girl from U.N.C.L.E.
>   April Dancer: played by Stefanie Powers

Girl Hunters, The
>   1964 movie in which detective Mike Hammer is played by his author, Mickey Spillane

Gish Sisters, The
>   Actresses, notably in silent movies: Lillian, Dorothy. Real name: De Guiche

Gladstone Gander
>   Donald Duck's lucky cousin (cartoon)

Gladys Ormphby
>   Purse-swinging old maid played by Ruth Buzzi, who is always slugging the dirty old man played by Arte Johnson (TV series "Laugh In")

Gleason, Jackie
>   His TV personalities: The bachelor, Charley the loudmouth, Joe the bartender, Ralph Kramden, The Poor Soul, Reginald Van Gleason III, Rudy the repairman, Stanley R. Soog (announcer of Mother Fletcher's products), Fenwick Babbit. Gleason also played Chester Riley in 1949 TV series "Life of Riley"

Glens Falls
>   Town, locale of radio serial "Big Sister"

Glinda
>   The good witch (*The Wizard of Oz*): played in 1939 movie by Billie Burke

Goat
>   Low man in marks in West Point graduating class

Gobo
>   Bambi's cousin

God Save the King (or Queen)
>   National anthem of Great Britain

Godfather, The
>   Don Vito Corleone (novel by Mario Puzo): played in 1971 movie by Marlon Brando

Godfrey Daniels
>   W. C. Fields' most popular exclamation

Godwin-Austin
>   Mountain in Karakoram range, also called K2

Godzilla
>   Sea monster (Japanese movies, 1956 and subsequent years): voice of narrator in English dubbing in original movie was Raymond Burr's; Burr also played a reporter

Goldbergs, The
>   Dramatic-comedy series written by Gertrude Berg
>   Radio series (from 1929):

Gertrude Berg—Molly
James R. Waters—Jake
Menasha Skulnik—Uncle David
Roslyn Siber—Rosalie
Alfred Ryder, Everett Sloane—Sammy
TV series:
Gertrude Berg—Molly
Philip Loeb—Jake
Eli Mintz—Uncle David
Arlene McQuade—Rosalie
Larry Robinson—Sammy

Gold Cup
Awarded annually to winner of unlimited hydroplane championship

Gold Diggers
Series of musical movies, stemming from Avery Hopwood's 1919 play *The Gold Diggers*:
Gold Diggers (1923)
Gold Diggers of Broadway (1929)
Gold Diggers of 1933 (1933), part of which is shown in the movie-show sequence of *Bonnie and Clyde* (1967)
Gold Diggers of 1935 (1935)
Gold Diggers in Paris (1938)
Painting the Clouds with Sunshine (1951) followed the original story line

Gold Dust Twins
Goldy and Dusty, two little boys on label of Gold Dust products: slogan "Let the twins do your work" (also a radio program)

Golden Hinde, The
Sir Francis Drake's ship, originally the "Pelican": circumnavigated globe 1577-1580

Goldenrod
The Summers brothers' land speed record autmobile: 409.227 mph, Nov. 12, 1965, Bonneville, Utah

Gold Record award
45 RPM's: million copies sold
33 RPM's (LP's): million dollars in sales (includes tapes and cassettes)

Golf's Big Four
United States Open, Masters, P.G.A., British Open.
The Grand Slam of Bobby Jones (1930), an amateur player, included the British Amateur, the British Open (291), the U.S. Amateur, and the U.S. Open (287). In the British Amateur final, he beat Roger Wethered 7 and 6; in the U.S. Amateur final, he defeated Gene Homans 8 and 7

Golf clubs

Woods	Irons
No. 1: Driver	No. 1: Driving iron/Cleek
No. 2: Brassie	No. 2: Midiron
No. 3: Spoon	No. 3: Mid mashie
No. 4: Baffy/Cleek	No. 4: Mashie iron
	No. 5: Mashie
	No. 6: Spade mashie
	No. 7: Mashie niblick
	No. 8: Pitching niblick/Lofter
	No. 9: Niblick
	No. 10: Wedge/Sand wedge
	— Putter

Only 14 clubs are allowed in tournament play; the No. 10 iron is usually omitted

Gone with the Wind

Novel (1936; Pulitzer Prize, 1937) by Margaret Mitchell; sold about 1,500,000 copies in its first year.

Movie roles (Oscar, best picture, 1939):

> Scarlett O'Hara, by Vivien Leigh (Oscar)
> Rhett Butler, Clark Gable
> Ashley Wilkes, Leslie Howard
> Melanie Hamilton, Olivia de Havilland
> Mammy, Hattie McDaniel (Oscar)

Goodrich, B. F.

Benjamin Franklin Goodrich (1841-1888), Ohio rubber manufacturer

Goody Two-Shoes

Children's story, published 1765 by John Newbery and said to have been written by Oliver Goldsmith, about a very poor little girl and her excitement over having a *pair* of shoes

Googol

One followed by 100 zeroes: word credited to the mathematician Edward Kasner's 9-year-old nephew Milton Sirotta

Gopher wood

Used to build Noah's Ark (Genesis 6:14)

Gordian Knot

Tied by Gordius, king of Phrygia, and cut by Alexander the Great (rather than untie it). He fulfilled the prophecy that whoever undid the knot would rule the East

Gorgons

Daughters of Phorcys and Ceto in Greek mythology:
Stheno, the mighty

Euryale, the wide-wandering

Medusa, the cunning one, also called The Gorgon, the sight of whom petrified mortals—literally

Gorilla

Played by Walter Pidgeon (in disguise) in the 1931 movie *The Gorilla*

Gorman, Margaret

First Miss America, 1921: blue-eyed blond, 5'1", 30-25-32, 108 lbs., 16 years old

Gort

Klaatu's 9-foot robot (1951 movie *The Day the Earth Stood Still*)

Gotham City

Hometown of Batman and Robin

Grable, Betty

Most popular pinup girl of World War II (closely followed by Rita Hayworth)

Graduate, The

Benjamin Braddock (Charles Webb's novel *The Graduate*): played in 1967 movie by Dustin Hoffman

Graf Spee

German pocket battleship and raider blown up and scuttled by her own crew, December 1939, outside Montevideo harbor. In the first major naval engagement of World War II, "Spee" had sought refuge there from the Royal Navy's "Achilles," "Ajax," and "Exeter"

Graf und Stift

Automobile, 1912 model, in which Archduke Ferdinand and his wife Sophie were riding when they were assassinated June 28, 1914, by Gavrilo Prinzip. The automobile became known as the car with a curse, since more than a dozen people have been killed by it or while riding in it

Graf Zeppelin

First lighter-than-air airship to fly around the world, completed trip in 21 days (1929)

Grail Knight

Sir Galahad, sinless son, in Arthurian legend, of Sir Lancelot and Elaine, daughter of King Pelles. In German literature and Wagnerian opera, the Grail Knight is Parsifal

Grand Fenwick

Tiny country that declares war on the United States (Leonard Wibberley's *The Mouse That Roared*)

Grand Old Man of Football, The

Nickname of football coach Amos Alonzo Stagg (1862-1965). As coach of Springfield, Chicago, and College of the Pacific, in 57 years he won 314 games, one more than Glenn "Pop" Warner, and the record number of wins for a coach

Grand Pooh-Bah

Headman of the Order of the Water Buffalo, fraternity of Fred Flintstone and Barney Rubble (TV cartoon series)

Grane

Siegfried's horse (German mythology)

Granny

The talking piano (radio series "The Buster Brown Show")

Grant, U. S.

Ulysses Simpson Grant (1822-1885), 18th president of the United States (1869-1877)

Grasshopper

Master Po's name for young Caine (TV series "Kung Fu")

Grauman's Chinese Theater

Movie theater on Hollywood Boulevard outside which stars have left footprints and other marks in wet cement since Norma Talmadge began the tradition in 1927

Graves, Leonard

Narrated TV series "Victory at Sea"

Graves, Peter

Actor in TV and movies, especially "Mission Impossible" on TV as Phelps; real name Peter Arness, brother of actor James Arness

Gray, Pete

One-armed outfielder (real name: Peter Wyshner) who played for the St. Louis Browns in 1945 and batted .218

Great Britain, India, Nepal

Three nations whose flags were set atop Mt. Everest, May 28, 1953, on its first ascent by Edmund Hillary and Tenzing Norkay; the UN emblem was also included

Great Gildersleeve, The

Throckmorton P. Gildersleeve, character originally in radio's "Fibber McGee and Molly" and later with his own show: played by Hal Peary. He was water commissioner of Summerfield

Great Imposter, The

Ferdinand Waldo Demara, Jr., alias: Ben W. Jones, Assistant Warden; Brother John Payne, Trappist monk; Dr. Cecil Boyce Hamann; Dr. Joseph C. Cyr, surgeon; Dr. Robert Linton French; Martin Godart

Great Seal, The

Adopted September 16, 1789 (both sides are shown on reverse of one-dollar bill): 13 stars, 13 stripes, 13 clouds, 13 arrows, 13 laurel leaves, 13 berries, 13 feathers in left wing, 13 feathers in right wing, 13 feathers in tail, 13 rows in pyramid, 13 letters each in the mottoes (*E pluribus unum* and *Annuit coeptis*)

Great White Fleet, The
American battleship fleet, painted white, circumnavigated the world in 1908 (December 16, 1907, to February 22, 1909), stopping in many foreign ports and covering 46,000 miles: "Connecticut" (flagship), "Georgia," "Illinois," "Kansas," "Kearsarge," "Kentucky," "Louisiana," "Minnesota," "Missouri," "Nebraska," "New Jersey," "Ohio," "Rhode Island," "Vermont," "Virginia," "Wisconsin"

Greek alphabet
Alpha, Beta, Gamma, Delta, Epsilon, Zeta, Eta, Theta, Iota, Kappa, Lambda, Mu, Nu, Xi, Omicron, Pi, Rho, Sigma, Tau, Upsilon, Phi, Chi, Psi, Omega

Greek orders
Architectural: Ionic, Doric, Corinthian

Green
Color of Mr. Spock's blood (TV series "Star Trek")

Green Arrow, The
Secret identity of Oliver Queen (comic book series)

Green Hornet, The
Secret identity of Britt Reid, grand-nephew of the Lone Ranger

Green Lantern, The
Secret identity of Alan Scott (comic book series). His creed: "In brightest day, in blackest night, no evil shall escape my sight. Let those who worship Evil's might, beware my power—Green Lantern's light"

Green Monster, The
Art Arfons' jet-powered car, held speed record 1964-1965

Green Monster, The
Nickname for Boston's Fenway Park's left-field fence

Grendel
Monster slain by Beowulf

Grimm Brothers
Linguists and compilers of children's fairy tales: Jacob Ludwig (1785-1863), Wilhelm Karl (1786-1859)

Groucho Marx
Stage name of Julius Marx, the brother with the mustache
His movie roles:
> *The Cocoanuts*, 1929, Mr. Hammer
> *Animal Crackers*, 1930, Captain Jeffrey T. Spaulding
> *Monkey Business*, 1931, no name
> *Horse Feathers*, 1932, Professor Quincey Adams Wagstaff
> *Duck Soup*, 1933, Rufus T. Firefly

A Night at the Opera, 1935, Otis B. Driftwood
A Day at the Races, 1937, Dr. Hugo Z. Hackenbush
Room Service, 1938, Gordon Miller
At the Circus, 1939, J. Cheever Loophole
Go West, 1940, S. Quentin Quale
The Big Store, 1941, Wolf J. Flywheel
A Night in Casablanca, 1946, Ronald Kornblow
Copacabana, 1947, Lionel Q. Devereaux
Love Happy, 1949, Sam Grunion
Double Dynamite, 1951, Emil J. Kech
The Story of Mankind, 1957, Peter Minuit

Grover

Stan Freberg's puppet

Grovers Mill

New Jersey fictional landing place of Martians (Orson Welles' radio broadcast "War of the Worlds," October 30, 1938): in the H. G. Wells novel the landing place was Horsell Common, near Woking, Surrey, England

Grumman F5F Skyrocket

The Blackhawks' first plane (comic book series "Blackhawk"): later they flew a Lockheed XF90

Guinevere

King Arthur's wife and Sir Lancelot's lover

Gulf of Tonkin

North Vietnam PT boats reported to have attacked the U.S.S. "Maddox" and "C. Turner Joy," August 2, 5, 1964

Gull Cottage

House haunted by Captain Gregg and inhabited by Mrs. Muir (TV series "The Ghost and Mrs. Muir")

Gulliver's Travels

Novel (originally published 1726) by Jonathan Swift. The lands and people Lemuel Gulliver visited were:

Lilliput, a nation of 6-inch-high people

Blefuscu, a country of 6-inch-high people at war with Lilliput

Brobdingnag, a nation of 60-foot-tall giants

Laputa, a flying island inhabited by forgetful, scientific quacks

Glubdubdrib, a land of magicians and sorcerers

Luggnag, an island where the inhabitants, the Struldbrugs, live forever

Houyhnhnms, a nation where rational, intelligent horses rule over human-like Yahoos

Balnibarbi, the land of inventors and projectors; capital: Lagado

GUM

Moscow's largest department store

Gumps, The

Comic strip (1917-1959) by Sydney Smith and then Gus Edson: Min, Andy, Chester, Uncle Bim, Tilda the maid

Gunga Ram

Indian elephant boy (TV series "Andy's Gang")

Gungnir

Odin's spear

Gunsmoke

Longest running TV Western

Radio series (1955):

Matt Dillon, played by William Conrad

Chester Proudfoot, Parley Baer

Kitty Russell, Georgia Ellis

Doc Galen Adams, Howard McNear

TV series (late 1955):

Matt Dillon, played by James Arness

Chester Goode, Dennis Weaver

Kitty Russell, Amanda Blake

Doc Galen Adams, Milburn Stone

Festus Haggin, Ken Curtis

Gus Goose

Grandma Duck's hired hand (cartoon)

Gypsy Moth IV

53-foot sailboat in which Sir Francis Chichester sailed around the world in 9 months (August 27, 1966, to May 28, 1967)

Gyro Gearloose

Donald Duck's inventor friend who has his friend the light bulb always with him (cartoon)

H

$100,000 infield

Philadelphia Athletics' infield (managed by Connie Mack) 1911-1914: John Phelan "Stuffy" McInnis, 1B; Edward Trowbridge Collins, 2B; John Joseph Barry, SS; John Franklin "Home Run" Baker, 3B

H A L 9000

Computer of spaceship "Discovery" (movie *2001: A Space Odyssey*)

H Bar O

Bobby Benson's ranch while Hecker's H-O Cereal was the program's sponsor

H Movies

Of Paul Newman: *Helen Morgan Story, The,* 1957; *Hustler, The,* 1961; *Hemingway's Adventures of a Young Man,* 1962; *Hud,* 1963; *Harper,* 1966; *Hombre,* 1967; *Hall of Mirrors,* 1969

H. M. S. Pinafore

Operetta by W. S. Gilbert and Arthur Sullivan: subtitle—*The Lass that Loved a Sailor*

Hail to the Chief

Official song of the President. Words by Sir Walter Scott (*The Lady of the Lake,* Canto II)

Hair Bear Bunch, The

TV cartoon series: Bubi, Hair, Square

Half Moon, The

Henry Hudson's ship (1609)

Hall of Fame

Gallery of busts or commemorative tablets "of Great Americans" (New York University, Washington Heights). Elections to the Hall of Fame occur every 5 years

Halley's Comet

Recurring, highly visible comet: it has been traced to 240 B.C. It is named for Sir Edmund Halley (1656-1742), astronomer royal, who calculated its 76-year period and predicted its return in 1758. It appeared the year of Mark Twain's birth (1835) and also the year of his death (1910).

Ham

Chimpanzee, first United States animal to orbit, Jan. 31, 1961

Hamburglar

Bad guy in McDonaldland (McDonald's Hamburgers ads)

Hamelin

Town in Germany from which the Pied Piper chased the mice

Hamilcar

Carthaginian general, father of Hannibal

Hamlet

Sarah Bernhardt's dog

Hancock, John

Boston merchant; first signer of the Declaration of Independence

Hand of God, The

Sculpture by Auguste Rodin, at Metropolitan Museum of Art, New York

Handsome Dan

The Yale football team's mascot bulldog

Handy, William C.

Father of the Blues (1873-1958): "St. Louis Blues," etc.

Hanging Judge, The

Isaac Parker, who sentenced 79 men to be hanged

Hanks

Country music fame: Hank Locklin; Hank Snow; Hank Thompson; Hank Williams; Hank Williams, Jr.

Hannibal

Missouri town in which Mark Twain grew up, 1839-1853. He was born in Florida, Missouri, in 1835

Hannibal 8

Automobile of Professor Fate (Jack Lemmon) (1965 movie *The Great Race*)

Hans und Fritz

The Katzenjammer Kids. Hans, the blond, and Fritz, the one with the dark brush cut, appeared first in 1897, drawn by Rudolph Dirks, later by Harold Knerr. During World War I, the strip was retitled "The Captain and the Kids"

Hanson, John

Maryland political leader (1721-1783), first "president of the United States Congress assembled" (Nov. 1781-Nov. 1782) under the Articles of Confederation and sometimes therefore considered first President of the United States: he presided, however, over the Congress, not over the United States

Hansons

Family in TV series "Mama," adapted from 1948 movie *I Remember Mama*: lived on Steiner Street, San Francisco

Happiness Boys, The

Early radio vocal duo: Ernie Hare, Billy Jones

Happy Hooker, The

Nickname of Xaviera Hollander, used as title of her best-selling autobiography

Happy McMann

Martin Kane's aide (radio series "Martin Kane, Private Eye"): played by Walter Kinsella

Happy Trails

Theme song of Roy Rogers and Dale Evans (when sponsored by Dodge automobiles). Before Dodge, it was "Smiles Are Made Out of Sunshine" and later "It's Roundup Time on the Double R Bar"

Happy Warrior

Nickname of Alfred E. Smith (1873-1944), four-time governor of New York State and 1928 Democratic candidate for President: noted for his brown derby hat

Hardy Boys, The

Stories written by Franklin W. Dixon about Frank and Joe

Harmony

Charles Starrett's sidekick, cowboy character played by Cliff Edwards

Harper Valley P. T. A.

Country and western song recorded by Jeanne C. Riley:

Mrs. Johnson, miniskirted mother who attacks the P.T.A.

P.T.A. members: Bobby Taylor, Mr. Baker, Widow Jones, Mr. Harper, Shirley Thompson

Harrison, William Henry

Nicknamed Tippecanoe, President of the United States (1841: died one month after inauguration) and grandfather of President Benjamin Harrison: oldest (68) president at inauguration

Harry Lime

The third man (Graham Greene's *The Third Man*): played in the 1949 Carol Reed-directed movie by Orson Welles

Hartford

Admiral D. G. Farragut's flagship at New Orleans and at Mobile Bay

Hartline, Mary

Blonde leader of the band (TV series "Super Circus," 1949)

Hartmann, Erich

World War II German fighter pilot: all-time ace of aces, with 352 confirmed victories on the Russian front

Harvey

Invisible 6-foot rabbit, friend of Elwood P. Dowd (play by Mary C. Chase)

Hatfields and McCoys

Famous feuding hillbilly families (Pike County, Kentucky, 1880's to 1890's)

Hathaway, Anne

Wife of William Shakespeare. They were married in November 1582. Children:

Susannah, born May 1583

Hamnet and Judith (twins), born January 1585

Hauptmann, Bruno Richard

German immigrant carpenter who kidnapped and murdered (1932) Charles Lindbergh's 20-month-old son. He was tried (1935) at Flemington, New Jersey, convicted, and electrocuted (April 3, 1936)

Hawaiian Islands

Eight largest: Hawaii, Kahoolawe, Kauai, Lanai, Maui, Molokai, Niihau, Oahu

Hawkeye

Natty Bumppo, the trapper (James Fenimore Cooper's *Last of the Mohicans* and other Leatherstocking novels)

Hawkgirl

Shiera Sanders (Carter Hall's girlfriend)

Hawkman

Secret identity of Carter Hall (comic book series)

Hayes, George "Gabby"

Played the sidekicks of Gene Autry, Hopalong Cassidy (as Windy Halliday), Roy Rogers, John Wayne, Bill Elliott, Randolph Scott

Hayworth, Rita

Actress (real name Marguerite Cansino)

Her husbands: Edward Judson, 1937-1943; Orson Welles, 1943-1947; Aly Khan, 1949-1951; Dick Haymes, 1953-1955; James Hill, 1958-1961

Hazel

Switchboard operator for Shell Scott, private eye (Richard S. Prather novel series)

He ain't heavy, he's my brother

Inscription on statue at Boys Town, Nebraska (statue of a boy carrying his younger brother on his shoulders)

Head

1969 movie starring the Monkees (their only movie)

Heavyweight boxing champions

1882-1892 John L. Sullivan

(Sullivan was the last bare-knuckle champion)

1892-1897 James J. Corbett, by decision, 21 rounds

1897-1899 Robert Fitzsimmons, by KO, 14

1899-1905 James J. Jeffries, by KO, 11

1905-1906 Marvin Hart, by KO, 12

(Defeated Jack Root)

1906-1908 Tommy Burns, by decision, 20

1908-1915 Jack Johnson, by KO, 14

1915-1919 Jess Willard, by KO, 26

1919-1926 Jack Dempsey, by KO, 3

1926-1928 Gene Tunney, by decision, 10

1930-1932 Max Schmeling, on foul, 4

(Defeated Jack Sharkey)

1932-1933 Jack Sharkey, by decision, 15

1933-1934 Primo Carnera, by KO, 6

1934-1935 Max Baer, by KO, 11

1935-1937 James J. Braddock, by decision, 15

1937-1949 Joe Louis, by KO, 8

(Louis defended his title 25 times)

1949-1951 Ezzard Charles, by decision, 15

(Defeated Joe Walcott)

1951-1952 Joe Walcott, by KO, 7

1952-1956 Rocky Marciano, by KO, 13

1956-1959 Floyd Patterson, by KO, 5
     (Defeated Archie Moore)
1959-1960 Ingemar Johansson, by KO, 3
1960-1962 Floyd Patterson, by KO, 5
     (Only heavyweight champion to regain a lost title)
1962-1964 Sonny Liston, by KO, 1
1964-1967 Cassius Clay (Muhammad Ali), by KO, 7
1970-1973 Joe Frazier, by KO, 5 (Defeated Jimmy Ellis)
1973-1974 George Foreman, by KO, 2
1974-   Muhammad Ali, by KO, 8
Champions who retired undefeated: James J. Jeffries, Gene Tunney, Joe Louis, Rocky Marciano

Heckle and Jeckle

Two magpies in movie cartoons

Hee Haw

TV series featuring country and western music and humor
Main characters: Roy Clark, Buck Owens, Buckaroos, Grandpa Jones, Cathy Baker, Archie Campbell, Jenifer Bishop, Susan Raye, Jeannine Riley, Lulu Roman, Junior Samples, Stringbean, Sunshine, Gordie Tapp, Sheb Wooley

Hegira

The flight of Mohammed from Mecca to Medina, September 13, 622 (Moslem calendar begins with this date)

Heidi Game

Football game (Nov. 17, 1968) between the New York Jets and the Oakland Raiders. The movie *Heidi* preempted the last two minutes of the game, New York ahead 32-29. In 2 minutes Oakland scored twice, to win 43-32.

Heisman Trophy

Awarded to most outstanding college football player of the year (first awarded in 1935 to Jay Berwanger of Chicago)

Helen of Troy

"The face that launched a thousand ships": her eloping with Paris of Troy caused her husband Menelaus to gather the Greeks and attack Troy in the Trojan War

Henderson

Town locale (TV serial "Search for Tomorrow")

Hendersons

Family for which Beulah worked (radio's "Beulah")

Henrietta

Ship bought by Phileas Fogg for $60,000 that gets him from New York to Liverpool (Jules Verne's *Around the World in 80 Days*)

Henry

Amos Burke's valet (TV series "Burkes Law")

Henry Fleming
>   Young soldier in Civil War (Stephen Crane's *The Red Badge of Courage*)

Henry Tremblechin
>   Little Iodine's father (comic strip). His boss is Mr. Bigdome

Henson, Matthew Alexander
>   Negro (1866-1955) who accompanied Admiral Robert Peary in 1909 journey to the North Pole. Henson reached the Pole first. Four Eskimos also reached the Pole with them: Ooqueah, Ootah, Egingwah, Seegloo

Herb and Tootsie Woodley
>   Dagwood and Blondie Bumstead's neighbors

Herbert Philbrick
>   American businessman, Communist agent, and FBI counterspy: played by Richard Carlson (TV series "I Led 3 Lives")

Herbert, Master/Sergeant Tony
>   Korean War's most decorated GI

Herbie
>   The Love Bug, a Volkswagen (Disney movies *The Love Bug* and *Herbie Rides Again*). Number 53 was painted on the side of the car

Hercule Poirot
>   Belgian detective created by Agatha Christie

Herman
>   The duck (voice by Clarence Nash) (radio "Burns and Allen Show")

Hero
>   The Phantom's horse (comic strip)

Heth, Joice
>   P. T. Barnum's fake 161-year-old Negro woman for whom it was claimed that she was a former slave of George Washington

Higgins
>   Pet dog (TV series "Petticoat Junction")

High Tower
>   Detective agency for which Tenafly works

Hillbillie Bears
>   TV cartoon: Pa Bear, Ma Bear, Floral, Shag

Hilltop House
>   Radio serial: "Dedicated to the women of America. The story of a woman who must choose between love and the career of raising other women's children." Program later called The Story of Bess Johnson

Him and Her
>   President Lyndon B. Johnson's two beagles

Hindenburg

Zeppelin that exploded at Lakehurst, New Jersey, May 6, 1937; 36 died

Hindu Trinity

Brahma, The Creator

Shiva, The Destroyer and Restorer

Vishnu, The Savior

Hippocrates

Father of medicine, Greek physician of 4th and 5th century B.C.

His Master's Voice

Slogan of RCA Victor, symbolized by a terrier listening to an old phonograph

Hispaniola

Captain Smollett's ship (Robert Louis Stevenson's *Treasure Island*)

Hitchcock, Alfred

Motion picture director, since 1925. He has made a cameo appearance in more than 30 of the 50 movies he has directed. Before each episode of his TV series ("Alfred Hitchcock Presents") he greeted viewers with "Good e-ve-ning"

Hitler, Adolf

Time magazine's "Man of the Year for 1938"

Hitless Wonders, The

1906 Chicago White Sox baseball team, who won the American League pennant (and the World Series against the Chicago Cubs) with a team batting average of only .230, no regular team member batting as high as .280

Ho Ho song

Red Buttons' theme

Hoboken Four, The

Singing group with which Frank Sinatra first sang. They made a famous appearance on Major Bowes' Amateur Hour

Hockey Hall of Fame

The Canadian museum is located at Toronto, Canada; the American is at Eveleth, Minnesota

Hodge

Dr. Samuel Johnson's cat

Holden Caulfield

Hero of J. D. Salinger's *The Catcher in the Rye*

Hole-in-the-Wall Gang

Butch Cavendish's gang: ambushed the Lone Ranger and his fellow Texas Rangers

Holiday Inn

Movie (1942) from which came the song "White Christmas" (by Irving Berlin)

Holliday, James Henry
> Known as "Doc" Holliday; a dentist, he took part with the Earp brothers in the O.K. Corral shootout in Tombstone, Arizona, Oct. 25, 1881. He died of tuberculosis in Colorado in 1897

Hollywood Ten
> Witnesses who invoked the 5th Amendment before the House Committee on Un-American Activities hearings (1947) to investigate alleged Communist activity. The ten were fired by their studios, fined, and sentenced to a year in jail. They and others accused of radical sympathies were not given work in Hollywood for more than a decade. They were: Alvah Bessie, Herbert Biberman, Lester Cole, Edward Dmytryk (served only two months), Ring Lardner, Jr., John Howard Lawson, Albert Maltz, Samuel Ornitz, Adrian Scott, Dalton Trumbo

Holy Moley!
> Favorite expression of Captain Marvel (comic book series)

Homer
> Father of poetry, reputed blind author of the *Iliad* and *Odyssey*

Homer Brown
> Henry Aldrich's friend, always reading the book "How to Win the Love of a Good Woman" (radio series "The Aldrich Family"): played by Jackie Kelk

Honeymoon
> Daughter of Moonmaid and Junior (Dick Tracy comic strip)

Honeymooners, The
> Domestic skit appearing regularly on TV series "The Jackie Gleason Show": Alice Kramden (Audrey Meadows); Ralph Kramden (Jackie Gleason); Ed Norton (Art Carney); Trixie Norton (Joyce Randolph). The sketches first appeared on "Cavalcade of Stars," with Pert Kelton playing Alice

Honeywell and Todd
> Company for which Vern Albright, Margie's father, worked (TV series "My Little Margie")

Honolulu
> City, state capital, on the island of Oahu, Hawaii

Honor Thompson
> Woman who shot Chief Robert Ironside, paralyzing him and putting him in a wheelchair (TV series "Ironside")

Hood, H.M.S.
> British battle cruiser of World War II: sunk by the German battleship "Bismarck," May 24, 1941, off Iceland

Hooterville
> Town (TV series "Petticoat Junction")

Hop Harrigan
> America's Ace of the Airways (radio serial)

Hop Sing

Chinese cook of the Cartwrights (TV series "Bonanza"): played by Victor Sen Yung

Hopalong Cassidy

Cowboy hero of novels written by Montgomery Mulford
In movies, played by William Boyd. His horse: Topper
Sidekicks (movies):

California Carlson (played by Andy Clyde)
Lucky Jenkins (Russell Hayden; real name: Pate Lucid)
Windy Halliday (George "Gabby" Hayes)
Johnny Nelson (James Ellison)

Sidekick (TV): Red Connors (Edgar Buchanan)

Hope

Only thing that remained in Pandora's box after she opened it

Hopkins, Oceanus

Only child born aboard the "Mayflower" at sea (1620); parents were Stephen and Elizabeth Hopkins

Hopper, William

Played private investigator Paul Drake (TV series "Perry Mason"). Hopper is the son of gossip columnist Hedda Hopper

Hoppy

Bunny who becomes Captain Marvel Bunny, the world's mightiest bunny when he says the magic word "SHAZAM" (comic book series)

Horace Horsecollar

The horse in early Mickey Mouse cartoons

Horatio Hornblower

Went from midshipman to Lord of the Admiralty (novel series by C. S. Forester)

Hornet, U.S.S.

Aircraft carrier from which Lt. Colonel James Doolittle led the attack of 16 B-25's on Tokyo: called "Shangri-La" by President Franklin D. Roosevelt

Horton

Dr. Seuss' egg-hatching elephant

Hot Springs

Town in New Mexico renamed Truth or Consequences as publicity for the radio game show "Truth or Consequences"

Hotel Carleton

Paladin's home in San Francisco (TV series "Have Gun Will Travel")

Houdini, Harry

Stage name of Ehrich Weiss (1874-1926), American magician and escape artist

House of Wax, The
   Second full-length 3-D movie in color: starred Vincent Price
House that Ruth Built, The
   Yankee Stadium, Bronx, New York: opened 1923
How Little We Know
   Song sung by Marie (Lauren Bacall: her movie debut) in Gerard's Cafe while Cricket (Hoagy Carmichael) plays the piano (1945 movie *To Have and Have Not*)
How to Win the Love of a Good Woman
   The book that Henry Aldrich's friend Homer was always reading
Howdy Doody Time
   TV series for children (1947-1960): Buffalo Bob Smith, Howdy Doody (the puppet star), Clarabelle the clown (Bob Keeshan), Chief Thunderthud ("Kowabonga"), Dilly Dally, Don Jose, Flub-A-Dub, John J. Fadoozle, Phineas T. Bluster (Mayor of Doodyville), Princess Summerfallwinterspring, Chief Thunderchicken, K. Cornelius Cobb
Howe, Julia Ward
   American poet (1819-1910), wrote the words of "The Battle Hymn of the Republic" to replace those of "John Brown's Body"
Hubbell, Carl
   New York Giants' southpaw pitcher; struck out in succession in the 1934 All Star game: Babe Ruth, Lou Gehrig, Jimmy Foxx, Al Simmons, Joe Cronin
Hudson High
   Jack Armstrong's school (radio series)
Hugin and Munin
   Two ravens that sit on the shoulders of Odin; they represent thought and memory
Hugo
   One award for the year's best science-fiction writing. Another award is the Nebula
Hull House
   Settlement house in Chicago founded by Jane Addams and Ellen Gates Starr (1889)
Human body
   Parts of the body that have only three letters: arm, ear, eye, gum, jaw, leg, lip, rib, toe
Human Bomb, The
   Roy Lincoln, member of the Justice League of America (comics)
Human psyche
   Theory of Sigmund Freud: Ego, Id, Superego
Human senses (traditional)
   Hearing, sight, smell, taste, touch

Humphrey Agnew

> Last passenger to board Flight 420, Hawaii to San Francisco (Ernest K. Gann's *The High and the Mighty*): in the 1954 movie played by Sidney Blackmer

Humphrey Pennyworth

> Joe Palooka's fat friend who drove a bicycle with house on it (comic strip)

Hymie

> Robot (TV series "Get Smart"): played by Dick Gautier

I

IBAC

> Villain (Captain Marvel comic strip adventures): gets his powers from (initials)
> Ivan the Terrible
> Borgia
> Attila the Hun
> Caligula

ICE

> Intelligence Coordination and Exploitation (Matt Helm novels)

I Am Woman

> Helen Reddy's theme song (TV show)

I Can't Get Started

> Theme song of Bunny Berigan's orchestra

I got a warrant right here, Sheriff

> Sole line of George Plimpton in movie *Rio Lobo*, spoken to John Wayne. Line originally read, "This here's your warrant, mister," but it was changed at the last minute

I Love a Mystery

> Radio adventure of Jack Packard; Doc Long, a Texan; Reggie York, an Englishman, who ran the A-1 Detective Agency, "just off Hollywood Boulevard and one flight up": "No job too tough, no mystery too baffling"

Ibistick

> Ibis the Invincible's magic wand (comic book series "Ibis")

Ichabod Crane

> Schoolteacher in village of Sleepy Hollow (Washington Irving's "The Legend of Sleepy Hollow")

Ichabod Mudd (Ikky)

> Captain Midnight's mechanic (radio series)

Idaho

> Only state in the U. S. over which no foreign flag has ever flown

Ides of March
>   March 15th

If I Didn't Care
>   Ink Spots' theme song

Ignatz
>   Pet monkey aboard the ship "Venture" (movie *King Kong*)

Ignatz Mouse
>   Krazy Kat's friend who is always throwing bricks

Igor
>   Pet bat (TV series "The Munsters")

Igor (Ygor)
>   Dr. Frankenstein's assistant (movie series). In the 1931 movie *Frankenstein* Dwight Frye plays a cripple named Fritz: in the 1939 *Son of Frankenstein*, Bela Lugosi plays Ygor, the mad shepherd twisted by an abortive hanging, who takes care of the unconscious Monster

Illustrated Press
>   Newspaper edited by Steve Wilson (TV series "Big Town")

I'm Getting Sentimental Over You
>   Theme song of Tommy Dorsey's orchestra

IMF Agents
>   Impossible Mission Force: James Phelps and his Mission Impossible crew (TV series "Mission Impossible") starring Steven Hill and later Peter Graves

Imperial Wizard
>   Title of leader of the Ku Klux Klan (leader of the original KKK—1865-1877—was the Grand Cyclops)

In God We Trust
>   Motto of the United States, adopted July 30, 1956; first appeared on U. S. coins, 1864

In This Style 10/6
>   Sign on the Mad Hatter's hat (as originally illustrated by Sir John Tenniel in Lewis Carroll's *Alice's Adventures in Wonderland*)

Incitatus
>   Caligula's horse. The Roman emperor is said to have wanted to bestow the rank of Consul upon this, his favorite steed

Incredible Journey, The
>   Pet animals in the novel (1961) by Sheila Burnford; Luath, bull terrier; Tao, Siamese cat; Bodger, retriever

Incredible Shrinking Man, The
>   Scott Carey, who keeps growing smaller each day (1957 movie by Richard Matheson): played by Grant Williams

Indian Love Call
>   Title of movie in TV release and of song in it (by Rudolf Friml,

Otto Harbach, and Oscar Hammerstein II) sung by Jeanette Mac-
Donald and Nelson Eddy (1936 movie *Rose Marie*)

Indianapolis 500

"Gentlemen, start your engines": 200-lap Decoration Day race
since 1911 (won then by Ray Harroun in a Marmon Wasp at
74.59 mph

Indomitable, H.M.S.

Ship upon which Billy Budd was the foretopman (novel by Herman Melville)

Information Please

Radio quiz program (1938-1952)

M. C.: Clifton Fadiman

Original panelists:

Clifton Fadiman (replaced by Oscar Levant when he became M.C.)

John Kieran

Franklin Pierce Adams (F.P.A.)

Ink Spots

Original members: Ivory (Deek) Watson, Orville (Hoppy) Jones,
Charlie Fuqua, Slim Green. Bill Kenny joined the group in 1934

Inka Dinka Doo

Jimmy Durante's theme song

Inky and Dinky

Nephews of Felix the Cat (comic books)

Inky and Tut

Sidekicks of Jet Jackson (TV series "Jet Jackson, Flying Commando")

Inn of the Eight Happinesses

Mission-hotel founded by Gladys Aylward (biographical movie
The Inn of the Sixth Happiness). The title of the story is from an
ancient Chinese wish for the five happinesses: tranquility, virtue,
position, wealth, and a peaceful death in old age (the sixth happiness must be found by everyone within himself)

Inspector Clouseau

French detective of great ineptness (movies *The Pink Panther*,
1964, and *A Shot in the Dark*, 1964): played by Peter Sellers. In
Inspector Clouseau (1968) Alan Arkin played the role

Inspector Faraday

Policeman on "Boston Blackie" series (radio/TV)

Inspector Fenwick

Dudley Do-right's boss in the Canadian Mounted Police (comics)

Inspector Fix

Scotland Yard detective who hounds Phileas Fogg around the
world under the impression that he is a bank robber (Jules

Verne's *Around the World in 80 Days*): in the 1956 movie played
by Robert Newton

Inspector Gerard (Lieutenant)

Pursuer of Dr. Richard Kimble (TV series "The Fugitive"):
played by Barry Morse

Inspector Henderson

Police detective in Metropolis (TV series "Superman")

Inspector Japp

Scotland Yard C.I.D. man and friend of Hercule Poirot

Inspector Javert

Policeman who tracks down Jean Valjean (Victor Hugo's *Les
Miserables*)

Inspector Lestrade

Scotland Yard detective who seeks the aid of Sherlock Holmes

Inspector Maigret

Chief of detectives in novels by Georges Simenon

Inspector Queen

Richard Queen, a New York City police officer, father of Ellery
Queen (novels of Frederic Dannay and Manfred B. Lee writing
as Ellery Queen)

Intertech

Computer agency for which Joe Mannix worked before he
opened his own private detective agency (TV series "Mannix").
His boss was Lou Wickersham (played by Joseph Campanella)

Intolerance

Epic motion picture (1916) by David Wark Griffith that told four
stories simultaneously:

The Modern Story (capital and labor)
The Babylonian Story (the fall of Babylon)
The French Story (the massacre of the Huguenots)
The Judean Story (the story of Christ)

Between episodes Lillian Gish appeared rocking a cradle in reference to Walt Whitman's "Out of the cradle endlessly rocking"

Intrepid

Apollo 12 lunar module; command module "Yankee Clipper"

I. Q.

(Lewis M.) Terman's classification:

Above 140—Genius	80-90—Dull
120-140—Very superior	70-80—Borderline
110-120—Superior	50-70—Moron
90-110—Average	25-50—Imbecile

Below 25—Idiot

Iron Mike

Automatic baseball pitching machine

Iron Mike

Epithet applied to Jack Dempsey's right hand

Ironman One

Apollo space capsule on which retrofire fails (1969 movie *Marooned*)

Ironside

Chief Robert Ironside of the San Francisco police department, confined to a wheelchair since being paralyzed after being shot by Honor Thompson; he works in the field from a specially fitted van (TV series "Ironside"): played by Raymond Burr

Is this the end of Rico?

Last line of Edward G. Robinson in the 1930 movie *Little Caesar*

Ishi

Lone survivor of a Yana tribe, the Yahi, he stumbled into Oroville, California, in 1911, his first contact with white people

Ishmael

Narrator in Herman Mellville's *Moby Dick*

It Girl, The

Clara Bc . (1905-1965), movie actress

Itasca, U.S.S.

Coast Guard cutter that last had communications with Amelia Earhart, July 3, 1937

It's All in the Game

Hit song, words by Carl Sigman, recorded (1951, 1958) by Tommy Edwards, (1963) by Cliff Edwards, based on a melody written (1912) by Charles G. Dawes, later U. S. Vice President under Coolidge

It's a Mad, Mad, Mad, Mad World

Comedy spectacular movie (1963) produced and directed by Stanley Kramer

Cast	Role
Spencer Tracy	Captain C. G. Culpeper
Milton Berle	J. Russell Finch
Sid Caesar	Melville Crump
Buddy Hackett	Benjy Benjamin
Ethel Merman	Mrs. Marcus
Dorothy Provine	Emmeline Finch
Edie Adams	Monica Crump
Mickey Rooney	Ding Bell
Phil Silvers	Otto Meyer
Dick Shawn	Sylvester Marcus
Jonathan Winters	Lennie Pike
Terry-Thomas	Lt. Col. J. Algernon Hawthorne

Cameo appearances were made by: Eddie "Rochester" Anderson, Peter Falk, Leo Gorcey, William Demarest, Alan Carney,

Andy Devine, Madlyn Rhue, Stan Freberg, Norman Fell, Nicholas Georgiade, Stanley Clements, Allen Jenkins, Tom Kennedy, Roy Engel, Paul Birch, Paul Ford, Charles McGraw, Ben Blue, Carl Reiner, Charles Lane, Jesse White, Bobo Lewis, Harry Lauter, Eddie Ryder, Don C. Harvey, ZaSu Pitts, Sterling Holloway, Moe Howard, Larry Fine, Joe DeRita (of The Three Stooges), Jim Backus, Barrie Chase, Edward Everett Horton, Buster Keaton, Don Knotts, Joe E. Brown, Marvin Kaplan, Arnold Stang, Lloyd Corrigan, Selma Diamond (voice only), Louise Glenn (voice only), Ben Lessy, Mike Mazurki, Nick Stewart, Sammee Tong, Jimmy Durante, Doodles Weaver, Jerry Lewis, Jack Benny, Dale Van Sickel, Roy Roberts, Barbara Pepper, Cliff Norton, Chick Chandler

It's Not Unusual
Tom Jones' theme song

Ivan
Cat in movie cartoon version of Prokofiev's "Peter and the Wolf"

Ivan Ivanovitch
Ethnic nickname applied to the average Russian

I've Got a Right to Sing the Blues
Theme song of Jack Teagarden's orchestra

Ivy League
Group of old, established Eastern colleges: so-called in athletic competition:

	Location	Date Founded	Football Nickname
Brown	Providence, R.I.	1764	Bruins
Columbia	New York, N.Y.	1754	Lions
Cornell	Ithaca, N.Y.	1865	Big Red
Dartmouth	Hanover, N.H.	1769	Big Green
Harvard	Cambridge, Mass.	1636	Crimson
Pennsylvania	Philadelphia, Pa.	1740	Red and Blue
Princeton*	Princeton, N.J.	1746	Tigers
Yale**	New Haven, Conn.	1701	Bulldogs

Iwo Jima
American flag was raised (Feb. 23, 1945) during World War II on Mount Suribachi by U. S. Marines: John H. Bradley, Michael Strank, Harlon H. Block, Franklin R. Sousley, Rene A. Gagnon, Ira H. Hayes***

The Pulitzer Prize winning photo was taken by Joe Rosenthal

---

* Known as Old Nassau

** Known as Old Eli

*** A movie, *The Outsider,* was made (1961) about Ira Hayes, starring Tony Curtis. A song was recorded by Johnny Cash, "Ballad of Ira Hayes"

A 78-foot bronze reproduction of the scene by Felix de Weldon, overlooking Washington, D. C., stands outside Arlington National Cemetery, Virginia

J

J

Joan Garrity, author of the best-seller *The Sensuous Woman*

J & B Rare Scotch

Justerini and Brooks

J. C. Penney

James Cash Penney, American businessman, retailer

J. W.

Little fat sheriff who sells Dodge automobiles (TV commercials): played by Joe Higgins

J. Fred Muggs

Chimpanzee on Dave Garroway's "Today Show" (TV)

J. Worthington Foulfellow

Fox (Disney feature cartoon movie *Pinocchio*)

Jabbar, Kareem Abdul-

Name adopted by basketball player Lew Alcindor as a practicing Muslim

Jabez Stone

New England farmer who sells his soul to the Devil and is defended by Daniel Webster (Stephen Vincent Benét's "The Devil and Daniel Webster"): played (in *All That Money Can Buy*) by James Craig

Jack

Sailor boy on Cracker Jacks box

Jack Griffin

Name of "The Invisible Man" in H. G. Wells's novel: in 1933 movie played by Claude Rains. In later "Invisible Man" movies, played by Vincent Price, Jon Hall, and Arthur Franz, the name became Geoffrey Radcliffe, Frank Raymond, Robert Griffin, and Tommy Nelson

Jack the Ripper

1888 London murderer of six prostitutes. First victim (August 7), Mary Anne Nicholls; last victim (November 9), Marie Kelly, though some attribute other victims before and after the 3-month period. He was never apprehended

Jack Tar

Nickname for a common sailor in the days of sailing ships, especially a British sailor: the name is either from "tarpaulin" or from the tar used on ropes that rubbed off on hands and clothing

Jackie Paper

Puff, the Magic Dragon's human friend (song by Peter, Paul, and Mary)

Jacko

The reversible dog, one of Paul Bunyan's three dogs

Jackson, Shoeless Joe

See *Shoeless Joe Jackson*

Jackson Five, The

Singing group: Marlon, Tito, Jackie, Jermaine, Michael

Jacob Marley

Ebenezer Scrooge's dead partner (Charles Dickens' *A Christmas Carol*): his ghost haunts Scrooge with clanking chains and other weird sounds

James Bond

Hero (secret agent) of novels written by Ian Fleming (1908-1964). Bond (C.M.G., R.N.V.R.) is a British secret agent in an organization headed by M. A gourmet, single and a womanizer, he marries Teresa Draco, who is killed soon after, though retaining a solid affection for Miss Moneypenny, M's secretary

Casino Royale (1954)
Diamonds Are Forever (1956)
Doctor No (1958)
For Your Eyes Only (1959)
From Russia, with Love (1957)
Goldfinger (1959)
Live and Let Die (1955)
The Man with the Golden Gun (1965)
Moonraker (1955)
Octopussy (1966)
On Her Majesty's Secret Service (1963)
The Spy Who Loved Me (1962)
Thunderball (1961)
You Only Live Twice (1964)

Movies (name of actor playing Bond in parentheses):

Dr. No, 1963 (Sean Connery)
From Russia with Love, 1964 (Sean Connery)
Goldfinger, 1965 (Sean Connery)
Thunderball, 1965 (Sean Connery)
You Only Live Twice, 1967 (Sean Connery)
Casino Royale, 1967 (David Niven)
On Her Majesty's Secret Service, 1970 (George Lazenby)
Diamonds Are Forever, 1971 (Sean Connery)
Live and Let Die, 1973 (Roger Moore)
The Man with the Golden Gun, 1974 (Roger Moore)

James T. Kirk

Captain and commander of the starship "Enterprise" (TV series "Star Trek"): played by William Shatner

Jamestown, Va.

Ships, under Christopher Newport, brought settlers to Jamestown (1607): "Sarah Constant," "Discovery," "Godspeed"

Jane Marple

Female detective created by Agatha Christie: played in motion pictures by Margaret Rutherford

Jane Porter

Tarzan's mate: in the 1932 *Tarzan the Ape Man* (the first Weissmuller picture) she is played by Maureen O'Sullivan and named Jane Parker

January 1, 2001

The first day of the 21st century

Jaq and Gus

Mice (Walt Disney's cartoon movie *Cinderella*)

Jasper

Family's pet dog (TV series "Bachelor Father")

Javert

French police inspector who hounds Jean Valjean (Victor Hugo's *Les Misérables*)

Jay, John

American diplomat (1745-1829), first chief justice of the Supreme Court (1789-1795), first (acting) secretary of state under the Constitution (1789-1790), author of some *Federalist* papers

Jazz Age, The

The 1920's: title coined by F. Scott Fitzgerald (*Tales of the Jazz Age,* 1922)

Jazz Singer, The

First "talkie" movie (1927, Warner Brothers): starring Al Jolson

Jean

Paul Bunyan's son

Jeeves

Butler of Bertie Wooster in P. G. Wodehouse novels

Jefferson City Junior High

School at which Mr. Peepers (Wally Cox) taught (TV series "Mr. Peepers")

Jefferson High

School at which Mr. Novak (James Franciscus) taught (TV series "Mr. Novak")

Jefferson High

School that the gang attends (TV series "Happy Days")

Jellystone Park

Home of Yogi Bear (TV cartoon)

Jennie

Thे mule of Jane Gibson (the Pig Woman) who discovered the bodies in the Hall-Mills murder case of the 1920's: every trivial thing in this case became subject for headlines

Jerry

Cartoon mouse (of "Tom and Jerry" series) who was Gene Kelly's dancing partner in *Anchors Aweigh* (1945)

Jersey Lily

Judge Roy Bean's saloon, named for actress Lily Langtry, in Langtry, Texas, where he was "the law west of the Pecos"

Jesus wept

Shortest verse in the Bible (John 11:35)

Jet Jackson

Hero of TV series "Jet Jackson, Flying Commando": played by Richard Webb

Jets and Sharks

Two rival gangs in movie *West Side Story*
Leader of the Jets—Riff: played by Russ Tamblyn
Leader of the Sharks—Bernardo: played by George Chakiris

Jim

Negro slave who accompanies Huckleberry Finn down the Mississippi on a raft

Jim Bell

Sky King's foreman (radio series)

Jim Hawkins

Boy hero of Robert Louis Stevenson's *Treasure Island*

Jiminy Cricket

Pinocchio's cricket friend (Disney cartoon feature movie): voice of Cliff Edwards

Jimmy the Greek

Nickname of Las Vegas odds-maker James Snyder (original name, before 1939: Dimitrios Synodinos)

Jimmy and Jane Webb

Tom Mix's wards (radio series)

Jimmy Olsen

Office boy for the *Daily Planet* ("Superman")

Jingles

Wild Bill Hickok's partner (TV series "Wild Bill Hickok"): played by Andy Devine

Joad

Name of migrant Okie family (John Steinbeck's *The Grapes of Wrath*)

Jock

Scottish terrier in *Lady and the Tramp* (Disney cartoon feature movie)

Joe Corntassel
Orphan Annie's boyfriend

Joe Mannix
Private eye (TV series "Mannix"): played by Mike Connors

Joe the Monster
Villain in Ian Fleming's *Chitty-Chitty-Bang-Bang*. His gang: Man-Mountain Fink, Soapy Sam, Blood-Money Banks

Joey
Dennis the Menace's younger friend (Hank Ketcham's comic strip)

Joey Chill
Shot and killed Mr. and Mrs. Thomas Wayne, the parents of Bruce Wayne (Batman)

John
Loretta Young's announcer (TV show "The Loretta Young Show")

John and Alice Clayton
Lord and Lady Greystoke, Tarzan's father and mother

John Birch Society
Named after United States missionary and intelligence officer killed (1945) by Chinese Communists: founded by Robert Welch, retired candy manufacturer, in 1958

John Brown's Body
Tune to which Julia Ward Howe's words for "Battle Hymn of the Republic" are sung

John Bull
Personification of the British people

John J. Malone
Detective in Craig Rice stories: played by Frank Lovejoy on radio

John Reid
Texas Ranger who became the Lone Ranger

Johnny
Señor Wences' hand puppet

Johnny
John Roventini, the Philip Morris page boy: "Call for Philip Morris" (sometimes played by Freddy Douglas)

Johnny Appleseed
Nickname of John Chapman, 1775-1845, who planted apple seeds throughout the Ohio Valley

Johnny Corkscrew
Pet name of the cutlass of Smee, Captain Hook's first mate (James M. Barrie's *Peter Pan*)

Johnny Yuma
"The Rebel" in TV series: starred Nick Adams

Johnson, Andrew

President of the United States after Lincoln's assassination (1865): also called Tennessee Johnson. Quarreling with the more severe wing of the Republican Party over Reconstruction tactics, he was impeached by the House of Representatives on March 4, 1868, on 11 counts, and was acquitted when the Senate failed by one vote to reach a ⅔ majority for conviction on the first 3 counts

Johnson, Lyndon B.

President of the United States after Kennedy's assassination (1963). His wife, Claudia Alta Taylor Johnson, was called Lady Bird. His children (married names): Lynda Bird Robb and Lucy (Luci) Baines Nugent

JoJo

The dog-faced boy, exhibited in the United States in 1885. Real name: Theodore Peteroff

Jolly Roger

Pirate flag of white skull and crossbones on a black field

Jolly Roger

Captain Hook's pirate ship (James M. Barrie's *Peter Pan*)

Jonathan Livingston Seagull

Best-selling novel by Richard Bach

Jones, John Luther

Casey Jones's real name

Jor-El and Lara

Superman's real parents, who died when the planet Krypton was destroyed

Jorgensen, George, Jr.

Christine Jorgensen's name before sex-change operation in Copenhagen, 1951

Jose Jimenez

Mexican-Spanish comic: played by Bill Dana ("My name Jose Jimenez")

Josephine

Widow of Alexandre, Vicomte de Beauharnais, who became Napoleon's first wife (married 1796, divorced 1809). He then married (1810) Princess Marie Louise of Austria

Josephine

Female plumber in TV Comet cleanser commercials: played by Jane Withers

Josh Randall

The bounty hunter (TV series "Wanted—Dead or Alive"): played by Steve McQueen. He called his 30-40 carbine "Mare's Laig"

Jot 'Em Down Store

In Pine Ridge, Arkansas, location of radio series "Lum and Abner"

Judah

Ben-Hur's first name (Lew Wallace's *Ben-Hur*)

Judge (James) Hardy

Andy Hardy's father: for most of the series played by Lewis Stone (in the first picture, *A Family Affair*, Lionel Barrymore was Judge Hardy)

Judy

Chimpanzee (TV series "Daktari")

Judy, Judy, Judy

Never said by Cary Grant in any movie: used by imitators as characteristic Grant exclamation

Judy Splinters

Shirley Dinsdale's dummy (radio/TV)

Jughead Jones

Archie Andrews' sidekick (comics)

Julius

Jeff's twin brother ("Mutt and Jeff" comic strip)

July 4

U. S. Independence Day, day on which ex-presidents Thomas Jefferson and John Adams (1826, 50th anniversary of Declaration of Independence) and James Monroe (1831) died. Stephen Collins Foster, popular song writer, was born the day Adams and Jefferson died, and George M. Cohan claimed July 4, 1878, as his birth date (actually July 3)

June Bug

Glenn Curtiss' first airplane, winner of the Aeronautical Trophy, 1908

June Taylor Dancers

Dancers on Jackie Gleason's TV show

Juneau, U.S.S.

United States cruiser on which the five Sullivan brothers lost their lives, Nov. 13, 1942, off Guadalcanal during the American landings

Jungle Jim

Movie series (1948) played by Johnny Weissmuller: Caw-Caw, pet crow; Skipper, pet dog; Tamba, pet chimp; Kolu, native companion

Jungle Twins, The

Tono and Kono (created by Edgar Rice Burroughs)

Junior

Chester Riley's son (radio/TV "Life of Riley")

Junior Woodchucks

Organization to which Donald Duck's nephews, Huey, Dewey, and Louie belong

Junkville

Bucky Bug and June Bug's home (Walt Disney cartoon characters)

Jupiter

Central Pacific wood-burning locomotive No. 60 that met the Union Pacific coal-burning locomotive No. 119 at Promontory, Utah, May 10, 1869

Justice, Inc.

Evil-fighting organization led by The Avenger (Richard Henry Benson): headquarters on Bleek Street, Manhattan (novel series created by Kenneth Robeson). Members of the organization: Fergus MacMaudie, Cole Wilson, Algernon Heathcote Smith (Smitty), Nellie Gray, Josh Newton, Rosabel Newton

Justice League of America

Comic book series featured:

Earth One

The Flash; Wonderwoman; Superman; Batman; Green Lantern

Earth Two

Hawkman; Black Canary; Doctor Fate; Doctor Midnite; Starman

Earth Three

Superwoman; Owlman; Ultraman; Johnny Quick; Power ring

Other members

Uncle Sam; The Ray (Happy Terrill); Doll Man (Darrell Dane); The Black Condor (Tom Wright); The Human Bomb (Roy Lincoln); The Phantom Lady (Sandra Knight)

K

K2

Mt. Godwin-Austen or Dapsang, 28,250 feet, second highest mountain in the world: in Himalayas (Karakorams)

K H A Q Q

Amelia Earhart's call sign on her last flight, July 3, 1937

K H W B B

Call sign of Toni Carter's Lockheed Electra NR16056 (1943 movie *Flight for Freedom*, based on Amelia Earhart's life)

Kaa

Python (Rudyard Kipling's *The Jungle Book*)

Kala

The ape that adopted and raised the baby Tarzan

Kal-El

Superman's name on the planet of his birth, Krypton

Kamikaze

The Divine Wind: name adopted by Japanese World War II suicide pilots

KAOS

Evil organization (TV series "Get Smart")

Karas, Anton

Zither player (only his hands appear) who plays theme song and a waltz (1949 movie *The Third Man*)

Kato

The Green Hornet's valet (TV series "The Green Hornet"): played by Bruce Lee. In the radio series earlier, Kato, played by several actors, is said to have changed from Japanese to Filipino when World War II broke out

Katzenjammer Kids

Comic strip begun (1897) by Rudolph Dirks and continued (from 1912) by Harold Knerr. Also known by the names "Hans und Fritz" (Dirks) and "The Captain and the Kids" (since World War I)

Kaw-Liga

Cigar-store wooden Indian (song written by Hank Williams)

Kearsarge, U.S.S.

Only U. S. battleship not named after a state. The screw sloop "Kearsarge" sank the Confederate raider "Alabama" in 1864. When that "Kearsarge" was lost in the West Indies in 1894, the name was given, because of popular demand, to one of the new battleships

Keeling, U.S.S.

Commander George Krause's destroyer (C. S. Forester's *The Good Shepherd*)

Keeshan, Bob

Played Clarabell the clown ("Howdy Doody Show") and Captain Kangaroo

Kelcy's Bar

Archie Bunker's favorite hangout (TV series "All in the Family")

Kelly, Alvin

See *Shipwreck Kelly*

Kelly, Mary

Jack the Ripper's last victim (London, 1888)

Kemo Sabe
>   Meaning "faithful friend": said of the Lone Ranger by Tonto

Kemp Morgan
>   The world's greatest oil well dweller (American folklore)

Ken
>   Barbie the doll's boyfriend doll

Ken Thurston
>   Identity of radio's "A Man Called X" (detective played by Herbert Marshall)

Kennedy children
>   The family of Joseph (1888-1969) and Rose Fitzgerald Kennedy:
>   Joseph, Jr., killed (1944) in World War II
>   Jack (John) (1917-1963), President of the United States, 1961-1963; assassinated
>   Rosemary, mentally retarded
>   Kathleen, killed (1948) in plane crash
>   Eunice, married R. Sargent Shriver
>   Patricia, married Peter Lawford
>   Robert (1925-1968), Attorney General of the United States (1961-1963) and United States Senator from New York (1965-1968); assassinated
>   Jean, married Stephen Smith
>   Edward, United States Senator from Massachusetts (1962-   )

Kennedy, John Fitzgerald
>   (1917-1963), youngest man elected President of the United States, 43 years old when elected in 1960 (Theodore Roosevelt was the youngest inaugurated, 42 years, 10 months, 18 days, when sworn in Sept. 14, 1901)
>   His children: Caroline (born 1957), John (born 1960), Patrick (born 1963; died soon after birth)

Kenny, Bill
>   Lead singer of the Ink Spots

Kent Allard
>   Secret identity of The Shadow, though he uses the guise of Lamont Cranston. The real Lamont Cranston, a world explorer, has given Allard permission to use his name (comic book series "The Shadow")

Kents
>   Martha (was Mary) and Jonathan: adopted infant Superman

Kentucky Derby
>   Annual horse race at Churchill Downs, Louisville, Kentucky (run on the first Saturday in May). First winner (1876): Aristides

Kermit
>   Frog (TV series "Sesame Street")

Kid Shelleen/Tim Strawn

Lee Marvin's dual role as good/bad twins (movie *Cat Ballou*): won Oscar as best actor 1965

Kienast Quintuplets

Born Feb. 24, 1970: Ted; Gordon; Abigail; Sara; Amy

Kigmy

Animal glad to have aggressions taken out on it ("Li'l Abner" comic strip)

KILLER

Flip Wilson's California automobile license plate

Kim

Kimball O'Hara, Irish orphan in Lahore, India (Rudyard Kipling's *Kim*): played in 1950 movie by Dean Stockwell

Kimba

The white lion (TV cartoon)

Kimba

Jungle Jim's pet chimpanzee (movie series)

King

Horse (TV series "National Velvet"): in the 1944 movie the horse was called The Pie, as he was in Enid Bagnold's 1935 novel (short for The Piebald)

King

Alaskan husky used as dog-team leader by Sergeant Preston of the Yukon

King, Billie Jean

Top U. S. women's tennis player, victor over former Wimbledon and Forest Hills winner Bobby Riggs in straight sets, 6-4, 6-3, 6-3, in the Houston Astrodome, Sept. 20, 1973. She is the sister of San Francisco Giants' pitcher Randy Moffitt

King Blozo

King of Nazilia (cartoon "Thimble Theatre")

King Cheops

Greek form of the Egyptian name Khufu, the pharaoh who built Egypt's largest pyramid (at Giza)

King of the Cowboys

Roy Rogers' title

King Creole

Title of 1958 movie made from Harold Robbins' *A Stone for Danny Fisher*: Elvis Presley played the role of Danny Finnell

King Kong

Giant gorilla brought from Skull Island by Carl Denham (Robert Armstrong) and John Driscoll (Bruce Cabot) to New York on Captain Englehorn's ship "Venture." Ann Darrow (Fay Wray) is later kidnapped by Kong. Kong climbs the Empire State building and is shot down by airplanes.

The 1933 movie, from a story by Edgar Wallace and Merian C. Cooper, was directed by Cooper and Ernest B. Schoedsack. The animation of the ape monster was by Willis O'Brien.

The monster ape's dimensions were supposedly:

Height, 50 ft.	Nose, 2 ft.
Reach, 75 ft.	Ear, 1 ft. long
Arm, 23 ft.	Eye, 10 in. long
Leg, 15 ft.	Chest, 60 ft.
Face, 7 ft.	Molar, 14 in. round, 4 in. high

King Lear's daughters

Goneril, wife of Duke of Albany

Regan, wife of Duke of Cornwall

Cordelia, the youngest daughter, wife of King of France

King Leonardo Lion

King of all Bongo Congo (comic strip)

King Sisters

Singers: Donna, Alyce, Louise, Maxine, Yvonne, Marilyn

King Solomon's Ring

Magic ring worn by Solomon that enabled him to understand the animals and gave him power over all things

King Timahoe

President Nixon's Irish setter

Kingdoms of Nature

Animal, Vegetable, Mineral (generally used as opening question of a twenty questions game)

Kingfish

George Stevens' title on "Amos 'n' Andy" (he was top man of The Mystic Knights of the Sea Lodge)

Kingston Trio

Group established in 1958. Original members: Bob Shane; Dave Guard (replaced by John Stewart); Nick Reynolds

Kitty

Girlfriend (Mae Clarke) who gets grapefruit shoved in her face by Tom Powers (James Cagney) (movie *The Public Enemy*, 1931)

Kiwi, The

Schooner (TV series "The Wackiest Ship In the Army")

Klaatu Borada Nikto

Words that stop the huge robot Gort from destroying the earth as he has been programmed to do (1951 movie *The Day the Earth Stood Still*): said by Patricia Neal

Klingons

Enemies of the Federation (TV series "Star Trek")

Knievel, Robert Craig

Daredevil motorcycle stunt rider, known as Evel Knievel: suffered many crashes and broken bones

Knighthood

Orders (9) of Great Britain (highest to lowest):
Garter (royalty or peerage), KG
Thistle (Scottish nobles), KT
St. Patrick (Irish nobles), KP
Bath (3 classes), GCB, KCB, CB
Star of India (3 classes), GCSI, KCSI, CSI
St. Michael and St. George (3 classes), GCMG, KCMG, CMG
Indian Empire (3 classes), GCIE, KCIE, CIE
Victorian Order (5 classes; open to women)
British Empire (5 classes; open to women)
(Baronets rank just below Knights of the Bath; Knights Bachelor are not members of any order)

Knights of the Round Table

The Round Table was given to Arthur by Leodegraunce, his father-in-law, whose men filled 100 seats; Merlin seated 28 more, Arthur 2, and 20 were left for worthy knights. The Siege Perilous, next to Arthur, was the death of any who sat in it except the Grail Knight

King Arthur's retainers and henchmen who sat at a smaller Round Table with him were: Sir Lancelot; Sir Galahad; Sir Gawain; Sir Percivale; Sir Kay; Sir Tor; Sir Gareth; Sir Tristram; Sir Palomides; Sir Lamorack; Sir Modred; Sir Mark; Sir Acolon; Sir Bors; Sir Floll; Sir Lionel

Knobby Walsh

Joe Palooka's trainer and manager (comic strip "Joe Palooka"). In a Monogram movie series, played by Leon Erroll and James Gleason

Kojak

Theo Kojak, New York City detective (TV series "Kojak"): played by Telly Savalas. To cut down smoking, he sucks Tootsie Roll pops

KoKo

Clown drawn "Out of the Inkwell" (movie cartoons) by Max Fleischer

Kolu

Jungle Jim's native companion (comics)

Kon-Tiki

Thor Heyerdahl's balsawood raft, sailed from Lima, Peru, to Tuamotu Islands (1947)

Konigin Luise

German patrol boat pursued by the "African Queen" (*The African Queen* by C. S. Forester)

Kookie

Parking lot attendant for Dino's Restaurant (TV series "77 Sunset Strip"): played by Edd Byrnes

Kor

Kingdom of the African sorceress "She" (Ayesha or "She Who Must Be Obeyed") in H. Rider Haggard's novel *She*

Krypto

Superman's superdog

Krypton

Superman's planet of birth

Kryptonite

Green metal that takes away Superman's magic powers

Kukla, Fran, and Ollie

Burr Tillstrom, puppeteer

Fran, Fran Allison

Puppets on the TV show: Kukla; Ollie; Madame Oglepuss; Beulah the Witch; "Dumb" Cecil Bill; Windbag Colonel Crackie; Dolores Dragon; Mercedes; Fletcher Rabbit; Ollie's Niece

L

L90

Police unit commanded by Sergeant MacDonald (Mac, played by William Boyett) (TV series "Adam 12")

LSD

Lysergic acid diethylamide

L.S./M.F.T.

Lucky Strike / Means Fine Tobacco

La Paloma

Ship that brought the Maltese Falcon from Hong Kong to San Francisco (Dashiell Hammett's *The Maltese Falcon*). The ship burns at its San Francisco pier, an occurrence unexplained in the movie

Ladadog

Family dog (TV series "Please Don't Eat the Daisies")

Laddie Boy

President Harding's airedale

Lady Be Good

World War II B-24 that landed in Libyan Desert after crew bailed out: plane found intact in 1959; none of the crew was ever found

Lady Bird

Nickname of Claudia Alta Taylor Johnson, wife of President Lyndon B. Johnson

Lady with the Lamp

Florence Nightingale (1820-1910), English nurse in Crimean War; first woman to receive Order of Merit (1907)

Laika

"Barker": first dog to orbit Earth, in Russian Sputnik II, November 1957

Lake of the Woods

Lake between Minnesota and Canada, contains the most northerly point of the 48 contiguous states

Lakeview

Locale of TV serial "How to Survive a Marriage"

Lambert

The sheepish lion (movie cartoon)

Lamont Cranston

Real identity of The Shadow. But compare *Kent Allard*

Lana Lang

Superboy's girlfriend when he lived and grew up in Smallville (comic book series "Superboy")

Lancelot Link

Chimpanzee that heads APE (Agency to Prevent Evil) (TV series "Lancelot Link"). CHUMP (Criminal Headquarters for Underworld Master Plan) is the evil organization with which APE is in constant battle

Land of Nod

Country east of Eden where Cain lived after killing Abel

Landon, Michael

Actor (real name: Orowitz) who was Little Jo in TV series "Bonanza"

In movies, played the Werewolf in 1957 *I Was a Teenage Werewolf* and Dave Dawson, the albino, in 1958 *God's Little Acre*

Lane Sisters

Actresses (real name: Mullican): Lola, Rosemary, Priscilla; appeared together (with Gail Page) in *Four Daughters* (1938), *Four Wives* (1940), *Four Mothers* (1941)

Langley, U.S.S.

First United States aircraft carrier, commissioned March 20, 1922 (ex coal carrier "Jupiter")

Larsen, Don

New York Yankee pitcher who on October 8, 1956, pitched the only perfect game in World Series history. It was at Yankee Stadium against the Brooklyn Dodgers, not one of whose batters reached first base. Final score: New York 2, Brooklyn 0. Larsen made only 97 pitches and struck out 7, including the last batter, Dale Mitchell, who batted for Larsen's opposing pitcher, Sal Maglie

Laser

Light Amplification by Stimulated Emission of Radiation

Lash La Rue

Movie cowboy Al La Rue who uses a 15-foot bullwhip as his primary weapon

Lassie

First animal named to Animal Hall of Fame

Last of the Red Hot Mamas

Nickname of singer Sophie Tucker (1884-1966)

Laugh-In

Original cast (1968) included: Dan Rowan, Dick Martin, Judy Carne, Arte Johnson, Jo Anne Worley, Henry Gibson, Ruth Buzzi, Garry Owens. Goldie Hawn joined in midseason

Law West of the Pecos

Judge Roy Bean

Lawrence, D. H.

David Herbert Lawrence (1885-1930), English novelist and poet: *Sons and Lovers* (1913), *Lady Chatterley's Lover* (1928)

Lawrence, (Captain) James

U. S. naval officer who said "Don't give up the ship," when he fell mortally wounded aboard the "Chesapeake" fighting the "Shannon," June 1, 1813

Lawrence of Arabia

Thomas Edward Lawrence (1888-1935), alias T. E. Shaw, alias Aircraftman Ross, English scholar, soldier, diplomat, and secret agent

Laws

Murphy's Law: "Whatever can be done wrong, eventually will be (at the worst possible time)"

Parkinson's Law: "Work expands so as to fill the time available for its completion"

Gresham's Law: "Bad money will drive good money out of circulation"

Worth's Law: "When something fails to work and you demonstrate it for a repairman, it works better than ever, as if it never failed to work at all"

Peter Principle: "In a hierarchy, every employee tends to rise to his level of incompetence"

Lazarus

The man Jesus Christ raised from the dead

Lazarus and Bummer
>Emperor Norton's two dogs

Leap Frog
>Theme song of Les Brown's orchestra

Leapin' Lizards
>Little Orphan Annie's favorite expression

Leatherstocking
>Natty Bumppo, hero of novels by James Fenimore Cooper. In the order in which they are supposed to have occurred, they are
>>*The Deerslayer* (1841)
>>*The Last of the Mohicans* (1826)
>>*The Pathfinder* (1840)
>>*Tne Pioneers* (1823)
>>*The Prairie* (1827)
>
>Natty Bumppo is also called Deerslayer, Hawkeye, Trapper, and Pathfinder, as well as Leatherstocking

Lee
>Charlie Chan's number one son

Legend of Sleepy Hollow, The
>Story by Washington Irving in *The Sketch Book (of Geoffrey Crayon)* (1819-20): The headless horseman, said to be the ghost of a Hessian soldier who lost his head by a cannonball in the Revolutionary War, was impersonated by Brom Bones who thus scared schoolmaster Ichabod Crane out of the village and won the hand of Katrina Van Tassel

Legs
>Insects, 6 legs; Spider, 8 legs; Octopus, 8 legs; Squid, 10 legs; Lobster, 8 legs

Lemuel Gulliver
>Hero of Jonathan Swift's *Gulliver's Travels*

Lemuel Q. Stoopnagle
>Col. Stoopnagle of "Col. Stoopnagle and Budd"

Lena the Hyena
>Ugliest woman in lower Slobbovia (comic strip series "Li'l Abner")

Lenin, Nikolai
>Pseudonym of Vladimir Ilyich Ulyanov (1870-1924), leader (1917) of Bolshevik (Communist) revolution in Russia: also called V. I. Lenin

Leningrad
>Formerly St. Petersburg (1703-1914) and Petrograd (1914-1924). Founded by Peter the Great in 1703, it was the Russian capital until after the 1917 Revolution

Lennie and George

Characters in John Steinbeck's *Of Mice and Men*: George tells Lennie "all about the rabbits"

Lennon Sisters

Singers: Dianne, Peggy, Janet, Kathy

Leo

The MGM lion (trademark)

Leper Colony

B-17 belonging to the 918th Bomber Group to which the misfits were assigned (1949 movie *Twelve O'Clock High*)

Lepidopterist

A collector of butterflies or moths

Leslie Special

Automobile driven by Leslie Gallant III (Tony Curtis) (movie *The Great Race*)

Lester

Willie Tyler's dummy (TV's "Laugh-In")

Lester

Family in Erskine Caldwell's *Tabacco Road*: Jeeter Lester is the poor-white father. Dramatized by Jack Kirkland, it ran on Broadway for 3,182 performances (1933-1941)

Lestrade

Scotland Yard man often seeking Sherlock Holmes' aid

Let's Dance

Theme song of Benny Goodman's orchestra

Levant, U.S.S.

Corvette upon which Philip Nolan died (Edward Everett Hale's "The Man Without a Country")

Lew Archer

Detective in Ross Macdonald's novels

Lewis and Clark

Captain Meriwether Lewis and Lieutenant William Clark who led expedition from St. Louis to Pacific Ocean and back (1804-1806)

Lewis, Jerry

American comedian, actor, and director (real name: Joseph Levitch)

"The _____" character movies: *The Stooge*, 1953; *The Caddy*, 1953; *The Delicate Delinquent*, 1957; *The Sad Sack*, 1958; *The Geisha Boy*, 1958; *The Bellboy*, 1960; *The Errand Boy*, 1961; *The Lady's Man*, 1961; *The Nutty Professor*, 1963; *The Patsy*, 1964; *The Disorderly Orderly*, 1964; *Big Mouth*, 1967 Lewis's partner until 1957 was Dean Martin.

Lewis, Shari
> Ventriloquist. Her puppets: Lamb Chop, Charlie Horse

Lexington
> George Washington's saddle horse

Lexington, U.S.S.
> Carrier lost in the Battle of the Coral Sea (May 1942)

Liberal Arts
> Trivium: Grammar, Logic, Rhetoric
> Quadrivium: Arithmetic, Geometry, Astronomy, Music

Liberty
> John Hancock's schooner

Liberty Island
> Location of the Statue of Liberty in New York harbor (formerly Bedloe's Island)

Liberty, U.S.S.
> United States ship attacked near Sinai Peninsula by Israeli planes and PT boats during Six Day War (June 8, 1967): 34 killed, 75 wounded

Lieutenant Colonel
> Permanent rank held by George Armstrong Custer when killed at the Little Big Horn (1876)

Lieutenant Flap
> Black lieutenant (cartoon series "Beetle Bailey")

Lieutenant Fuzz
> Young lieutenant (cartoon series "Beetle Bailey")

Lieutenant Jacoby
> Peter Gunn's police friend (on TV played by Herschel Bernardi)

Lieutenant Pinkerton
> Madame Butterfly's lover, an American Navy officer (opera by Giacomo Puccini, 1904-1905)

Lieutenant Rip Masters
> Commander of Fort Apache (TV series "Rin-Tin-Tin")

Life Savers candy
> Order of colors in five-flavor roll: Yellow, Red, Orange, Green, White, Red, Yellow, Green, White, Red, Orange

Light Horse Harry
> General Henry Lee (1756-1818), American cavalry officer in the Revolutionary War, father of General Robert E. Lee

Lightnin'
> Janitor of Amos 'n' Andy's Mystic Knights of the Sea Lodge

Lightning Lad
> Native of the planet Winath (true name: Garth Ranzz) he creates lightning in fight against evil: charter member of the Legion of Super-Heroes (comic books)

Li'l Abner

Hero of comic strip by Al Capp, begun August 12, 1935. He and his father and mother, Pappy and Mammy Yokum, live in Dogpatch, somewhere in the Appalachian mountains. Li'l Abner marries Daisy Mae Scraggs

Li'l Abner was played in the movies by Buster Keaton (1940: *Li'l Abner* or *Trouble Chaser*) and in musical film by Peter Palmer, who also played the part in the New York stage musical

Lilliput

Land of the small people (Swift's *Gulliver's Travels*)

Linc Case

One of the automobilists in TV's "Route 66" (replaced by Buz Murdock): played by Glenn Corbett

Lincoln Highway

First coast-to-coast paved road in the United States (New York to California), opened in 1913

Lincoln International

Airport of Arthur Hailey's *Airport*

Lincoln Island

Name of "The Mysterious Island" in the novel (1870) by Jules Verne

Lincoln Memorial

Classical building (architect Henry Bacon, 1922) west of The Mall, Washington, D.C., with monumental statue of seated Lincoln by Daniel Chester French: first appeared on reverse of Lincoln penny in 1959

Lindbergh, Charles

Made solo flight, May 20-21, 1927, in Ryan monoplane, "The Spirit of St. Louis," from Roosevelt Field, Long Island, New York, to Le Bourget Air Field, Paris, France, 33 hours, 39 minutes

Lipton Tea Girl, The

Mary (radio commercials)

Little Beaver

Sidekick of Red Ryder

Little Black Sambo

Black Jumbo was his father, Black Mumbo his mother

Little Boy

Code name for the atomic bomb dropped on Hiroshima

Little boys

Made of "frogs and snails and puppy dog tails"

Little Caesar

Caesar Enrico Bandello, central gangster role (1930 movie *Little Caesar*): played by Edward G. Robinson

Little Corporal
Nickname of Napoleon Bonaparte, who was 5 ft. 6 in. tall

Little Egypt
Pseudonym of Catherine Devine, who danced at the Chicago World's Fair in 1893

Little girls
Made of "sugar and spice and everything nice"

Little Green Sprout
The Jolly Green Giant's little helper (advertisement)

Little League World Series
Played at the home of Little League baseball, Williamsport, Pa.

Little Lulu's Friends
Tubby Tompkins, Gloria, Iggy, Annie (comic book)

Little Mermaid, The
Statue by Edvard Ericksen at the water's edge in Copenhagen Harbor, depicting the heroine of one of Hans Christian Andersen's stories

Little Rascals, The
"Our Gang" movies shown on TV

Little Red-haired Girl
Girl Charlie Brown is in love with (Charles "Sparky" Schulz says that he will never draw her)

Little Richard
Pseudonym of rock 'n' roll singer Richard Penniman

Little Tough Guys
Group formed from Dead End Kids to work at Universal. It included Huntz Hall, Gabriel Dell, Billy Halop, and Bernard Punsley

Little Tramp, The
A nickname of Charles Chaplin

Little White Dove
Running Bear's little Indian maiden (song "Running Bear" by Johnny Preston)

Little Wise Guys
Crime-fighting kids: Meatball, Scarecrow, Pee Wee, Jock (comic book series): their mentor is Daredevil

Lizzy
Douglas "Wrong Way" Corrigan's airplane: also known as "The Flying Crate"

Llanview
Locale of TV serial "One Life to Live"

Lobo
The trained dog with Horace Heidt's band

Lockard, Joe
>   The radar operator at Pearl Harbor who spotted the approaching Japanese planes but was told to ignore it, December 7, 1941

Lockheed XF90
>   Plane flown by the Blackhawks, after they flew the Grumman F5F (comic book series "Blackhawk")

Loco
>   Horse ridden by Pancho (Cisco Kid's partner)

Lois Lane
>   Superman's girlfriend who works as a reporter for the "Daily Planet"

Lollipops
>   Tootsie Roll pops, substitute for cigarettes adopted by Lt. Kojak (Telly Savalas) (TV series "Kojak")

Lombardo brothers
>   Guy (leader of the "Royal Canadians," who play "the sweetest music this side of heaven"); Carmen (whose flute training gave his saxophone playing a distinctive sound); Lebert (trumpet), Victor (saxophone)

Lon, Alice
>   Lawrence Welk's original Champagne Lady (TV)

London Bridge
>   Re-erected at Lake Havasu City, Arizona

Londonderry Air
>   Tune to which the words of "Danny Boy" are sung"

Lone Eagle, The
>   Nickname of Charles Lindbergh

Lone Ranger
>   Secret identity of Texas Ranger John Reid
>   His horse is named Silver
>   His sidekick is an Indian named Tonto, whose horse is named Scout (or, earlier, White Feller or Paint)
>   Radio, played by Jack Deeds, George Seaton (Stenius), Brace Beemer, Earle Graser, John Todd
>   Movies, played by Robert Livingston, 2nd, Lee Powell
>   TV, played by Clayton Moore, John Hart

Lone Wolf, The
>   Nickname of Michael Lanyard in TV series

Lonesome George
>   Nickname adopted by George Gobel (TV)

Long Branch
>   Dodge City saloon owned by Miss Kitty (Amanda Blake) (TV series "Gunsmoke")

Long Count, The

Occurred in the Jack Dempsey-Gene Tunney heavyweight championship fight, Sept. 22, 1927, at Soldier Field, Chicago. Tunney, on the canvas for thirteen seconds in the seventh round, went on to win the 10-round decision (Referee Dave Barry began counting only when Dempsey had gone to a neutral corner, as the rules required)

Long John Silver

Peg-legged pirate (Robert Louis Stevenson's *Treasure Island*): formerly Captain Flint's quartermaster

Long Tom

Captain Hook's ship's cannon (James M. Barrie's *Peter Pan*)

Looney Tunes

Cartoon series by Warner Brothers (together with "Merrie Melodies"): "That's All, Folks"

Lord Greystoke

Tarzan's true identity

Lord Haw-Haw

Nickname for William Joyce (1906-1946), Irish-American who broadcast for the Germans during World War II: he was tried, convicted of treason, and hanged

Lord of San Simeon

William Randolph Hearst (1863-1951), California newspaper publisher who built palace-like estate at San Simeon

Lorelei Kilbourne

Steve Wilson's society editor and girlfriend (radio/TV series "Big Town"): played on radio by Claire Trevor, Ona Munson, and Fran Carlon

Lost Horizon

Novel (1933) by James Hilton: the first paperback book issued by Pocket Books (1939), cost 25¢

Lothar

Mandrake the Magician's giant partner (comics)

Lou Wickersham

Mannix's former boss (TV series "Mannix"): played by Joseph Campanella

Louie's Sweet Shop

Bowery Boys' hangout run by Louis Dumbrowsky (played by Bernard Gorcey, Leo Gorcey's father)

Louis XIV candelabra (or candelabrum)

Liberace's constant companion (placed on his piano)

Louisville Lip

Nickname of boxer Cassius Clay (Muhammad Ali), noted for his volubility

Love Bug, The

A Volkswagen named Herbie (Disney movies *The Love Bug* and *Herbie Rides Again*)

Love in Bloom

Jack Benny's theme song: originally sung by Bing Crosby in *She Loves Me Not* (1934)

Love Nest

Theme song of George Burns and Gracie Allen

Love Story

Novel (1970) by Erich Segal (when the movie made from it was shown on TV nearly 72 million people watched, the largest audience ever for one TV show)

Lovelace, Linda

Female star of X-rated movie *Deep Throat*

Low, Juliette Gordon

Founded the Girl Scouts (originally Girl Guides) in the United States, 1912

Lubanski, Ed

Bowled two consecutive 300-point games at Miami's Bowling Palace, June 22, 1959

Luce, Henry Robinson

American publisher (1898-1967), founder of *Time* (1923), *Fortune* (1930), and *Life* (1936) magazines

Lucifer

Cinderella's stepmother's cat (Disney cartoon movie)

Lucille

B. B. King's red electric guitar

Lucille McGillicuddy

Lucy Ricardo's maiden name (TV series "I Love Lucy")

Lucky

The *National Enquirer's* dog

Lucky Lady II

First round-the-world nonstop airplane flight (1949): B-50 Superfortress (refueled four times)

Lucky Pup

TV puppet show (puppeteers: Hope and Morey Bunin)
Featured puppets: Lucky Pup, Pinhead, Foodini

Lucky Smith

Detective in series on radio: played by former heavyweight champion Max Baer

Lucy

Guitar of Albert King (blues singer)

Lucy

Goose (Walt Disney's cartoon movie feature *101 Dalmatians*)

Lucy

Elephant led to safety across the Alps to Switzerland by a British soldier (movie *Hannibal Brooks*)

Luke the Drifter

Nickname of Hank Williams

Lulubelle

Bongo the Bear's girlfriend

Luno

Winged stallion of Mighty Mouse cartoons (comic book/TV series)

Lupus, Peter

Actor who played Willie Armitage in TV series "Mission Impossible." He was winner of titles Mr. Indianapolis, Mr. Indiana, Mr. Hercules, Mr. International Health

Lurch

Butler of the Addams family (TV series "The Addams Family"): played by Ted Cassidy

Lusitania

Cunard liner, torpedoed and sunk May 7, 1915, off Old Head of Kinsale, Ireland, in a voyage from New York. Some 1,198 lives were lost

Lydia, H.M.S.

Captain Horatio Hornblower's ship (C. S. Forester's novel series)

M

M

Admiral Sir Miles Messervy, K.C.M.G., James Bond's supervisor in His Majesty's Secret Service

M

Author of the best-selling book *The Sensuous Man*

M*A*S*H

Mobile Army Surgical Hospital: title of 1970 movie starring Donald Sutherland, Elliott Gould, and Sally Kellerman, and subject of 1952 *Battle Circus* starring Humphrey Bogart and June Allyson

The TV series features Alan Alda

M-G-M

Metro-Goldwyn-Mayer: Metro being Marcus Loew's early film company; Goldwyn being Samuel Goldwyn; Mayer being Louis B. Mayer

M-G-M's lion is called Leo

The company motto, *Ars Gratia Artis* ("Art for Art's Sake"), appears in the circular band framing the lion's head

MV

Secret identification signal of the French fleet, discovered and used by Captain Horatio Hornblower (1951 movie *Captain Horatio Hornblower*)

Ma Barker

Kate Barker, born (1872) Arizona Donnie Clark in Springfield, Mo.; she married George Barker, who died in 1932; an outlaw, she was reputed head of gang which included her boys (sons) Arthur, Fred, Herman, Lloyd

Ma and Pa Kettle

Movie series in which principal roles were played by Marjorie Main and Percy Kilbride as a pair of rustics
Originally in *The Egg and I*, 1947
Ma and Pa Kettle, 1949
Ma and Pa Kettle Go to Town, 1950
Ma and Pa Kettle at the Fair, 1952
Ma and Pa Kettle Go on Vacation, 1953
Ma and Pa Kettle Back on the Farm, 1954
Ma and Pa Kettle at Home, 1954
Ma and Pa Kettle at Waikiki, 1955
The Kettles in the Ozarks, 1956
The Kettles on Old MacDonald's Farm (Parker Fennelly as Pa), 1957

Ma Perkins

Ran a lumberyard in Rushville Center (radio series, 1933-1960). Daughters: Fay, Evey

Mac

The 97-pound weakling who gets sand kicked in his face prior to taking the Charles Atlas course in physique-building

Macaroni

Caroline Kennedy's pony

MacDougal

Philip Boynton's frog (TV series "Our Miss Brooks")

Mach Five, The

Speed Racer's racing car (TV cartoon)

Mack Bolan

Detective created by Don Pendleton

MacLaine, Shirley

Actress; sister of actor Warren Beatty

MacNeill, Don

Host of "The Breakfast Club" (radio series). MacNeill also was host of "Tea Time at Morrell's," one afternoon a week

Macy's

New York-based department store; main store was setting for the movie *Miracle on 34th Street*

Mad Hatter's tea party

Attended by the Hatter, the March Hare, Dormouse, Alice (Lewis Carroll's *Alice's Adventures in Wonderland*)

Mad Monk, The

Epithet applied to Rasputin (1871-1916), Russian monk at the court of Czar Nicholas II

Mad Russian, The

Radio comedian Bert Gordon (radio series "The Eddie Cantor Show")

Madame Queen

Andrew H. Brown's girlfriend ("Amos 'n' Andy"): played on radio by Harriet Widmer

Madge

Manicurist in Palmolive dishwashing liquid TV commercials

Madison High

School at which Miss Brooks teaches (TV series "Our Miss Brooks")

Maggie

Jiggs' wife (comic strip "Bringing Up Father")

Magnificent Seven, The

1960 movie following 1954 Japanese *The Seven Samurai* (directed by Akira Kurosawa and starring Toshiro Mifune). The seven were played by Charles Bronson, Yul Brynner, James Coburn, Horst Buchholz, Steve McQueen, Robert Vaughn, Brad Dexter

Maharishi Mahesh Yogi

The Beatles' guru

Maid Marian

Robin Hood's companion

Maid of Orleans

One appellation of Joan of Arc

Maigret

French police official in novels of Georges Simenon

Main Street

Novel (1920) by Sinclair Lewis. The street characterizes the small-town narrowness of Gopher Prairie, Minnesota

Maine, U.S.S.

First U. S. battleship (actually a battle cruiser), launched Nov. 18, 1890, sank after explosion in Havana Harbor, Feb. 15, 1898, with 250 killed

Major

Old horse turned into a coachman for Cinderella's carriage (Walt Disney's cartoon feature movie)

Major Seth Adams

Wagonmaster (TV series "Wagon Train"): originally played by Ward Bond

Major William Martin

"The Man Who Never Was": fictitious World War II British courier (Operation Mincemeat)

Malcolm X

Name adopted by Malcolm Little (1925-1965), black nationalist, founder of Organization of Afro-American Unity

Man on the Street

Skit on Steve Allen's "Tonight Show" (TV), in which were interviewed: Don Knotts, Louis Nye, Tom Poston, Bill Dana, Gabe Dell

Man O'War

Race horse (1917-1947) defeated only once in 20 starts (by Upset, 1919). Among the horses he sired was War Admiral

The Man with a Horn

Theme song of Ray Anthony's orchestra

Manassa Mauler

Nickname of Jack Dempsey, world heavyweight champion 1919-1926; he was born in Manassa, Colorado, in 1895

Manhattan District

Code name for development of the A-Bomb

Manhunter

Secret identity of Dan Richards (comic book series)

Mannix

TV series about a private eye. Joe Mannix was played by Mike Connors

Manor Farm

Farm on which the animals live (George Orwell's *Animal Farm*)

Mantle, Mickey

New York Yankee switch-hitting outfielder, credited with hitting (batting left-handed) the longest home run, 565 feet: off Chuck Stobbs of the Washington Senators in Griffith Stadium, April 1953

Mantz, Paul

Stunt pilot killed when the "Phoenix" crashed in making the movie *The Flight of the Phoenix*

March Sisters

In Louisa May Alcott's *Little Women*: Amy, Beth, Jo, Meg

March 21

> Beginning of astrological year

Marciano, Rocky

> World heavyweight champion 1952-1956, called the Brockton Bomber, won all his 49 professional bouts, 43 by KOs: killed in a plane crash in Iowa, Aug. 31, 1969

Marengo

> Napoleon Bonaparte's horse

Mare's Laig

> Pet name for Josh Randall's 30-40 sawed-off carbine (TV series "Wanted—Dead or Alive")

Margaret

> Dennis the Menace's girlfriend

Margo Lane

> Girlfriend of the Shadow (Lamont Cranston)

Mariner's rule of thumb

> "Red sky at night, sailor's delight,
> Red sky in morning, sailor take warning"

Mark Twain

> Pseudonym of Samuel Langhorne Clemens (1835-1910), American writer, who took the name from the cry of the leadsman sounding the depth of the river, Sam Clemens having been a Mississippi River pilot 1859-1861

Mark Twain

> Disneyland's three-deck stern-wheeler steamboat on the Frontierland River

Marlin

> The Kennedys' 52-foot cabin cruiser

Marmon Wasp

> Car (Number 32) driven (1911) by Ray Harroun in winning the first Indianapolis 500 race

Marriages

> Entertainment:*
> John Agar—Shirley Temple
> Eddie Albert—Margo
> Steve Allen—Jayne Meadows
> Desi Arnaz—Lucille Ball
> Lew Ayres—Ginger Rogers
> Bert Bacharach—Angie Dickinson
> Lex Barker—Arlene Dahl
> Lex Barker—Lana Turner

---

*Multiple marriages listed under the person's name

John Barrymore—Dolores Costello
Wallace Beery—Gloria Swanson
Jack Benny—Mary Livingstone
Ernest Borgnine—Ethel Merman
George Brent—Ann Sheridan
George Burns—Gracie Allen
Jack Cassidy—Shirley Jones
Jackie Coogan—Betty Grable
Joseph Cotten—Patricia Medina
Tony Curtis—Janet Leigh
Bobby Darin—Sandra Dee
Sammy Davis, Jr.—May Britt
Troy Donahue—Suzanne Pleshette
Howard Duff—Ida Lupino
Douglas Fairbanks—Mary Pickford
Douglas Fairbanks, Jr.—Joan Crawford
Jose Ferrer—Rosemary Clooney
Mel Ferrer—Audrey Hepburn
Eddie Fisher—Debbie Reynolds
Eddie Fisher—Elizabeth Taylor
Phil Harris—Alice Faye
Harry James—Betty Grable
Al Jolson—Ruby Keeler
George Jones—Tammy Wynette
Steve Lawrence—Eydie Gorme
John Lennon—Yoko Ono
Vincente Minnelli—Judy Garland
Laurence Olivier—Vivien Leigh
John Payne—Gloria De Haven
Dick Powell—Joan Blondell
Dick Powell—June Allyson
William Powell—Carole Lombard
Prince Rainier—Grace Kelly
Ronald Reagan—Jane Wyman
Roy Rogers—Dale Evans
Gilbert Roland—Constance Bennett
Tommy Sands—Nancy Sinatra
Raymond Scott—Dorothy Collins
David O. Selznick—Jennifer Jones
Roger Smith—Ann-Margret
Robert Taylor—Barbara Stanwyck

Marryin' Sam
Married Li'l Abner to Daisy Mae

Marseillaise, La

French national anthem, words by Claude Joseph Rouget de Lisle: originally titled "War Song of the Army of the Rhine" ("Chant de Guerre de l'Armée du Rhin")

Marshall, James Wilson

Pioneer (1810-1885) who discovered gold at Sutter's Mill, Coloma, California, Jan. 24, 1848

Martin Kane

Detective created for radio by Ted Hediger: played on radio by William Gargan and on TV by Gargan, Lee Tracy, Lloyd Nolan, and Mark Stevens

Martinez

Ferryboat sunk in San Francisco harbor; the schooner "Ghost" (captain Wolf Larsen) picked up survivor Humphrey Van Weyden (Jack London's *The Sea Wolf*)

Marvel Family

(Comic book series) Captain Marvel, Billy Batson; Captain Marvel, Jr., Freddy Freeman; Mary Marvel, Mary Batson; Uncle Marvel, Dudley Batson

Marx Brothers

Sons of Sam and Minnie Schoenberg Marx (she was sister of Al Shean of Gallegher and Shean, famous vaudeville team):

     Chico (Leonard, 1891-1961)

     Harpo (Adolph, afterwards Arthur, 1893-1964)

     Groucho (Julius, born 1895)

     Zeppo (Herbert, born 1901)

     Gummo (Milton, not part of the comedy team)

Groucho's roles are listed separately, under his name

Mary

Boston Blackie's helpful heroine (radio and TV)

Mary

The Lipton Tea Girl (radio)

Mary Bromfield

Mary Marvel's adopted name, given her when she was separated at birth from her twin brother, Billy Batson (Captain Marvel). See *Marvel Family*

Mary Celeste

Ship that left Boston for Genoa in November 1872, found abandoned in Atlantic four weeks later, all sails set and the crew completely disappeared

Mary Nestor

Girlfriend (eventually wife) of Tom Swift

Mary Poppins

Nanny to Jane and Michael Banks (movie *Mary Poppins*)

Mascots

    Military academy football teams:

    Army, Mule; Navy, Goat; Air Force, Falcon

Mason-Dixon Line

    Boundary between Pennsylvania and Maryland, surveyed (1763-1767) by Charles Mason and Jeremiah Dixon. As the line separating the free and the slave states, it became the traditional division between North and South

Master Chen Ming Kan

    Monk in charge of Shaolin Monastery, Hunan, China, where young Kwai Chang Caine becomes a Shaolin priest and master of Kung Fu (TV series "Kung Fu"). Caine's other masters were Master Po, Master Sun, Master Wong, Master Yuen, Master Teh, Master Shun

Master Po

    Blind monk in Shaolin Monastery, China, young Caine's master and friend (TV series "Kung Fu"): played by Keye Luke. Po called Caine Grasshopper, Caine called Po Old Man. Po was killed by the Emperor's nephew, who was in turn slain by Caine, who then fled from China to America

Masterson, Bat

    Pseudonym of William Barclay Masterson (1853-1921), U. S. marshal in frontier area, later a sports writer

Mata Hari

    Pseudonym of Gertrude Margarete Zelle, World War I spy, executed (1917) by the French

Mata Hari

    Lancelot Link's girlfriend (TV monkey series)

Match King, The

    Nickname of Ivar Kreuger (1880-1932), Swedish entrepreneur and monopolist

Matt Helm

    Detective created in satirical novels by Donald Hamilton

Matt Helm movies

    Dean Martin starred as Matt Helm: *The Silencers*, 1966; *Murderers' Row*, 1966; *The Ambushers*, 1967; *The Wrecking Crew*, 1968

Mauch Chunk

    Town in Pennsylvania renamed (1954) Jim Thorpe after the Olympic champion who had died the year before

Mauretania

    Sister ship of the "Lusitania"

Maverick

    Brothers living in the frontier West (TV series "Maverick"):

played by Jack Kelly (Bart) and James Garner (Bret), the unstable one

Max Brand

Pseudonym of Frederick Schiller Faust (1892-1944), Western adventure novel writer

Maxwell

Make of Jack Benny's antique automobile

Mayflower

Ship that carried the Pilgrims from Southampton, England, to Plymouth, Massachusetts, September to November 1620; her companion ship, "Speedwell," could not make the voyage

Maynard G. Krebs

Dobie Gillis' beatnik buddy (TV series "The Many Loves of Dobie Gillis"): played by Bob Denver

Mayo Brothers

Famous American surgeons at Rochester, Minn.: Charles Horace (1865-1939), William James (1861-1939), sons of William Worrall Mayo (1819-1911), American surgeon

Mayor La Trivia

Caller at 79 Wistful Vista (radio's "Fibber McGee and Molly"): played by Gale Gordon

McCall, Jack

Shot and killed Wild Bill Hickok in the Bella Donna Saloon, Deadwood City, Black Hills, Dakota Territory, August 2, 1876

McConnell, James

Top American ace of the Korean War: 16 victories

McDaniel, Hattie

First Negro to win an Oscar (1939), for the role of Mammy in *Gone with the Wind*

McGill

Montreal university, first to play, against Harvard, at Harvard, May 1874 or 1875, an intercollegiate football match under "Harvard rules," a mixture of rugby and soccer

McGregor

Farmer whose garden Peter Rabbit invades

McGuire Sisters

Singing group: Christine, Dorothy, Phyllis

McKean, Thomas

Delaware jurist (1734-1817), President of the Continental Congress when the Articles of Confederation were adopted (1781) on Maryland's ratification (sometimes called first President of the United States)

McMahon, Ed

Announcer of TV's Johnny Carson show (circus clown in early 1950's on TV show "Big Top")

Mean Mary Jean

Chrysler-Plymouth girl (TV ads)

Meathead

Archie's nickname for Michael (Rob Reiner) (TV series "All in the Family")

Mehitabel

Cat friend of archy the cockroach, whose battle cry was "toujours gai" (created by Don Marquis)

Melody Ranch

Home of Gene Autry (radio)

Mel's

The 1950's drive-in (movie *American Graffiti*)

Memphis, U.S.S.

Cruiser that brought Charles Lindbergh home from France after his famous flight (1927)

Merrie Melodies

Movie cartoon series by Warner Brothers (as well as "Looney Tunes"): "That's All, Folks"

Merrimack

Confederate ship, renamed the "Virginia" as an ironclad, that fought "Monitor" 5 hours on March 9, 1862, at Newport News, Va.

Merry Men

Robin Hood's band in Sherwood Forest. Among them: Alan-a-Dale, George-a-Green, Little John (John Little), Friar Tuck, Will Scarlet, Will Stutely, Midge (Much) the Miller's Son, David of Doncaster, Arthur-a-Bland

Messala

Ben Hur's rival in the great chariot race (Lew Wallace's *Ben-Hur*)

Me.262

German twin-jet Messerschmitt aircraft that flew during World War II

Methuselah

Lived 969 years (Genesis 5:27)

Metropolis

Superman's hometown on Earth (he lived in Smallville when he was Superboy)

Mexican Spitfire

Movie series starring Lupe Velez and Leon Errol:
(*The Girl from Mexico*, 1939)
Mexican Spitfire, 1939
Mexican Spitfire Out West, 1940
Mexican Spitfire's Baby, 1941
Mexican Spitfire at Sea, 1942

>*Mexican Spitfire's Elephant*, 1942
>*Mexican Spitfire Sees a Ghost*, 1942
>*Mexican Spitfire's Blessed Event*, 1943

Michael
Pet bee of The Red Bee, kept in Rick Raleigh's belt (comic book series)

Michael Anthony
The Millionaire's executive secretary who delivers the checks (TV series "The Millionaire"): played by Marvin Miller

Michael Lanyard
The Lone Wolf, TV detective from a character created by Louis Joseph Vance in a 1914 novel

Michael Shayne
Hardboiled detective in novels by Brett Halliday

Mickey Mouse's nephews
Ferdy, Morty

Midnight
Black cat with diamond-studded collar in introduction to TV series "Mannix" and "Barnaby Jones"

Midnight
Violin-playing cat on the "Smilin' Ed Show" and "Andy's Gang"

Midnight Cowboy
Adventures of Joe Buck (novel by James Leo Herlihy)

Midshipmen
U. S. Naval Academy's football team

Mighty Manfred
Tom Terrific's dog (cartoon)

Mighty Mo
Nickname for the battleship Missouri

Mighty Thor
Secret identity of Dr. Don Blake (comic book series)

Mike Hammer
Detective created by Mickey Spillane, originally in *I the Jury* (1948): played by Darren McGavin on TV

Mike Waring
Real name of the Falcon

Miles Archer
Sam Spade's partner, killed in *The Maltese Falcon*

Military Aircraft

Designator	Name	Manufacturer
Attack Bomber:		
A1	Skyraider	Douglas
A2	Savage	North American

Designator	Name	Manufacturer
A3	Skywarrior	Douglas
A4	Skyhawk	Douglas
A5	Vigilante	North American
A6	Intruder	Grumman
A7	Corsair 2	Ling-Temco-Vought
A12	Shrike	Curtiss
A20	Havoc	Douglas
A26	Invader	Douglas
(later B26)		
A37	Dragonfly	Cessna

Bomber:

B17	Flying Fortress	Boeing
B18	Digby	Douglas
B24	Liberator	Consolidated (Convair)
B25	Mitchell	North American
B26	Marauder	Martin
B29	Fortress	Boeing
B36	Peacemaker	Convair
B45	Tornado	North American
B47	Stratojet	Boeing
B50	Superfortress	Boeing
B52	Stratofortress	Boeing
B57	Canberra	Martin
B58	Hustler	Convair
B66	Destroyer	Douglas

Cargo:

C1	Trader	Grumman
C2	Greyhound	Grumman
C4		Grumman
C5	Galaxy	Lockheed
C7	Caribou	DeHavilland
C9	Skytrain II	Douglas
C46	Commando	Curtiss-Wright
C47	Skytrain-Dakota	Douglas
C54	Skymaster	Douglas
C97	Stratocruiser	Boeing
C117	Super DC3	Douglas
C118	Liftmaster	Douglas
C119	Packet/Friendship	Fairchild-Hiller
C121	Warning Star	Lockheed
C123	Provider	Fairchild-Hiller
C124	Globemaster	McDonnell-Douglas

Designator	Name	Manufacturer
C130	Hercules	Lockheed
C131	Samaritan	Convair
C133	Cargomaster	Douglas
C135	Stratolifter	Boeing
C137	Stratoliner	Boeing
C140	Jet Star	Lockheed
C141	Starlifter	Lockheed

Electronic:

E1	Tracer	Grumman
E2	Hawkeye	Grumman

Fighter:

F1		North American
F3	Demon	McDonnell-Douglas
F4	Phantom II	McDonnell-Douglas
F5	Freedom Fighter	Northrop
F6	Skyray	Northrop
F8	Crusader	Ling-Temco-Vought
F9	Cougar	Grumman
F10	Skynight	McDonnell-Douglas
F11	Tiger	Grumman
F12		Lockheed
P38	Lightning	Lockheed
P39	Airacobra	Bell
P40	Tomahawk	Curtiss
P43	Lancer	Republic
P47	Thunderbolt	Republic
P51	Mustang	North American
P61	Black Widow	Northrop
F80	Shooting Star	Lockheed
F84	Thunderstreak/ Thunderjet/ Thunderflash	Republic
F86	Sabre	North American
F89	Scorpion	Northrop
F100	Super Sabre	Northrop
F101	Voodoo	McDonnell
F102	Delta Dagger	Convair
F104	Starfighter	Lockheed
F105	Thunderchief	Republic
F106	Delta Dart	Convair
F111		General Dynamics

Refueler:

KC135	Stratotanker	Boeing

Designator	Name	Manufacturer
Observation:		
OV1	Mohawk	Grumman
OV10	Bronco	North American
Patrol:		
P2	Neptune	Lockheed
P3	Orion	Lockheed
Trainer:		
T1	Sea Star	Lockheed
T2	Buckeye	North American
T28	Trojan	North American
T29	Flying Classroom	Convair
T33	Shooting Star	Lockheed
T34	Mentor	Beech
T37		Cessna
T38	Talon	Northrop
T39	Sabreliner	North American
T41	Skyhawk	Cessna
T42	Baron	Beech
Search:		
S2	Tracker	Grumman
Utility:		
U1	Otter	DeHavilland
U2		Lockheed
U3	Model 310	Cessna
U4	Commander 560	Aero
U6	Beaver	DeHavilland
U8	Queen Air	Beech
U9	Grand Commander	Aero
U10	Super Courier	Helio
U11	Aztec	Piper
U16	Albatross	Grumman
U17	Skywagon	Cessna
U18	Rangemaster	Navion
U19	Sentinel	
U20	Model 195	Cessna

Millionaire, The

John Beresford Tipton (TV series "The Millionaire"): Marvin Miller as Michael Anthony delivered the checks for him

Mills Brothers

Singing group: John, Jr. (John, Sr., after John, Jr.'s death in 1935); Herbert; Harry; Donald

Milo

Ape scientist (played by Sal Mineo) and then baby (chimpanzee)

named for him, born to Zira and Cornelius, the two simian scientists (1971 movie *Escape from the Planet of the Apes*, in the series based on Pierre Boulle's *Planet of the Apes*). The baby grows up to become Caesar, leader of the revolt in the next film, *Conquest of the Planet of the Apes*

Milton
Kellogg's cartoon toaster

Minden, The
English ship (flag of truce boat) aboard which Francis Scott Key wrote "The Star Spangled Banner" (Sept. 13-14, 1814, in Baltimore Harbor)

Minerva
Cat belonging to landlady Mrs. Davis (TV series "Our Miss Brooks")

Ming the Merciless
Emperor of the planet Mongo, Flash Gordon's foe: played by Charles Middleton

Mingo
Daniel Boone's Indian companion (TV series "Daniel Boone"): played by singer Ed Ames

Minnehaha
Hiawatha's wife in H. W. Longfellow's poem "Hiawatha"

Minnelli, Liza
Actress and singer (born 1946), daughter of Vincente Minnelli and Judy Garland: Oscar as best actress (for Sally Bowles in *Cabaret*), 1972

Minnesota Fats
Pool champ (1961 movie *The Hustler*): played by Jackie Gleason

Minnie
Paul Bunyan's wife

Minnie the Moocher
Theme song of Cab Calloway's band

Minnie Mouse
Mickey Mouse's girlfriend

Minnow, S.S.
Boat that ran aground (TV series "Gilligan's Island")

Mint marks
United States coins:

	Mark
Philadelphia	None
Denver	D
San Francisco	S

(Obsolete mints and marks: New Orleans [O], Carson City [CC])

Minuit, Peter
>Dutch governor who purchased Manhattan Island from the Indians for 60 guilders, the equivalent of $24, in beads and other geegaws (1626)

Minute Man
>Secret identity of Private Jack Weston (comic book character)

Misfits, The
>1961 motion picture, written by Arthur Miller, directed by John Huston, last movie for Clark Gable and Marilyn Monroe
>
>Lead actors: Montgomery Clift (Perce Howland); Clark Gable (Gay Langland); Marilyn Monroe (Roslyn Taber); Thelma Ritter (Isabelle Steers); Eli Wallach (Guido)

Mishe-Mokwa
>Great bear in H. W. Longfellow's *Hiawatha*

Mishe-Nahma
>Sturgeon in H. W. Longfellow's *Hiawatha*

Miss (Genevieve) Blue
>Andy's secretary (radio series "Amos 'n' Andy"): played by Madaline Lee

Miss Burbank
>Winner (1948): Debbie Reynolds

Miss Columbia
>First airplane purchased by the United States government: from the Wright Brothers, 1909

Miss Frances
>Dr. Frances Horwich, host of TV series "Ding Dong School" (1952-1956)

Miss Grundy
>Archie Andrews' teacher at Riverdale High (comic strip series "Archie")

Miss Hungary
>Winner (1936): Zsa Zsa Gabor

Miss Jameson
>Private secretary of Billy Batson (Captain Marvel) (comic books)

Miss Josephine Ford
>Fokker trimotor airplane in which Lt. Commander (later Admiral) Richard E. Byrd flew over the North Pole on May 9, 1926: piloted by Floyd Bennett

Miss Moneypenny
>Secretary to M (James Bond's boss)

Miss Nell
>Dudley Do-Right's girlfriend (TV cartoon series)

Miss New Orleans
>Winner (1931): Dorothy Lamour

Mission Impossible

TV series opening with "self-destruct" tapes and dealing with hard espionage and counterespionage

Original cast included Steven Hill, Martin Landau, Barbara Bain, Peter Lupus, Greg Morris. Replacing Hill, Landau, and Bain, the latter couple leaving the show in 1970, were Peter Graves, Leonard Nimoy, Lesley Warren, Lynda Day George, and Barbara Anderson

Missions of California

From the south to north:

1769*	San Diego de Alcala (San Diego)	
1798	San Luis Rey de Francia	
1776*	San Juan Capistrano	
1771	San Gabriel Arcangel (San Gabriel)	
1797	San Fernando Rey de España (San Fernando)	
1782*	San Buenaventura (Ventura)	
1786	Santa Barbara Virgen y Martir (Santa Barbara)	
1804	Santa Ynez Virgen y Martir (Santa Inez)	
1787	La Purisima Concepcion	
1772*	San Luis Obispo de Tolosa (San Luis Obispo)	
1797	San Miguel Arcangel (San Miguel)	
1771*	San Antonio de Padua	
1791	Nuestra Señora de la Soledad (Soledad)	
1770*	San Carlos Borromeo del Carmelo (Carmel)	
1797	San Juan Bautista	
1791	Santa Cruz	
1777*	Santa Clara de Asis	
1797	San Jose de Guadalupe	
1776*	San Francisco de Asis (Mission Dolores)	
1817	San Rafael Arcangel (San Rafael)	
1823	San Francisco Solano (Sonoma)	

Mississippi, U.S.S.

Commodore Matthew Calbraith Perry's flagship on his voyage (1852-1854) to open Japan's ports to American trade

Missouri, U.S.S.

Battleship upon which the Japanese signed surrender terms in Tokyo Bay, September 2, 1945, ending World War II

Mitzi

Mighty Mouse's girlfriend (comic book /TV series)

Moby Dick

Pet Pelican of Kate Fairchild (Stefanie Powers) (movie *The Beatniks*)

---

* Founded by Father Junipero Serra

Mod Squad

Three young reformed delinquents active on the police force (TV series): Julie Barnes, played by Peggy Lipton; Linc Hayes, by Clarence Williams III; Pete Cochran, by Michael Cole

Molink

Hot line between Washington and Moscow

Molly Byrd

Head nurse of Blair General Hospital (Doctor Kildare movie series): played by Alma Kruger

Mongo

Evil planet ruled by Emperor Ming in Flash Gordon series

Monitor

Union ironclad ship that fought the Confederate ship "Merrimack" ("Virginia") at Hampton Roads, Va., March 9, 1862: sank off Cape Hatteras, December 1862, but was pattern for 60 more Union ironclads before Civil War ended

Monkees, The

TV series: Micky Dolenz (formerly of TV series "Circus Boy"); Davy Jones; Mike Nesmith; Peter Tork

Monopoly

Real estate board game invented (1933) by Charles Darrow, American heating engineer

All places named on the game board are in Atlantic City, N. J. Starting from GO (collect $200.00 salary as you pass), the squares are, in order:

Mediterranean Ave.	Kentucky Ave.
Community Chest	Chance
Baltic Ave.	Indiana Ave.
Income Tax	Illinois Ave.
Reading Railroad	B & O Railroad
Oriental Ave.	Atlantic Ave.
Chance	Ventnor Ave.
Vermont Ave.	Water Works
Connecticut Ave.	Marvin Gardens
Jail (a corner square)	Go To Jail (a corner square)
St. Charles Place	Pacific Ave.
Electric Company	North Carolina Ave.
States Ave.	Community Chest
Virginia Ave.	Pennsylvania Ave.
Pennsylvania Railroad	Short Line Railroad
St. James Place	Chance
Community Chest	Park Place
Tennessee Ave.	Luxury Tax ($75.00)
New York Ave.	Boardwalk
Free Parking (a corner square)	(and so back to GO)

Monroe, Marilyn

American actress (1926-1962): real name, Norma Jean Baker (Mortenson)

Her husbands: James Dougherty, 1942-1946; Joe DiMaggio, 1954 (9 months); Arthur Miller, 1956-1962

Monsieur Bon-Bon's Secret "Fooj"

Recipe given at end of Ian Fleming's *Chitty-Chitty-Bang-Bang*

Monster Society of Evil

Comic book series featuring Captain Nazi, Nippo, Ibac, Dr. Smash, Mr. Mind, The Orange Octopus, Herkimer the Crocodile Man

Montague

Romeo's family name (Shakespeare's *Romeo and Juliet*)

Monticello

Thomas Jefferson's home, near Charlottesville, Virginia: the mansion was designed by Jefferson

Monticello

Town, location of TV serial "The Edge of Night"

Montini, Giovanni Battista

Pope Paul VI

Moo

Land ruled by King Guzzle (comic strip "Alley Oop")

Moon Plaque

Placed by crew of Apollo 11: "Here men from the planet Earth first set foot upon the Moon July 1969, A. D. We came in peace for all mankind"

Moonlight Serenade

Theme song of the Glenn Miller orchestra

Moons

Planet	Moon	Planet	Moon
Mercury	None	Saturn	Dione
Venus	None	(cont.)	Rhea
Earth	Moon (Luna)		Titan
Mars	Phobos		Hyperion
	Deimos		Iapetus
Jupiter	Io		Phoebe
	Europa	Uranus	Miranda
	Ganymede		Ariel
	Callisto		Umbriel
	(8 others, all numbered)		Titania
Saturn	Janus		Oberon
	Mimas	Neptune	Triton
	Enceladus		Nereid
	Tethys	Pluto	None

Moose
> Midge's boyfriend (Archie comics)

Morgan, J. P.
> John Pierpont Morgan (1837-1913), American financier

Morgan, Linda
> "The Miracle Girl" who was aboard the "Andrea Doria" when that ship collided, July 26, 1956, with the "Stockholm," and was found alive on the "Stockholm" when the ships separated and the "Andrea Doria" sank

Morgiana
> Ali Baba's woman slave, who discovered and killed the 40 thieves hiding in the oil jars

Morlands
> Company—of Grosvenor Street, London—that makes the special Balkan and Turkish mixture cigarettes smoked by James Bond: the cigarette has 3 gold rings

Morlocks
> Dominant group of people of 802,701 A.D. (H. G. Wells' *The Time Machine*)

Morris
> Cat in "Nine Lives" cat food advertisements (TV commercial)

Morro Castle, S.S.
> Passenger ship that burned off Asbury Park, N. J., Sept. 8, 1934, with loss of 125 lives

Mortimer Mouse
> Mickey Mouse's original name

Mortimer Snerd
> One of Edgar Bergen's dummies

Morton Girl
> Girl on front of Morton Salt packages: "When it rains, it pours." Four different girls have appeared: drawing changed in 1914, 1921, 1956, 1972

Mother
> The Avengers' boss (TV series): played by Patrick Newell

Mother Fletcher
> Products sold by Stanley R. Soog (Jackie Gleason)

Mother Goose
> Said to be nickname of Mrs. Isaac Goose of colonial Boston, but the name has been traced back to centuries before (Perrault's fairy tales of 1697 were titled *Mother Goose Stories*)

Mother's
> Peter Gunn's favorite nightclub

Mothra
> Monster moth (Japanese movie, 1962)

Motown

Detroit record company, founded by Berry Gordy, Jr., in 1963. Motown recording artists include: Supremes, Four Tops, Miracles, Temptations, Marvelettes, Diana Ross, Contours, Martha and the Vandellas, Mary Wells, Marvin Gaye, Jr. Walker and the All Stars, Stevie Wonder, Gladys Knight and the Pips, Smokey Robinson

Mouse Series, The

Novels by Leonard Wibberley. The series concerns the adventures of the people of Grand Fenwick.

The Mouse that Roared (1955)
Beware of the Mouse (1958)
The Mouse on the Moon (1962)
The Mouse on Wall Street (1969)

Mouseketeers, The

Members of the Mickey Mouse Club (TV program series), included Cheryl, Bobbie, Annette, Karen, Cubby, Darlene, Sharon, Tommy, Doreen, Jimmy (adult), Roy (adult), among others

Mowgli

Boy hero of Rudyard Kipling's The Jungle Books

Mr. Beasley

Mailman who delivers to Dagwood and Blondie Bumstead

Mr. Blooper

Kermit Schafer, who presents the gold statuette Bloopy to the best bloopers (verbal or other errors that are broadcast)

Mr. Bojangles

Nickname of Bill Robinson (1878-1949), Negro tapdancer popular in the 1920's and 1930's

Mr. C

Name Perry Como's announcer, Frank Gallop, would call him on his TV program

Mr. Chipping

Full last name of Mr. Chips (James Hilton's *Goodbye, Mr. Chips*)

Mr. (Longfellow) Deeds

Millionaire hero of movie *Mr. Deeds Goes to Town* (1936); played by Gary Cooper

Mr. Dirt

Embodiment of dirty engines (Mobil Oil TV commercials); played by Ronnie Graham

Mr. District Attorney

Radio program pledge:

"And it shall be my duty as District Attorney not only to prosecute to the limit of the law all persons accused of crimes perpetrated within this county but to defend with equal vigor the rights and privileges of all its citizens"

Mr. J. C. Dithers
    Dagwood Bumstead's boss

Mr. Ed
    Talking horse of Wilbur (Alan Young) (TV series "Mr. Ed")

Mr. Green Jeans
    Captain Kangaroo's friend

Mr. Hooper
    Owner of the soda fountain on Sesame Street

Mr. Hyde
    Edward Hyde, the "evil" side of the split person in Robert Louis Stevenson's *Dr. Jekyll and Mr. Hyde*

Mr. Inside and Mr. Outside
    Felix "Doc" Blanchard and Glenn Davis, fullback and halfback of Army (U. S. Military Academy) football teams, 1944-1946

Mr. Jinks
    Cartoon cat that chases after Pixie and Dixie (mice)

Mr. Keen
    Tracer of lost persons (radio program): played by Bennett Kilpack, Phil Clarke, and Arthur Hughes

Mr. Limpet
    Man who turns into a fish (1962 movie *Mr. Limpet*): played by Don Knotts

Mr. Lucky
    Nickname of Joe Adams (1943 movie *Mr. Lucky*): played by Cary Grant; on TV, the role of Lucky Santell was played by John Vivyan

Mr. Magoo
    Near-sighted cartoon character in movies: voice by Jim Backus

Mr. (Wilkins) Micawber
    Played by W. C. Fields in 1935 movie *David Copperfield*

Mr. Moto
    Japanese detective in novels by John Phillips Marquand (5 written between 1936 and 1942). In the novels he is Mr. I. A. Moto. In the movies he was played by Peter Lorre.

> *Think Fast, Mr. Moto*, 1937
> *Thank You, Mr. Moto*, 1938
> *Mr. Moto's Gamble*, 1938
> *Mr. Moto Takes a Chance*, 1938
> *The Mysterious Mr. Moto*, 1938
> *Mr. Moto's Last Warning*, 1939
> *Mr. Moto in Danger Island*, 1939
> *Mr. Moto Takes a Vacation*, 1939
> *The Return of Mr. Moto*, 1965*

---

* Starring Henry Silva as Mr. Moto

Mr. MXYZPTLK
Superman's foe from the fifth dimension (get him to say his name backwards KLTPZYXM and he will return to the fifth dimension for 90 days)

Mr. Peabody
Sherman's superintelligent genius of a dog, who wears a red bow tie and glasses (TV cartoon series)

Mr. Peanut
Planters Peanuts' trademark

Mr. Peepers
TV series starring Wally Cox, who played a junior high school English teacher

Mr. Sanders
Name over the door of Winnie-the-Pooh's house (A. A. Milne's children's books)

Mr. Scratch
Name of the Devil in Stephen Vincent Benét's "The Devil and Daniel Webster"

Mr. Slate
Fred Flintstone's boss (movie cartoon series)

Mr. (Jefferson) Smith
Naive politician hero of 1939 movie *Mr. Smith Goes to Washington*: played by James Stewart

Mr. Spock
Science officer, second in command of the starship "Enterprise" (TV series "Star Trek"): played by Leonard Nimoy. He is half human and half Vulcan. His parents, Amanda and Sarek, were played by Jane Wyatt and Mark Lenard

Mr. Stubbs
Toby Tyler's chimpanzee

Mr. Tawny
Talking tiger (Tawky Tawny) who dresses in human clothes in Captain Marvel comics

Mr. Terrific
TV comedy show of 1967 starring Stephen Strimpell

Mr. Walker
Real name of the Phantom (comic strip/books)

Mr. Weatherbee
Principal of Riverdale High (Archie comics)

Mr. Wizard
Science explicator (Don Herbert) on TV educational series "Mr. Wizard"

Mr. and Mrs. North
Pamela and Jerry, the mystery-busting pair: played on radio by Joseph Curtin and Alice Frost; played on TV by Richard Den-

ning and Barbara Britton. The characters originally appeared in
novels by Richard and Francis Lockridge

Mr. and Mrs. Polka
Little Dot's parents (comic book cartoon series "Little Dot")

Mr. and Mrs. Silo
Little Orphan Annie's adoptive parents (comic strip by Harold Gray)

Mr. and Mrs. Wilson
Dennis the Menace's neighbors

Mrs. Bloom
Molly Goldberg's friend across the areaway (radio/TV series "The Goldbergs")

Mrs. Calabash
Said to be Jimmy Durante's first wife Maude Jean Olson, who died in 1943: his TV shows closed with his line, "Good night, Mrs. Calabash, wherever you are"

Mrs. Hudson
Sherlock Holmes' housekeeper at 221B Baker Street, London

Mrs. Muir
Widow who inhabits Gull Cottage, haunted by the ghost of Captain Gregg (movie and TV series "The Ghost and Mrs. Muir"): played in 1947 movie by Gene Tierney and in TV series by Hope Lange

Mrs. O'Leary's cow
Traditionally said to have started the Chicago fire of October 8, 1871, when it kicked over a lantern in Mrs. O'Leary's barn on De-Koven Street

Mrs. Olson
Proponent of Folger's Coffee (TV commercials): she apparently knows hundreds of young, married couples

Mt. Ararat
Traditional landing place of Noah's Ark, in Armenia

Mt. Blanc
Highest mountain (15,771 feet) in Europe (eastern border of France)

Mt. Calvary
Hill in Jerusalem where Jesus was crucified

Mt. Everest
Highest mountain (29,028 feet) in the world: Nepal-Tibet border in Asia
First conquered by Edmund Hillary and Tenzing Norkay, May 29, 1953

Mt. Idy
Hometown of Charley Weaver (role played by Cliff Arquette): its inhabitants include Grandma Og, Leonard Box, Elsie Crack

Mt. Kilimanjaro

Highest mountain in Africa, 19,340 feet, in Tanzania: now called Mt. Kibo

Mt. Nebo

Mountain from which Moses viewed the Promised Land

Mt. Olympus

Home of the gods (Greek mythology)

Mt. Pisgah

Where Moses died

Mt. Rushmore

Black Hills peak sculptured by Gutzon Borglum (1927-1941). The presidential faces are those of George Washington, Thomas Jefferson, Abraham Lincoln, Theodore Roosevelt

Mt. Sinai

Desert mountain where Moses received the Ten Commandments

Mt. Suribachi

Elevation on Iwo Jima, in the Volcano Islands, south of Japan, where the U. S. flag was raised during a fierce battle of World War II, March 15, 1945

Mt. Vernon

Virginia home of George Washington, 15 miles south of Washington, D. C.

Mt. Vesuvius

Volcano on the Bay of Naples that erupted in 79 A.D. and buried the towns of Pompeii and Herculaneum

Mudville

Home town of Casey's baseball team ("Casey at the Bat," poem by Ernest L. Thayer, 1888): said to be Boston

Muhammad Ali

Religious name adopted by Cassius Clay (born 1942), world heavyweight champion boxer

Mulligan

Milligan the detective's sidekick (radio series "Milligan and Mulligan")

Mummy movies

The Mummy, Karloff as Im-Ho-Tep, 1932

Mummy's Boys (Wheeler & Woolsey comedy), 1935

Mummie's Dummies (3 Stooges comedy), 1938

The Mummy's Hand, Tom Tyler as The Mummy, 1940

The Mummy's Tomb, Lon Chaney, Jr., as Kharis, 1942

The Mummy's Ghost, Lon Chaney, Jr., as Kharis, 1944

The Mummy's Curse, Lon Chaney, Jr., as The Mummy, 1945

Abbott and Costello Meet the Mummy, Edwin Parker as The Mummy, 1955

The Mummy, Christopher Lee as Kharis, 1959
The Curse of the Mummy's Tomb, 1964
The Mummy's Shroud, Toolsie Persand as Kah-To-Bey, 1967
Blood from the Mummy's Tomb, Valerie Leon as Tera, 1972

Munchkins
Little people who live in Munchkinland (*The Wizard of Oz*): played by the Singer Midgets in 1939 movie

Murania
Underground scientific city visited by Gene Autry (movie serial *The Phantom Empire*, also called, as a feature picture, *Men with Steel Faces*)

Murderer's Row
Heavy hitters of the 1927 New York Yankees: in order, the key players were Babe Ruth, Lou Gehrig, Bob Meusel, Tony Lazzeri

Murphy, Bridey
Virginia Tighe (Ruth Simmon was her real name) under hypnosis said that she was a girl living in Ireland in the year 1806, named Bridey Murphy (Doctor Morey Bernstein conducted the sessions)

MUrrayhill 8-9933
Telephone number for Major Bowes' "Original Amateur Hour"

Mutiny on the Bounty
1935 movie: William Bligh (Charles Laughton), Fletcher Christian (Clark Gable)
1962 movie: William Bligh (Trevor Howard), Fletcher Christian (Marlon Brando)

Muttley
Dick Dastardly's snickering dog (TV cartoon series "Wacky Races")

My Country 'Tis of Thee
One name for "America," patriotic anthem

My Day
Eleanor Roosevelt's newspaper column

My Fair Lady
Adaptation to musical stage of George Bernard Shaw's play *Pygmalion* (1912)
Eliza Doolittle, the heroine, was played by Julie Andrews in the theater; in the movie version she was played by Audrey Hepburn, whose songs were sung by Marni Nixon

My Mother the Car
A 1928 Porter (in TV series): voice by Ann Sothern
The surviving members of the Crabtree family were played by Jerry Van Dyke, Maggie Pierce, Randy Whipple, and Candy Eilbacher

My son
   Answer to the riddle, "Brothers and sisters I have none, but this man's father is my father's son"

Mycroft Holmes
   Sherlock Holmes' brother, supposed to have been even more clever than Sherlock

Mystery Ship
   Airplane that was the first Thompson Trophy Race winner (1929)

Mystic Knights of the Sea
   Fraternal lodge to which Amos and Andy belonged: George Stevens was the Kingfish

N

9
   Weight in pounds of hammer swung by John Henry (American folk ballad)

9 to 0
   Score of a forfeited baseball game

Nine Muses
   Clio, History
   Melpomene, Tragedy
   Thalia, Comedy and Burlesque
   Calliope, Epic Poetry
   Urania, Astronomy
   Euterpe, Lyric Poetry
   Terpsichore, Dancing and Choral Song
   Polymnia, Song and Oratory
   Erato, Love Poetry

90
   Distance in feet between bases in baseball

97
   Weight in pounds of weakling who gets sand kicked in his face before he takes the Charles Atlas course

98.6
   Normal human body temperature in degrees Fahrenheit

918th Bomber Group
   B-17 squadron in the 8th Air Force (movie/TV series "12 O'Clock High")

999
   Henry Ford's racing car

NATO

North Atlantic Treaty Organization, established **March 1949.** Member countries at present are:

        Belgium*
        Canada*
        Denmark*
        France**
        Greece
        Iceland*
        Italy*
        Luxembourg*
        Netherlands*
        Norway*
        Portugal*
        United Kingdom*
        United States*
        Turkey
        West Germany

NCC-1701

Registration number of the U.S.S. "Enterprise" (TV series "Star Trek")

NR 16020

Registration number of Amelia Earhart's lost Lockheed Electra

NR 16056

Registration number of Toni Carter's airplane in 1943 movie *Flight for Freedom* (based on Amelia Earhart's life)

Nairobi Trio

Comic musical group created by Ernie Kovacs (gorilla band)

Naismith, James

Physical education teacher at Springfield College, Mass.; inventor (1891) of the game of basketball; first game played Jan. 20, 1892

Namor

Sub Mariner's name (comic book)

Nana

Dog who guarded the Darling children (James Barrie's *Peter Pan*)

Nancy with the Laughin' Face

Song written by Jimmy Van Heusen and comedian Phil Silvers for Nancy Sinatra when she was five years old; afterwards recorded by her father, Frank Sinatra

---

  * Original member
** Resigned 1967

Nanu
> World's greatest athlete (Walt Disney movie *The World's Greatest Athlete*)

Napoleon
> Born on the island of Corsica (1769)
> Exiled to the island of Elba (1814)
> Died on the island of St. Helena (1821)

Napoleon
> Uncle Elby's 250-pound Irish wolfhound (comic strip by Clifford McBride)

Napoleon
> Leader of the animals, a pig (George Orwell's *Animal Farm*)

Narcissus
> Tugboat (TV series "Tugboat Annie")

Nash, Clarence
> Voice of Donald Duck

Natasha
> Spy antagonist of Rocky and Bullwinkle (cartoon series)

National Airways
> Airline for which pilot Jimmie Allen flew (radio series "The Air Adventures of Jimmie Allen")

National Baseball League

Eastern Division	Western Division
Chicago Cubs	Atlanta Braves
Montreal Expos	Cincinnati Reds
New York Mets	Houston Astros
Philadelphia Phillies	Los Angeles Dodgers
Pittsburgh Pirates	San Diego Padres
St. Louis Cardinals	San Francisco Giants

National Basketball Association

Atlantic Division (Eastern Conference)
> Boston Celtics
> Buffalo Braves
> New York Knick(erbocker)s
> Philadelphia 76ers

Central Division (Eastern Conference)
> Atlanta Hawks
> Baltimore Bullets
> Cleveland Cavaliers
> Houston Rockets

Midwest Division (Western Conference)
> Chicago Bulls
> Detroit Pistons
> Kansas City-Omaha Kings
> Milwaukee Bucks

Pacific Division (Western Conference)
   Golden State (San Francisco) Warriors
   Los Angeles Lakers
   Phoenix Suns
   Portland Trail Blazers
   Seattle Supersonics

National Football League

American Conference:

Central Division
   Cincinnati Bengals
   Cleveland Browns
   Houston Oilers
   Pittsburgh Steelers

Eastern Division
   Baltimore Colts
   Buffalo Bills
   Miami Dolphins
   New England Patriots
      (Foxboro, Mass.)
   New York Jets

Western Division
   Denver Broncos
   Kansas City Chiefs
   Oakland Raiders
   San Diego Chargers

National Conference:

Central Division
   Chicago Bears
   Detroit Lions
   Green Bay Packers
   Minnesota Vikings

Eastern Division
   Dallas Cowboys
   Philadelphia Eagles
   New York Giants
   St. Louis Cardinals
   Washington Redskins

Western Division
   Atlanta Falcons
   Los Angeles Rams
   New Orleans Saints
   San Francisco 49ers

National Hockey League

East Division
   Boston Bruins
   Buffalo Sabres
   Detroit Red Wings
   Montreal Canadiens
   New York Rangers (Madison Square Garden)
   New York Islanders (Carle Place, Long Island)
   Toronto Maple Leafs
   Vancouver Canucks

West Division
   Atlanta Flames
   California Golden Seals (Oakland)
   Chicago Blackhawks
   Los Angeles Kings
   Minnesota North Stars (Bloomington)
   Philadelphia Flyers
   Pittsburgh Penguins
   St. Louis Blues

Nautilus

Captain Nemo's submarine (Jules Verne's *20,000 Leagues under the Sea*): the world's first atomic submarine, U.S.S. "Nautilus," 1955, was named after it

Navy rank

Rank	Stars	Stripes (2 inch, ½ inch)
Fleet Admiral	5	1-4-0
Admiral	4	1-3-0
Vice Admiral	3	1-2-0
Rear Admiral	2	1-1-0
Commodore	1	1-0-0

Nazerman

Name on pawnshop in New York in the 1965 movie *The Pawnbroker*. The owner, Sol Nazerman, was played by Rod Steiger

Neal

St. Bernard who drank dry martinis (TV series "Topper")

Near You

Milton Berle's theme song

Nearer My God to Thee

Hymn played by the band aboard the "Titanic" as it sank, April 15, 1912

Nebuchadnezzar

Babylonian emperor: said to have built the Hanging Gardens of Babylon

Nebula

One science-fiction annual writing award: another is the Hugo

Nectar

Drink of the gods

Ned Buntline

Pseudonym of Edward Zane Carroll Judson (1823-1886), American writer and promoter, especially of Buffalo Bill Cody

Nellybelle

Pat Brady's jeep (TV series "Roy Rogers")

Nelson, Horatio

British admiral and lord (Viscount Nelson)

His commands:

Battle		Ship
Toulon, Corsica	1793	H.M.S. "Agamemnon"
Cape St. Vincent	1797	H.M.S. "Captain"
The Nile (Aboukir)	1798	H.M.S. "Vanguard"
Copenhagen	1801	H.M.S. "Elephant"
Trafalgar	1805	H.M.S. "Victory"

Nelson, Jimmy

His dummies: Danny O'Day; Farfel (dog) who sang the "N-E-S-T-L-E-S" song

Nerka, U.S.S.
> Submarine of Commander "Rich" Richardson (Clark Gable) (movie *Run Silent, Run Deep*)

Nero the Bear
> One of Paul Bunyan's three dogs (the hounddog)

Nero Wolfe
> Corpulent detective created (*Fer-de-Lance*, 1934) by Rex Stout; he raises orchids as a hobby. His assistant is Archie Goodwin.
> In the movies Wolfe was played by Edward Arnold (Archie by Lionel Stander); on radio by Santos Ortega and Sydney Greenstreet.

Nessie
> Nickname of the Loch Ness monster

Nevada Smith
> Role (his last) created by Alan Ladd (1964 movie *The Carpetbaggers*). His early years are told in 1966 movie *Nevada Smith*, starring Steve McQueen

Never, Never Land
> Peter Pan's home

Nevermore
> The one word spoken and repeated by the Raven (Edgar Allan Poe's poem "The Raven")

New Colossus, The
> Poem by Emma Lazarus inscribed on the pedestal of the Statue of Liberty

New Deal agencies
> AAA, Agricultural Adjustment Administration
> CCC, Civilian Conservation Corps
> FDIC, Federal Deposit Insurance Corporation
> FHA, Federal Housing Administration
> NLRB, National Labor Relations Board
> NRA, National Recovery Administration
> NYA, National Youth Administration
> SEC, Securities and Exchange Commission
> SSA, Social Security Administration
> TVA, Tennessee Valley Authority
> WPA, Works Progress Administration

New England states
> Maine, New Hampshire, Vermont, Massachusetts, Connecticut, Rhode Island

New Years Eve
> The day the passenger ship S.S. "Poseidon" is hit by a gigantic 90-foot tital wave (1972 movie *The Poseidon Adventure*)

New York City's rhyming pro teams
> Jets: football (NFL)

Mets: baseball (NL)
Nets: basketball (ABA)
Sets: tennis (WTT)

New York Knickerbockers
First organized baseball team, 1845

New York Loons
Baseball team inherited by Rhubarb the cat (H. Allen Smith's *Rhubarb*)

New York Times
Motto: "All the news that's fit to print"

New York World's Fair, 1939
Name of Howard Hughes' airplane in which he set a record by flying around the world, July 10-14, 1938 (91 hours, 14 min., 10 sec.)

New York World's Fair, 1939-1940
Theme center: Trylon and perisphere

New Zoo Review
Characters in TV series: Freddie the Frog, Henrietta the Hippo, Charlie the Owl
Hosts: Doug and Emily

Newsboy Legion
Crimefighting newsboys (comic book series): Big Words, Gabby, Scrapper, Tommy
Their guardian (at night): Officer Jim Harper

Nicholls, Mary Anne
Jack the Ripper's first victim (London, 1888)

Nick Adams
Narrator in Ernest Hemingway short stories

Nick Carter
Dime-novel detective in some 1,000 first-person novels from about 1880: begun by John R. Coryell and published by Street and Smith

Nicknames
Cities:

Nickname	City
Alamo City	San Antonio, Texas
Biggest Little City in the World	Reno, Nevada
Birthplace of American Liberty	Lexington, Massachusetts
Bison City	Buffalo, New York
Canoe City	Old Town, Maine
Celery City	Kalamazoo, Michigan
Cement City	Allentown, Pennsylvania
Chocolate Capital of the World	Hershey, Pennsylvania
City of Brotherly Love	Philadelphia, Pennsylvania
City by the Golden Gate	San Francisco, California

Nickname	*City*
City of Light	Paris, France
Crescent City	New Orleans, Louisiana
Eternal City	Rome, Italy
Film Capital of the World	Hollywood, California
Glass Capital of the World	Toledo, Ohio
Gulf City	Mobile, Alabama
Hub of the Universe	Boston, Massachusetts
Insurance City	Hartford, Connecticut
Motor City	Detroit, Michigan
Orchid Capital	Hilo, Hawaii
Palmetto City	Charleston, South Carolina
Peanut City	Suffolk, Virginia
Pittsburgh of the South	Birmingham, Alabama
Pretzel City	Reading, Pennsylvania
Railroad City	Indianapolis, Indiana
Rubber Capital of the World	Akron, Ohio
Silk City	Paterson, New Jersey
Windy City	Chicago, Illinois

States:

State	*Nickname*
Alabama	Cotton State / Yellowhammer State / Heart of Dixie
Alaska	The Last Frontier / Land of the Midnight Sun
Arizona	Grand Canyon State / Sunset State
Arkansas	Wonder State / Land of Opportunity
California	Golden State
Colorado	Centennial State / Silver State
Connecticut	Nutmeg State / Constitution State / Land of Steady Habits
Delaware	Blue Hen State / First State / Diamond State
Florida	Sunshine State
Georgia	Peach State / Empire State of the South
Hawaii	Aloha State / Paradise of the Pacific
Idaho	Gem State / Gem of the Mountains / Spud State / Panhandle State
Illinois	Land of Lincoln / Prairie State
Indiana	Hoosier State
Iowa	Hawkeye State
Kansas	Sunflower State / Jayhawk State / Wheat State
Kentucky	Bluegrass State

State	*Nickname*
Louisiana	Creole State / Sugar State / Pelican State
Maine	Pine Tree State
Maryland	Free State / Old Line State
Massachusetts	Bay State / Old Colony State
Michigan	Wolverine State
Minnesota	North Star State / Land of 10,000 Lakes / Gopher State
Mississippi	Magnolia State
Missouri	Show-Me State
Montana	Treasure State
Nebraska	Cornhusker State / Beef State
Nevada	Sagebrush State / Silver State / Battle-Born State
New Hampshire	Granite State
New Jersey	Garden State
New Mexico	Cactus State / Land of Enchantment / Sunshine State
New York	Empire State
North Carolina	Tar Heel State / The Old North State
North Dakota	Sioux State / Flickertail State / Old Colony State
Ohio	Buckeye State
Oklahoma	Sooner State
Oregon	Beaver State
Pennsylvania	Keystone State
Rhode Island	Little Rhody
South Carolina	Palmetto State
South Dakota	Coyote State / Sunshine State
Tennessee	Volunteer State
Texas	Lone Star State
Utah	Beehive State
Vermont	Green Mountain State
Virginia	The Old Dominion / Cavalier State / Mother of Presidents
Washington	Chinook State / Evergreen State
West Virginia	Mountain State
Wisconsin	Badger State
Wyoming	Equality State

Nightmare
Horse ghost, friend of Casper the friendly ghost (comic book/TV cartoon series)

Nightmare
Theme song of Artie Shaw's orchestra

Nikki Porter
> Ellery Queen's private secretary

Nipper
> RCA Victor dog in the trademark "His Master's Voice"

Nippy Weston
> One of G8's battle aces

Nixon, Marni
> Soprano who sang the parts for Margaret O'Brien in 1948 movie *Big City*, for Deborah Kerr in 1956 *The King and I*, for Natalie Wood in 1961 movie *West Side Story*, and for Audrey Hepburn in 1964 movie *My Fair Lady*

Nixon, Richard Milhous
> 37th President of the United States, first to resign (August 9, 1974) the office. He married Thelma Catherine Patricia Ryan. Their children: Tricia (Patricia), married Edward Finch Cox; Julie, married David Eisenhower

Noah Bain
> Head of SIA (TV series "It Takes a Thief"): played by Malachi Throne

Noah's Ark
> 300 x 50 x 30 cubits (Genesis 6:15): cubit = 18 inches

Noah's sons
> Ham, Shem, Japheth

Nobel Prizes
> Established by will of Alfred Nobel (1833-1896), Swedish inventor of dynamite, and first given in 1901
> Awarded for:
> Chemistry
> Economics (first awarded in 1969)
> Literature
> Medicine / physiology
> Physics
> Promotion of Peace

Nola
> Theme song of Vincent Lopez's orchestra

Noonan, Fred
> Amelia Earhart's co-pilot on her last flight, June 1-July 2, 1937

Nora
> Jiggs and Maggie's daughter (comic strip "Bringing Up Father")

North Manual Trades
> Fictitious high school in New York City that is the setting for Evan Hunter's novel *Blackboard Jungle*

North Star
> Cornelius Vanderbilt's 256-foot yacht

Numbers

United States and France: 1 followed by

6 zeroes, million	36 zeroes, undecillion
9 zeroes, billion	39 zeroes, duodecillion
12 zeroes, trillion	42 zeroes, tredecillion
15 zeroes, quadrillion	45 zeroes, quattuordecillion
18 zeroes, quintillion	48 zeroes, quindecillion
21 zeroes, sextillion	51 zeroes, sexdecillion
24 zeroes, septillion	54 zeroes, septendecillion
27 zeroes, octillion	57 zeroes, octodecillion
30 zeroes, nonillion	60 zeroes, novemdecillion
33 zeroes, decillion	63 zeroes, vigintillion

In British usage, a million is 1000 x 1000, or 1 followed by 6 zeroes, as in American and French usage. But a billion is a million millions, or 1 followed by 12 zeroes, and a trillion is 1 followed by 18 zeroes, etc. A British quadrillion (1 followed by 24 zeroes) is equivalent to the American/French septillion

Numismatist

A collector of coins or medals

Nurse Jane Fuzzy Wuzzy

Uncle Wiggily's housekeeper

O

007

James Bond's number as a secret agent (Ian Fleming novel series): the 00 / prefix gives the agent license to kill. It is the number of seconds left until the A-bomb was to explode in Fort Knox when it was shut off (1964 movie *Goldfinger*)

1/9

Part of iceberg above the water

1/6

Moon's surface gravity in relation to Earth's

One

Buck Rogers' robot (radio series)

1 Cherry Street

Address in New York City of first presidential mansion

One O'Clock Jump

Theme song of Count Basie's orchestra

$1.98

Price on Minnie Pearl's hat

100

Number of years Sleeping Beauty slept

$100

Fine paid by John T. Scopes when he was found guilty in the Scopes "Monkey" trial in Dayton, Tennessee, 1925

101 Dalmatians

Walt Disney cartoon feature movie: The Colonel and Towser (older dogs), Pongo and Perdita (parent dogs)

105

Elements discovered to date (1974): adopted as standard in 1968

132

Germans captured by Sgt. Alvin York in the battle of the Argonne (October 8, 1918) in World War I

138

Elevation in feet of Disneyland (shown on the Railroad Station sign at entrance to Disneyland)

$162.39

Weekly pay of officer Virgil Tibbs of the Philadelphia Police Department (1967 movie *In the Heat of the Night*)

1003.16

First Dow-Jones closing average over 1000 (N. Y. Stock Exchange) in history, November 14, 1972

137596

Sam Spade's license number as a private investigator (radio series "Sam Spade")

186,272

Speed of light in miles per second

O Canada

Canadian national anthem

O. Henry

Pseudonym of William Sydney Porter (1862-1910), short story writer who created The Cisco Kid among many other characters. The "O. Henry ending" to a story incorporates an unexpected twist

O. K. Corral

Site of famous gunfight, Tombstone, Arizona, Oct. 25, 1881:

Virgil Earp		Frank McLowery (killed)
Wyatt Earp	against	Tom McLowery (killed)
Morgan Earp		Billy Clanton (killed)
Doc Holliday		Ike Clanton

On trial in November, the Earps were acquitted as law officers

Oakdale

Town location of TV serial "As the World Turns"

Oceans
> Arctic
> Atlantic
> Indian
> Pacific

Odd Couple, The
> Oscar Madison, the good-natured sports writer and slob, and Felix Ungar, the prissy news writer, characters in 1965 play by Neil Simon: played by Walter Matthau and Art Carney. In 1967 movie played by Walter Matthau and Jack Lemmon. In TV series, played by Jack Klugman and Tony Randall, who became a commercial photographer

Oddjob
> Korean with steel derby hat (movie *Goldfinger*): played by Harold Sakata

Offissa B. Pupp
> Policeman in "Krazy Kat" (cartoon series by George Herriman)

Ohio
> State in which 7 United States Presidents were born:
>> Ulysses Simpson Grant, born 1822, Point Pleasant
>> Rutherford Birchard Hayes, born 1822, Delaware, Ohio
>> James Abram Garfield, born 1831, Cuyahoga County
>> Benjamin Harrison, born 1833, North Bend
>> William McKinley, born 1843, Niles
>> William Howard Taft, born 1857, Cincinnati
>> Warren Gamaliel Harding, born 1865, Morrow County

Ol' Bullet
> Dog (comic strip "Barney Google and Snuffy Smith")

Ol' Man River
> Mississippi River: title of song by Jerome Kern and Oscar Hammerstein II in *Show Boat*

Old Betsy
> Davy Crockett's rifle

Old Faithful
> Geyser in Yellowstone National Park, Wyoming: erupts every 64.5 minutes (average)

Old Hickory
> Nickname of President Andrew Jackson

Old Ironsides
> Nickname of the U.S.S. "Constitution"

Old Joe
> Camel Cigarettes' camel depicted on the package

Old MacDonald
> In children's nursery rhyme, had a farm (E-I-E-I-O) and on this

farm he had some chicks, ducks, turkeys, pigs, cows, donkeys, sheep

Old Noll

Nickname of Oliver Cromwell

Old North Church

Steeple from which Paul Revere is supposed to have received the signal (2 lights) for his famous ride, April 18, 1775: actually Revere was in the steeple when the signal was set and rode out toward Concord later

Old Ranger, The

Stanley Andrews (TV series "Death Valley Days")

Old Rough and Ready

Nickname of President Zachary Taylor

Old Whitey

President Zachary Taylor's horse

Old Wrangler

Tom Mix's sidekick: later on TV his pal was Mike Shaw

Olive Oyl

Popeye's girlfriend: sister of Castor Oyl, daughter of Cole and Nana Oyl

Ollie

Glasses-wearing little owl who is the friend of Henery Hawk (comic book cartoon character)

Olsen and Johnson

Zany comedy team: Ole Olsen, Chick Johnson, popular in 1940s

Olympia, U.S.S.

Admiral Dewey's flagship

Olympic

Sister ship of the "Titanic"

Olympic Games

	Year	Location	Year	Location
Summer				
	1976	Montreal	1928	Amsterdam
	1972	Munich	1924	Paris
	1968	Mexico City	1920	Antwerp
	1964	Tokyo	1912	Stockholm
	1960	Rome	1908	London
	1956	Melbourne	1906	Athens
	1952	Helsinki	1904	St. Louis
	1948	London	1900	Paris
	1936	Berlin	1896	Athens
	1932	Los Angeles		
Winter				
	1976	Innsbruck, Austria		

Year	Location
1972	Sapporo, Japan
1968	Grenoble, France
1964	Innsbruck, Austria
1960	Squaw Valley, California
1956	Cortina d'Ampezzo, Italy
1952	Oslo, Norway
1948	St. Moritz, Switzerland
1936	Garmisch-Partenkirchen, Germany
1932	Lake Placid, New York
1928	St. Moritz, Switzerland
1924	Chamonix, France

Olympic Rings

Colors (one of which appears on every national flag in the world) of interlocking circles: Black, Blue, Red, Green, Yellow

Once in Love With Amy

Ray Bolger's theme song

One-Armed Man

Killer of Dr. Richard Kimble's wife (TV series "The Fugitive")

Oola

Alley Oop's girlfriend

Open Sesame

Magic words that opened the secret treasure cave: "Ali Baba and the Forty Thieves," a tale from *The Arabian Nights*

Operation Crossbow

World War II Allied air attack on German V-bomb rocket sites

Operation Detachment

Invasion of Iwo Jima (February-March 1945)

Operation Grand-Slam

Auric Goldfinger's code name for his break-in of Fort Knox to make the gold radioactive for 58 years (novel/movie *Goldfinger*)

Operation Overflight

Gary Powers' U-2 mission over Russia (shot down May 1, 1960)

Operation Overlord

Allied invasion of Europe, June 6, 1944 (D-Day)

Operation Sea Lion

World War II projected German invasion of Great Britain (1940)

Operation Soapsuds

World War II Allied air attack on Ploesti oil field in Romania, August 1, 1943

Operation Torch

World War II Allied landings along the coast of North Africa, begun November 8, 1942

Operation Vittles

Berlin Air Lift (June 1948-October 1949)

Orange Bird
> Sunshine Orange Juice's bird (TV commercials)

Oranges
> Top producing states: California, Florida, Texas

Oregon Trail
> Pioneer route from Independence, Missouri, to Fort Vancouver, Washington, in Oregon Territory. Francis Parkman's book (1849) was originally titled *The California and Oregon Trail*

Orient Express
> Train that runs from Paris, France, to Istanbul, Turkey

Original Amateur Hour
> Variety show featuring non-professional specialty acts.
> Radio series hosts: Major Edward Bowes, Jay C. Flippen, Ted Mack
> TV series host: Ted Mack; announcer: Dennis James

Oriole
> Beulah's friend (radio/TV series "Beulah"): on radio played by Ruby Dandridge

Osborne Brothers
> Country and western group: Bob, Sonny, Benny Birchfield

Oscar
> Annual award, in several categories, of the Academy of Motion Picture Arts and Sciences: named for the uncle of Miss Margaret Herrick (she later became executive director of the Academy), after her 1931 remark "Why, it looks like my Uncle Oscar." Bette Davis (who "renounces" the claim) and Sidney Skolsky have also been credited as originator; H. L. Mencken also ties the story to the Academy, but differently

Oscar
> St. Bernard (Thorne Smith's *Topper*)

Oscar II
> Henry Ford's peace ship of 1915

Oscar the Grouch
> "Sesame Street" muppet that lives in a garbage can

Osgood Conklin
> Principal of Madison High (radio and TV series "Our Miss Brooks"): played by Gale Gordon

Osmond Brothers
> Singing group: Alan, Donny, Jay, Jimmy, Merrill, Wayne

Ostfriesland
> First battleship, a captured German ship, sunk by an airplane (experiment in bombing by General William "Billy" Mitchell, July 21, 1921): the heavily armored warship sank in 21½ minutes

Oswald the Rabbit
> Walt Disney's first cartoon character

Otis B. Driftwood

Groucho Marx's role in 1935 movie *A Night at the Opera*. Fiorello was played by Chico; Tomasso by Harpo

Otto

Sgt. Snorkel's dog (comic strip "Beetle Bailey")

Our American Cousin

English comedy (1859) by Tom Taylor, starring Laura Keene, given at Ford's Theatre, Washington D. C., the night Abraham Lincoln was shot by John Wilkes Booth (April 14, 1865)

Our Gal Sunday

Daytime radio series:

"The story that asks the question: Can this girl from a mining town in the West find happiness as the wife of a wealthy and titled Englishman?"

Our Gang

Comedy series (1922-1944) by Hal Roach and later MGM: called "The Little Rascals" in TV showings.

Something like 200 "Our Gang" kids appeared in literally hundreds of the comedies, among them:

Carl (Alfalfa) Switzer	Mickey Daniels
George (Spanky) McFarland	Jackie (Toughie) Davis
Billy (Buckwheat) Thomas	Eugene (Pineapple) Jackson
Darla Hood	Joe (Wheezer) Cobb
Eugene (Porky) Lee	Johnny Downs
Baby Patsy	Allen Clayton (Farina) Hoskins
Matthew (Stymie) Beard	Darwood K. (Waldo) Smith
Jackie Lynn Taylor	Walton (Wally) Albright, Jr.
Jean Darling	Scotty Beckett
Mickey Gubitosi (Bobby Blake)	Jackie Cooper
Mary Kornman	Mickey McGuire (Mickey Rooney)
Ernie (Sunshine Sammy) Morrison	Jackie Condon

Our Lady of Guadalupe

Patron saint of Mexico

Over-the-Hill Gang

Three retired Texas Rangers: Pat O'Brien, as Oren; Walter Brennan, as Nash; Edgar Buchanan, as Jason (1969 TV movie). In *The Over-the-Hill Gang Rides Again*, Chill Wills and Fred Astaire join Brennan and Buchanan

Overland Stage Line

Stagecoach company in 1939 movie *Stagecoach*

Owens, Jesse

Broke or tied six world track records in one afternoon on May 25, 1935 at Ann Arbor, Michigan:

> 100-yard dash (9.4 seconds: tied)
> Broad jump (26 feet, 8¼ inches)
> 220-yard dash (20.3 seconds)
> 220-yard low hurdles (22.6 seconds)

The records for the 200-meter dash and the 220-meter low hurdles were broken in the equivalent non-metric races.

Owens won 4 gold medals and set 3 Olympic records in the 1936 Berlin Olympics

Ozzie and Harriet

Ozzie Nelson and his wife, Harriet Hilliard Nelson, who had been the vocalist with a band led by Ozzie. "The Adventures of Ozzie and Harriet" became a big radio hit, with their sons David and Ricky also members of the cast. Then the show was transferred (1952-1966) to TV. It reappeared in the 1973-74 season without the sons, and with title changed to "Ozzie's Girls"

P

PATSY

Annual Award to animal performers in movies (beginning 1951) and TV (beginning 1958)

Acronym for either Picture Animal Top Star of the Year *or* Performing Animal Television Star of the Year

First winner: Francis the Talking Mule, 1951

PBX

Private Branch Exchange (telephone switchboard)

PT-73

Torpedo boat on "McHale's Navy" (TV series)

PT-109

Lt. John F. Kennedy's torpedo boat, sunk in the Solomons during World War II

Title of 1963 movie starring Cliff Robertson as Kennedy

Pablo

The cold-blooded penguin (cartoon movie)

Pacific Coast Baseball League

One of baseball's AAA leagues (just below the major-league classification)

Teams in 1940's and 1950's:

> Hollywood Stars
> Los Angeles Angels
> Oakland Oaks
> Portland Beavers

Sacramento Solons
San Diego Padres
San Francisco Seals
Seattle Rainiers

Packy
Straight Arrow's sidekick

Pagan Zeldschmidt
Ken Thurston's sidekick (radio series "A Man Called X"):
played by Leon Belasco

Pahoo Ka-ta-wah
Yancy Derringer's Indian companion (TV series "Yancy Derringer"): played by X. Brands

Painted Valley Ranch
Home of Red Ryder, Little Beaver, and the Duchess (radio series
"Red Ryder")

Paladin
Mercenary gun-fighter in the West (TV series "Have Gun Will
Travel"): played by Richard Boone. From his business card, reading "Have Gun Will Travel, Wire Paladin, San Francisco," the
gag arose that Paladin's first name was Wire

Palindromes
Sentences (or words) that can also be read the same backwards:
Madam, in Eden, I'm Adam
Egad, a base tone denotes a bad age
Evil I did dwell; lewd did I live
Poor Das is a droop
Able was I ere I saw Elba
Tini saw drawer, a reward was in it
Taem, no Devil lived on meat
Ten animals I slam in a net
Otto saw pup; pup was Otto
A man, a plan, a canal—Panama!
No, it is open on one position
Was it a car or a cat I saw?
Gateman sees name, garageman sees name tag
Draw pupil's lip upward
Straw? No, too stupid a fad, I put soot on warts
Pa's a sap
Won't lovers revolt now?
A dog! A panic in a pagoda
Draw no dray a yard onward
Zeus was deified, saw Suez
Draw putrid dirt upward
"Do nine men interpret?" "Nine men," I nod
I roamed under it as a tired, nude Maori

Pam and Jerry

Mr. and Mrs. (or rather Mrs. and Mr.) North (radio and TV series): on radio played by Joseph Curtin and Alice Frost; on TV by Richard Denning and Barbara Britton

Panama

Where Atlantic Ocean is west of Pacific Ocean

Pancho

Cisco Kid's partner (TV series "The Cisco Kid"): played by Leo Carrillo

Pandas

Given to United States by China (1973), kept at Washington, D. C. zoo: Ling-Ling, Hsing-Hsing

Pandemonium

Capital of Satan (John Milton's *Paradise Lost*)

Papillon (Butterfly)

Nickname of Henry Charrière, prisoner in French penal colony on Devil's Island, French Guiana

Papoose

Little Beaver's horse

Paradise Island

Home of Wonder Woman and her mother: no man has ever set foot on this all-female island (comic book): perhaps an echo of the land of the Amazons in Greek mythology, where no man until Hercules was permitted to remain

Paramount News

Motto: "The Eyes and Ears of the World"

Pard

Dog befriended by Roy Earle (Humphrey Bogart) in 1941 movie *High Sierra*

Paret, Benny "Kid"

Former welterweight boxing champion who died after being knocked out by Emile Griffith in the 12th round of their fight March 24, 1962, at Madison Square Garden: Ruby Goldstein was the referee

Paris and London

The two cities of Charles Dickens' *A Tale of Two Cities*

Paris Opera House

Setting of *The Phantom of the Opera*

Parker, Colonel Tom

Elvis Presley's manager: also was manager of Eddy Arnold and Hank Snow

Parker, Isaac Charles

Oklahoma judge (1838-1896), noted as the "Hanging Judge." In his 21 years on the bench, there were 172 capital convictions in his court

Parker Pyne

Detective invented by Agatha Christie

Partridge Family, The

TV series: Shirley (played by Shirley Jones); Keith (David Cassidy); Laurie (Susan Dey); Danny (Danny Bonaduce); Chris (Brian Foster); Tracy (Suzanne Crough)

Pasha

President Richard Nixon's Yorkshire terrier

Passepartout

Phileas Fogg's French valet (Jules Verne's *Around the World in 80 Days*)

Pat Aloysius Brady

Roy Rogers' sidekick, who drove his jeep "Nellybelle"

Pat Novak

Detective (radio series "Pat Novak for Hire"): played by Jack Webb

Patent

Good for 17 years (U. S. law)

Pathfinder, The

Nickname of John C. Fremont (1830-1890), American Army officer, explorer, and politician

Patna

Ship abandoned by its crew before it sank (Joseph Conrad's *Lord Jim*)

Patrick Henry

First Liberty ship of World War II

Patton, George Smith, Jr.

American general (1885-1945) known as "Old Blood and Guts," leader of the 3d Army in the break-out after the Normandy landings in June 1944 in World War II

Patton became notorious for slapping Pvt. Paul G. Bennett at the 93d Evacuation Hospital on August 10, 1943, 8 days after he had slapped and kicked Pvt. Charles H. Kuhl in the 3d Battalion Aid Station, in each instance presumably in a rage at what he considered malingering

Subject of 1970 movie *Patton*, directed by Franklin Schaffner, in which George C. Scott played the title role

Paul Bunyan

His dogs: Elmer the moose—terrier; Nero the bear—hound; Jacko the reversible dog

Paul Jones

River boat upon which Mark Twain received his training as a cub pilot

Peanut Gallery

Bleachers where the child guests sat on the Howdy Doody Show

Peanuts

Characters (in Charles Schulz's cartoon strip and motion picture features for TV), among others:

Charlie Brown, "Good grief," the put-upon
Linus, with the security blanket, Lucy's brother
Lucy van Pelt, the militant
Peppermint Patty
Pig-Pen
Schroeder, the toy-piano player and Beethoven fanatic
Sherman
Snoopy, the beagle who plays at fighting the Red Baron
Violet
Woodstock, Snoopy's bird secretary

Pearl Harbor's battleships

In Pearl Harbor December 7, 1941:

Arizona - sunk
California - sunk (salvaged)
Maryland - damaged
Nevada - beached (salvaged)
Oklahoma - sunk
Pennsylvania - damaged
Tennessee - damaged
Utah (target ship) - sunk
West Virginia - sunk (salvaged)

Pecos Williams

One of Tom Mix's sidekicks (radio): played by Joe "Curley" Bradley

Peeping Tom

Tailor struck blind after peeping at the nude Lady Godiva

Peg

Chester Riley's wife (radio/TV series "Life of Riley")

Pegasus

Winged horse (Greek mythology): sprang from the blood of Medusa

Peggy Fair

Joe Mannix's secretary (TV series "Mannix"): played by Gail Fisher

Peko

Pet marmoset of Dr. Fu Manchu

Pelé

Nickname of Edson Arantes do Nascimento (born 1941), Brazilian (Santos) soccer player (inside forward), called "The Black Pearl." A high-scoring, spectacular player, he became the highest paid athlete in the world before he retired from international competition in 1974. In the 1958 World Cup quarterfinals he scored the goal that beat Wales 1-0; in the semifinals he scored 3 times in defeating France 5-2; in the finals at Stockholm his 2 goals helped defeat Sweden 5-2

Penelope

Odysseus' wife (Homer's *The Odyssey*): every night she un-raveled the wedding gown she spent all day making, to the grow-ing impatience of her many suitors

Penfold Hearts

Brand of golf ball used by James Bond when he played against Auric Goldfinger (1964 movie *Goldfinger*)

PEnnsylvania 6-5000

Hit instrumental by Glenn Miller: the phone number is that of New York's Pennsylvania Hotel (now the Statler) which people would dial for reservations for the Cafe Rouge in which Miller made many appearances

Pennsylvanians, The

Fred Waring's orchestra

Penny

Sky King's niece (radio and TV)

Pentathlon

Men's: Riding, Fencing, Shooting, Swimming, Running (cross-country)
Women's: 100-meter hurdles, Shot put, High jump, Long jump, 200-meter dash

Pepe Le Pew

French skunk (character in Warner Brothers' cartoons)

Pepperland

Home of the Lonelyhearts Band (Beatles) which is attacked by the Blue Meanies (1968 cartoon feature movie *The Yellow Sub-marine*)

Peppermint Lounge

1960's New York nightclub where the twist fad started. The house band, Joey Dee and Starlighters, recorded a number of twist records including "Peppermint Twist"

Pepsi Twins

For Pepsi Cola: Pepsi, Pete

Percy Dovetonsils

Poet who wore very thick eyeglasses: played on TV by Ernie Kovacs, who created Percy

Perfect Fool, The

Stage appellation for comedian Ed Wynn

Perfect Song, The

Opening theme song of Amos 'n' Andy

Perils of Pauline

Motion picture serial (1914) starring Pearl White. A movie-biography in which Betty Hutton played Pearl White was made in 1947 and bore this title, too .

Perkins, Frances

First woman to hold a cabinet post: Secretary of Labor (1933-1945) under F. D. Roosevelt

Perry Mason

Sharp lawyer-detective created by Erle Stanley Gardner (1880-1970), himself a lawyer

Radio:

> CBS (October 18, 1943-1955) sponsored by Procter and Gamble:
>
> Perry Mason: John Larkin, Bartlett Robinson, Santos Ortega, Donald Briggs, John Larkin
>
> Della Street: Joan Alexander, Gertrude Warner, Jan Miner
>
> Paul Drake: Matt Crowley, Charles Webster
>
> Lt. Tragg: Mandel Kramer, Frank Dane

Television:

> Original series (1957-1965):
>
> > Perry Mason: Raymond Burr
> >
> > Della Street: Barbara Hale
> >
> > D.A. Hamilton Burger: William Talman
> >
> > Detective Arthur Tragg: Ray Collins
> >
> > Paul Drake: William Hopper
>
> Second series (1973):
>
> > Perry Mason: Monte Markham
> >
> > Della Street: Sharon Acker
> >
> > Hamilton Burger: Harry Guardino
> >
> > Sgt. Tragg: Dane Clark
> >
> > Paul Drake: Albert Stratton

Perry Mason cases

Novels by Erle Stanley Gardner, the titles all beginning "*The Case of the*":

Velvet Claws, 1933	*Perjured Parrot,* 1939
Sulky Girl, 1933	*Rolling Bones,* 1939
Curious Bride, 1934	*Baited Hook,* 1940
Howling Dog, 1934	*Silent Partner,* 1940
Lucky Legs, 1934	*Empty Tin,* 1941
Caretaker's Cat, 1935	*Haunted Husband,* 1941
Counterfeit Eye, 1935	*Careless Kitten,* 1942
Sleepwalker's Niece, 1936	*Drowning Duck,* 1942
Stuttering Bishop, 1936	*Buried Clock,* 1943
Dangerous Dowager, 1937	*Drowsy Mosquito,* 1943
Lame Canary, 1937	*Black-Eyed Blonde,* 1944
Shoplifter's Show, 1938	*Crooked Candle,* 1944
Substitute Face, 1938	*Golddigger's Purse,* 1945

Half-Wakened Wife, 1945   *Lucky Loser,* 1957
Borrowed Brunette, 1946   *Daring Decoy,* 1957
Fan-Dancer's Horse, 1947   *Screaming Woman,* 1957
Lazy Lover, 1947   *Calendar Girl,* 1958
Lonely Heiress, 1948   *Footloose Doll,* 1958
Vagabond Virgin, 1948   *Long-Legged Models,* 1958
Cautious Coquette, 1949   *Deadly Toy,* 1959
Dubious Bridegroom, 1949   *Mythical Monkeys,* 1959
Negligent Nymph, 1950   *Singing Skirt,* 1959
Angry Mourner, 1951   *Duplicate Daughter,* 1960
Fiery Fingers, 1951   *Shapely Shadow,* 1960
One-Eyed Witness, 1951   *Waylaid Wolf,* 1960
Grinning Gorilla, 1952   *Bigamous Spouse,* 1961
Moth-Eaten Mink, 1952   *Spurious Spinster,* 1961
Green-Eyed Sister, 1953   *Blonde Bonanza,* 1962
Hesitant Hostess, 1953   *Ice-Cold Hands,* 1962
Fugitive Nurse, 1954   *Reluctant Model,* 1962
Restless Redhead, 1954   *Amorous Aunt,* 1963
Runaway Corpse, 1954   *Mischievous Doll,* 1963
Glamorous Ghost, 1955   *Stepdaughter's Secret,* 1963
Nervous Accomplice, 1955   *Daring Divorcee,* 1964
Sun Bather's Diary, 1955   *Horrified Heirs,* 1964
Demure Defendant, 1956   *Phantom Fortune,* 1964
Gilded Lily, 1956   *Troubled Trustee,* 1965
Terrified Typist, 1956

Perry White
Clark Kent's editor at the *Daily Planet*

Pete
"Our Gang's" dog: with a ring around his eye

Pete Smith Specialties
Produced (1935-1955) for MGM; special Oscar, 1953

Peter Gunn
TV detective: played by Craig Stevens. Theme song by Henry Mancini sold over 1,000,000 records

Peter, Paul, and Mary
Folk singing group: Peter Yarrow, Paul Stookey, Mary Travers

Peter Quill
Radio detective and scientist: played by Marvin Miller

Peter Rabbit
His brothers and sisters: Flopsy, Mopsy, Cotton-tail

Peter Wimsey
Lord Peter Death Bredon Wimsey, 2d son of (and brother of) the Duke of Devon: detective invented by Dorothy Sayers, beginning with *Whose Body?* (1923). Married Harriet Vane (*Gaudy Night, Busman's Honeymoon*)

Petticoat Junction

Three sisters (TV series "Petticoat Junction"): Bobbie Jo, Billie Jo, Betty Jo

Petunia

Porky Pig's girlfriend

Pew

Blind beggar (Robert Louis Stevenson's *Treasure Island*): he gives the "Black Spot" to Billy Bones

Phantom, The

Masked seeker after justice (comic strip by Lee Falk and Ray Moore): he is the latest of a dynasty of Phantoms ruling an African jungle area

Phantom Lady

Sandra Knight, member of the Justice League of America (comics)

Phantom of the Opera

Acid-scarred Erique (Erik) Claudin
Played in movies by: Lon Chaney, 1925 (silent); Claude Rains, 1943; Herbert Lom, 1962

Pharaon

Cargo ship on which Edmond Dantès was first mate (Alexandre Dumas' *The Count of Monte Cristo*): the spelling is the French for "pharaoh"

Philatelist

A collector of postage stamps

Phileas Fogg

Englishman who bet he could travel around the world in 80 days (Jules Verne's *Around the World in 80 Days*)

Philip Marlowe

Private eye created by Raymond Chandler

Philip Nolan

"The Man Without a Country" in story (1863) by Edward Everett Hale

Philo Vance

Affected detective in very popular novels by S. S. Van Dine: played in movies by William Powell, Basil Rathbone, Warren William, Paul Lukas, Edmund Lowe, Grant Richards, William Wright, and others

Philosopher's stone

A substance the alchemists believed could turn metal into gold

Phiz

Charles Dickens' illustrator, Hablot K. Browne

Phoebe B. Beebee

Chimpanzee companion of J. Fred Muggs (Dave Garroway's TV show "Today")

Phoenix

Fabled bird that after a period of time (a century usually) sets fire to its nest, burns itself to ashes, and then springs out of the ashes to a new life

Phonetic alphabet

See the entry for *Alphabet, spoken*

Phyllis

Pet pig of circus clown Felix Adler

Pi

3.14159265+ (Ludolph's number): in 1873 computed to 707 places by William Shanks; in 1961 an IBM 7090 computed pi to 100,265 places

Pianola

Statuette awarded annually to composers and lyric writers of hit songs who are chosen for the Songwriters' Hall of Fame (beginning 1970)

Piccaninnies

Tribe of redskins at war with Captain Hook's pirates (James M. Barrie's *Peter Pan*)

Piccard brothers

Twins who made scientific explorations in stratospheric balloons and bathyscaphic diving vehicles: Auguste (1884-1962), Jean Felix (1884-1963)

Pie, The

Race horse belonging to Velvet (1944 movie *National Velvet*)

Pig Woman, The

Jane Gibson, chief witness in the 1926 Halls-Mills murder trial

Pigasus the Pig

Prank 1968 Presidential candidate

Piglet

Pig who is Winnie-the-Pooh's friend

Pilgrim

Brig on which Richard Henry Dana sailed (August 14, 1834) to California (*Two Years Before the Mast*): his return voyage was on the "Alert" (1836)

Pilot License No. 1

Issued to Glenn Curtiss

Piltdown Man

Supposed species of prehistoric (early Pleistocene) man found in Piltdown, England, in 1911: exposed as a hoax in 1953

Pine Ridge

Arkansas town, locale of radio's "Lum and Abner." In 1936, Waters, Ark., changed its name to Pine Ridge in tribute to the popular show

Pine Valley
>   Town, locale of daytime serial "All My Children"

Ping and Pong
>   Two little penguin friends of Chilly Willy, the "cold" penguin (comic book series)

Pinhead
>   Puppet on "Lucky Pup" show (TV)

Pink Panther
>   Priceless gem sought by the Phantom, who is in turn sought by Inspector Clouseau (1964 movie *The Pink Panther*)

Pinkie
>   Portrait of Miss Sarah Moulton-Barrett by Sir Thomas Lawrence

Pinky
>   Mr. Scarlet's boy sidekick (comic strip series "Mr. Scarlet")

Pinochle
>   Combination of Jack of Diamonds and Queen of Spades: scores 40

Pin-up girls
>   The two most popular of World War II: Betty Grable, Rita Hayworth

Pirate, The
>   The old bearded man who collected and sold kindling for a quarter a load (John Steinbeck's *Tortilla Flat*). His dogs were Enrique, Rudolph, Fluff, Pajarito, and Senor Alec Thompson

Pitcairn Island
>   South Pacific island settled by H.M.S. "Bounty" mutineers in 1790: it was discovered by Carteret in 1767 and named for the midshipman who sighted it. This sailor, Robert Pitcairn, was the son of Major John Pitcairn, who commanded the British troops at Lexington, April 19, 1775, and is said to have given the famous order, "Disperse, ye rebels!"

Pixie and Dixie
>   Mice, friends of Mr. Jinks the cat (TV cartoon)

Planets
>   (In order from the Sun)
>   Mercury
>   Venus
>   Earth
>   Mars
>   Jupiter
>   Saturn
>   Uranus
>   Neptune
>   Pluto

Plastic Man
> Secret identity of Eel O'Brian (comic book series "Plastic Man")

Platinum Record
> Award for LP record selling 1,000,000 copies, grossing approximately $5,000,000 (gold record is for LP with $1,000,000 sales)

Play It Again, Sam
> Line *not* said by Rick Blaine (Humphrey Bogart) to Sam (Dooley Wilson) in *Casablanca*. Ilsa Laszlo (Ingrid Bergman) gets him to play "As Time Goes By" by saying "Play it, Sam." Rick later says, "You played it for her, you can play it for me. . . . If she can stand it, I can; play it."

Plimpton, George
> American writer (born 1927): the Professional Amateur.
> Books: *Out of My League* (1961), *Paper Lion* (1966)
> Practiced as quarterback with Detroit Lions and Baltimore Colts
> Boxed 3 rounds with Archie Moore
> Pitched in a pre-season game in Yankee Stadium
> Played percussion in a session with the New York Philharmonic
> Performed comedy routine in Caesar's Palace, Las Vegas
> Performed as trapeze artist with circus
> Drove in an actual auto race
> Acted as guard at Buckingham Palace
> Participated in an African safari
> Rode in a steeplechase
> Acted in 1970 John Wayne movie *Rio Lobo*

Pluto
> Mickey Mouse's dog

Pogo
> Possum that lives in Okefenokee swamp (cartoon strip by Walt Kelly)

Poil
> Redheaded guest, girlfriend of Spooky, the Tuff Little Ghost (comic book series)

Point Maley
> Coast Guard cutter in Walt Disney movie *The Boatniks*

Poker Hands
> (in order of value, most to least value)
> Royal Flush
> Straight Flush
> Four of a Kind
> Full House
> Flush
> Straight
> Three of a Kind

Two Pairs
One Pair
High Card (no pair)

Pokey

Gene Autry's sidekick: played by Sterling Holloway

Po-Ko

Little Beaver's little Indian girlfriend (comic book)

Polly

Jack Benny's parrot (radio)

Polygons

Sides		Sides	
3	Triangle	8	Octagon
4	Quadrilateral	9	Nonagon
5	Pentagon	10	Decagon
6	Hexagon	12	Dodecagon
7	Heptagon		

Polynesia

Parrot that taught Doctor Dolittle to talk to the animals

Ponderosa

Ranch home of the Cartwright family (TV series "Bonanza")

Pony Express

Between St. Joseph, Missouri, and Sacramento, California: April 1860 to October 1861

Pool Balls

Pocket Pool

1 - Yellow	solid
2 - Blue	solid
3 - Red	solid
4 - Purple	solid
5 - Orange	solid
6 - Green	solid
7 - Plum	solid
8 - Black	solid
9 - Yellow	stripe
10 - Blue	stripe
11 - Red	stripe
12 - Purple	stripe
13 - Orange	stripe
14 - Green	stripe
15 - Plum	stripe
Cue ball - White	solid

Poole

Dr. Jekyll's butler (Robert Louis Stevenson's *Dr. Jekyll and Mr. Hyde*)

Poopsy

Seagull in the comic strip "Half Hitch" by Hank Ketcham

Popeye's Nephews

Peepeye; Pipeye; Poopeye; Pupeye

Poppin Fresh

Pillsbury's little dough boy

Poppy

Pillsbury's little dough girl

Porsche Spider

$7000 sports car in which James Dean was killed, Sept. 30, 1955

Potsdam Conference

International meeting at end of World War II in Europe (July 17 - August 2, 1945): attended by Harry S. Truman (U. S.); Joseph Stalin (U.S.S.R.); Winston Churchill/Clement Atlee (U.K.)

Potted palm tree

Tree belonging to Captain Morton thrown overboard by Lt. Roberts (Thomas Heggen's *Mr. Roberts*)

Potts Twins

Commander Caractacus and Mimsie Potts' twin boy and girl: Jeremy (black-haired boy), Jemima (golden-haired girl) (Ian Fleming's *Chitty-Chitty-Bang-Bang*)

Pottsylvania

Home country of Boris and Natasha (arch-enemies of Bullwinkle and Rocky)

Powerfull Puss

Mighty Mouse's foe (comic book cartoon)

Powers, Gary F.

U-2 pilot, shot down over Russia, May 1, 1960: later exchanged for Russian spy Colonel Rudolf Abel. The U-2 incident caused cancellation of a scheduled conference between President Eisenhower and Premier Khrushchev

Powhatan

Father of Pocahontas

Presidents of the United States

		Birthplace	Birth/Death Dates
1	George Washington	Virginia	1732-1799
2	John Adams	Massachusetts	1735-1826
3	Thomas Jefferson	Virginia	1743-1826
4	James Madison	Virginia	1750/51-1836
5	James Monroe	Virginia	1758-1831
6	John Quincy Adams	Massachusetts	1767-1848
7	Andrew Jackson	South Carolina	1767-1845
8	Martin Van Buren	New York	1782-1862

		Birthplace	Birth/Death Dates
9	William Henry Harrison	Virginia	1773-1841
10	John Tyler	Virginia	1790-1862
11	James Knox Polk	North Carolina	1795-1849
12	Zachary Taylor	Virginia	1784-1850
13	Millard Fillmore	New York	1800-1874
14	Franklin Pierce	New Hampshire	1804-1869
15	James Buchanan	Pennsylvania	1791-1868
16	Abraham Lincoln	Kentucky	1809-1865
17	Andrew Johnson	North Carolina	1808-1875
18	Ulysses Simpson Grant	Ohio	1822-1885
19	Rutherford Birchard Hayes	Ohio	1822-1893
20	James Abram Garfield	Ohio	1831-1881
21	Chester Alan Arthur	Vermont	1830-1886
22	Stephen Grover Cleveland*	New Jersey	1837-1908
23	Benjamin Harrison	Ohio	1833-1901
24	Stephen Grover Cleveland*	New Jersey	1837-1908
25	William McKinley	Ohio	1843-1901
26	Theodore Roosevelt	New York	1858-1919
27	William Howard Taft	Ohio	1857-1930
28	Thomas Woodrow Wilson	Virginia	1856-1924
29	Warren Gamaliel Harding	Ohio	1865-1923
30	John Calvin Coolidge	Vermont	1872-1933
31	Herbert Clark Hoover	Iowa	1874-1964
32	Franklin Delano Roosevelt	New York	1882-1945
33	Harry S. Truman	Missouri	1884-1972
34	Dwight David Eisenhower	Texas	1890-1969
35	John Fitzgerald Kennedy	Massachusetts	1917-1963
36	Lyndon Baines Johnson	Texas	1908-1973
37	Richard Milhous Nixon	California	1913-
38	Gerald Rudolph Ford**	Nebraska	1913-

Pride, The
    Jean Laffite's pirate ship

Prince Charming
    Woke Snow White with a kiss

Prince Philip
    Woke Sleeping Beauty with a kiss (Walt Disney cartoon movie)

Professor Edam
    Famed mouse scientist, father of Mighty Mouse's girlfriend,
    Mitzi (comic book series "Mighty Mouse")

---

   * The State Department has declared that Cleveland's non-consecu-
   tive terms make him both 22d and 24th president
  ** Born Leslie King, Jr.; name changed when his mother remarried

Professor Fate
> Villain who drove the car Hannibal 8 (1965 movie *The Great Race*): played by Jack Lemmon

Professor (Henry) Higgins
> Phonetics expert who taught Eliza Doolittle to be a lady (G. B. Shaw's play *Pygmalion* and stage/movie musical *My Fair Lady*)

Professor Horton
> Scientist who created the Human Torch (comic book series "The Human Torch")

Professor Marvel
> Itinerant salesman who becomes the Wizard of Oz in Dorothy's dream (L. Frank Baum's *The Wizard of Oz*)

Professor (James) Moriarty
> Sherlock Holmes' arch-rival

Professor Ohm
> Enemy of Mighty Mouse (comic book cartoon)

Professor Pierre Aronnax
> Narrator of Jules Verne's novel *20,000 Leagues Under the Sea*

Professor Quiz
> One of the earliest radio quiz programs (1936): Craig Earl was the quizmaster

Professor S. F. X. Van Dusen
> The Thinking Machine: detective created by Jacques Futrelle

Promontory Point
> Place north of Salt Lake, Utah, where were linked the Union Pacific and Central Pacific Railroads May 10, 1869. The Golden Spike was first hit by Leland Stanford at 2:47 P.M. EST (first swing missed the spike); spike was made by Schultz, Fisher and Machling of San Francisco. The weight was 18 oz. with a 6-inch nugget attached to the head. Union Pacific locomotive was No. 119, Central Pacific locomotive was No. 60 named "Jupiter"

Proteus
> Nuclear-powered submarine miniaturized so that it can travel through the bloodstream of a human patient (Isaac Asimov's *Fantastic Voyage*)

Proxima Centauri
> Faint star near Alpha Centauri, 4.16 light years distant: nearest star (except for the Sun) to the Earth

Pseudonyms

Pseudonym	Original name
June Allyson	Ella Geisman
Eve Arden	Eunice Quedens
Fred Astaire	Frederick Austerlitz

Pseudonym	*Original name*
Lauren Bacall	Betty Jolan Perske
Anne Bancroft	Annemarie Italiano
Jack Benny	Joseph Kubelsky
Irving Berlin	Israel Baline
Max Brand	Frederick Faust
George Burns	Nathan Birnbaum
Red Buttons	Aaron Chwatt
Rory Calhoun	Francis Timothy Durgin
Eddie Cantor	Israel Itskowitz
Cyd Charisse	Tula Ellice Finklea
Mike Connors	Krekor Ohanian
Joan Crawford	Billie Cassin/Lucille Le Sueur
Tony Curtis	Bernard Schwartz
Vic Damone	Vito Farinola
Bobby Darin	Robert Walden Cassotto
Doris Day	Doris Van Kappelhof
Kirk Douglas	Issur Danielovitch Demsky
Melvyn Douglas	Melvin Hesselberg
Bob Dylan	Robert Zimmerman
George Eliot	Mary Ann Evans
Douglas Fairbanks	Julius Ullman
Rhonda Fleming	Marilyn Louis
Redd Foxx	John Sanford
Arlene Francis	Arlene Kazanjian
Connie Francis	Concetta Franconero
Judy Garland	Frances Gumm
Stewart Granger	James Stewart
Cary Grant	Archibald Leach
Buddy Hackett	Leonard Hacker
Laurence Harvey	Larushka Skikne
Susan Hayward	Edythe Marrener
Rita Hayworth	Margarita Cansino
William Holden	William Beedle
Harry Houdini	Ehrich Weiss
Rock Hudson	Roy Fitzgerald
Tab Hunter	Arthur Gelien
Al Jolson	Asa Yoelson
Boris Karloff	William Henry Pratt
Danny Kaye	David Daniel Kaminsky
Billy the Kid	William Bonney
B. B. King	Riley E. King
Piper Laurie	Rosetta Jacobs

Pseudonym	Original name
Steve Lawrence	Sidney Leibowitz
Gypsy Rose Lee	Louise Hovick
Janet Leigh	Jeanette Morrison
Lenin	Vladimir I. Ulyanov
Jerry Lewis	Joseph Levitch
Joe Louis	Joe L. Barrow
Jane Mansfield	Vera Jane Palmer
Dean Martin	Dino Crocetti
Marilyn Monroe	Norma Jean Baker
Edward G. Robinson	Emanuel Goldenberg
Sugar Ray Robinson	Walker Smith
Ginger Rogers	Virginia McMath
Roy Rogers	Leonard Slye
Lillian Russell	Helen Louise Leonard
Artie Shaw	Abraham Isaac Arshawsky
Luke Short	Frederick Glidd
Belle Starr	Myra Belle Shirley
Robert Taylor	Spangler Arlington Brugh
John Wayne	Marion Morrison
Tennessee Williams	Thomas Lanier Williams
Shelley Winters	Shirley Schrift
Stevie Wonder	Steveland Morris
Natalie Wood	Natasha Gurdin
Danny Thomas	Amos Jacobs

Pueblo, U.S.S.

Electronics surveillance ship commanded by Commander Lloyd Bucher when captured by North Korea January 23, 1968

Puff

Magic dragon who lived in a land called Honalee: song by Peter, Paul, and Mary

Puff

Dick and Jane's cat (primary readers)

Pulitzer Prizes

Awards in journalism, creative writing, music, and related areas, established under the will of Joseph Pulitzer (1847-1911), first made in 1917

Puller, Chesty

Only marine to win 5 Navy Crosses (Lt. Gen. Lewis B. Puller)

Punctuation Marks

Period	.	Quotation mark	" "
Comma	,	Colon	:
Question mark	?	Semicolon	;

Exclamation point	!	Abbreviation point	.
Parentheses	( )	Braces	{ }
Dash	—	*Diacritical Marks:*	
Brackets	[ ]	Circumflex accent	^
Apostrophe	'	Acute accent	´
Hyphen	-	Grave accent	`
Asterisk	*	Dieresis	¨
Slash (obolus)	/	Tilde	~

Punjab

Henchman of Oliver "Daddy" Warbucks (Little Orphan Annie's foster father) in Harold Gray's comic strip

Purple Onion

San Francisco North Beach club where the Kingston Trio (1958), the Smothers Brothers, Pat Paulsen, and Phyllis Diller, among others, first made their appearance

Pushmi-Pullyu

Dr. Dolittle's two-headed llama

Pussy Galore

Goldfinger's lesbian accomplice who runs a flying school for female pilots (1964 movie *Goldfinger*): played by Honor Blackman

Put Your Dreams Away

Frank Sinatra's theme song

Pyewacket

Cat supposedly a witch's familiar (1958 movie *Bell, Book and Candle*)

Pyncheon

Name of family living in the House of the Seven Gables (novel by Nathaniel Hawthorne)

Pythagoras

Greek mathematical philosopher of 6th century B.C. His 4 basic elements and their qualities:

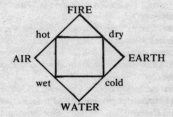

Q

Q Bomb
Quadium bomb stolen by the soldiers of Grand Fenwick from the United States (*The Mouse that Roared*)

Q and Z
Letters not on the telephone dial

QB VII
Novel (1970) by Leon Uris meaning Queen's Bench Number 7, the court in which the libel trial takes place. Most expensive movie ever made for TV: $2.5 million

Quarrymen, The
First group founded 1955 by John Lennon, with Paul McCartney, before establishing the Beatles

Quasimodo
The Hunchback of Notre Dame: played in movies by Lon Chaney, Sr. (1923), Charles Laughton (1939), and Anthony Quinn (1957) (from Victor Hugo's *The Hunchback of Notre Dame*)

Que Sera Sera
Doris Day's theme song

Queen Anne's Revenge
Blackbeard's pirate ship

Queen of Diamonds
The playing card that causes Raymond Shaw (Laurence Harvey) to go into a hypnotic trance leaving him open to external suggestions (1962 movie *The Manchurian Candidate*)

Queen Elizabeth I
Daughter of Anne Boleyn and Henry VIII: born 1533, reigned 1558-1603

Queen of Hearts
Ruler of Wonderland who demands "off with their heads" (Lewis Carroll's *Alice's Adventures in Wonderland*)

Queen Hippolyte
Wonder Woman's mother, who lives on Paradise Island (comic book series)

Queen Mary
Cunard ocean liner, now moored at Long Beach, California, as a floating hotel

Queen Tika
Ruler of the underground city Murania (Gene Autry serial *The Phantom Empire*)

Queen of the West
Dale Evans (Roy Rogers' wife)

Queequeg

> Harpooner on board the "Pequod" (Herman Melville's *Moby Dick*)

Question Mark, The

> First plane to fly (1930) non-stop from Europe to the United States: pilot was Captain Dieudonné Coste; mechanic was Maurice Bellonte

Quincy

> Mr. Magoo's first name (movie cartoon)

Quiz and game shows, television:

Name	Host
Answer Yes or No	Moss Hart
Baffle	Dick Enberg
Bank on the Stars	Jack Paar
Beat the Clock	Bud Collyer, Gene Wood
Brains and Brawn	Fred Davis, Jack Lescoulie
Break the Bank	Bert Parks
Charade Quiz	Bill Slater
Concentration	Hugh Downs, Jack Narz
Dating Game, The	Jim Lange
Dr. I. Q.	James McLain
Dollar a Second	Jan Murray
Double or Nothing	Bert Parks
Down You Go	Dr. Bergen Evans
Earn Your Vacation	Johnny Carson
Everybody's Talking	Lloyd Thaxton
Eye Guess	Bill Cullen
Family Game, The	Bob Barker
G. E. College Bowl	Allen Ludden, Robert Earle
Gambit	Wink Martindale, Dealer: Elaine Stewart
Girl in My Life	Fred Holliday
Hollywood Squares	Peter Marshall
Honeymoon Race	Bill Malone
It's Your Bet	Lyle Waggoner
I've Got a Secret	Garry Moore
Jeopardy	Art Fleming
Joker's Wild	Jack Barry
Judge for Yourself	Fred Allen, Dennis James
Jukebox Jury	Peter Potter
Juvenile Jury	Jack Barry
Laugh Line	Dick Van Dyke
Let's Make a Deal	Monty Hall

Name	Host
Life Begins at Eighty	Jack Barry
Match Game	Gene Rayburn
Name That Tune	George Dewitt, Bill Cullen, Red Benson
Name's the Same, The	Robert Q. Lewis, Dennis James
Newlywed Game	Bob Eubanks
Oh My Word	Jim Lange
$100,000 Big Surprise	Jack Barry, Mike Wallace
Pantomime Quiz	Mike Stokey
Parent Game	Clark Race
Password	Allen Ludden
Place the Face	Bill Cullen
Play Your Hunch	Merv Griffin
Price Is Right, The	Bill Cullen, Bob Barker, James Fenneman, Dennis James
Quiz Kids, The	Clifton Fadiman
Sale of the Century	Joe Garagiola
$64,000 Challenge, The	Sonny Fox, Ralph Story
$64,000 Question, The	Hal March
Snap Judgment	Ed McMahon
Split Second	Tom Kennedy
Stop the Music	Bert Parks
Strike It Rich	Warren Hull
$10,000 Pyramid	Dick Clark
Three on a Match	Bill Cullen
To Tell the Truth	Garry Moore
Truth or Consequences	Ralph Edwards, Jack Bailey, Bob Barker
Twenty-One	Jack Barry
Twenty Questions	Bill Slater
What's My Line	John Daly, Wally Bruner
Who, What, Where	Art James
Wizard of Odds	Alex Trebek
You Bet Your Life	Groucho Marx

Quotations

Agent 86, Maxwell Smart: "Sorry about that, Chief"

Alphonse and Gaston (comic strip by Frederick Burr Opper): "You first, my dear Alphonse"; "After you, my dear Gaston"

Neil Armstrong: "That's one small step for a man, one giant leap for mankind"

P. T. Barnum: "There's a sucker born every minute"

Rhett Butler: "Frankly, my dear, I don't give a damn" (*to Scarlett O'Hara in Gone with the Wind*)

Senator Claghorn (Fred Allen's radio show): "That's a joke, Son"

Cool Hand Luke (movie): "What we have here is a failure to communicate"

Jimmy Durante: "Everybody wants to get into de act"

W. C. Fields: "Any man who hates dogs and children can't be all bad"

Greta Garbo: "I want to be alone"

Jackie Gleason (as Ralph Kramden): "One of these days, Alice, pow, right in the kisser"

George Gobel: "Well, I'll be a dirty bird"

Oliver Hardy: "This is another fine mess you've gotten me into" (said to Stan Laurel)

Gabriel Heatter: "Ah, there's good news tonight"

Al Jolson: "You ain't heard nothing yet, folks" (*The Jazz Singer*)

Little Beaver: "You betchum, Red Ryder"

Baron Munchhausen (Jack Pearl): "Vas you dere, Sharlie?"

Joe Penner: "Wanna buy a duck?"

Sergeant Preston: "On, King! On, you huskies"

Chester Riley: "What a revoltin' development this is" (*Life of Riley*)

Knute Rockne: "When the going gets tough, the tough get going"

Will Rogers: "I never met a man I didn't like"

Red Ryder: "Roll, Thunder, roll"

Sam Spade (radio): "Period. End of report"

Little man in Bill Holman comic strip: "Nov Shmoz Kapop"

Mae West: "Beulah, peel me a grape"

Mae West: "Come up and see me sometime" (*Diamond Lil*)

Ella Wheeler Wilcox: "Laugh and the world laughs with you, weep and you weep alone"

R

R

Initial on Archie Andrews' sweater (letter of Riverdale High)

RKO

Radio-Keith-Orpheum, Hollywood picture production company

Ra II

Thor Heyerdahl's raft that sailed from Safi, Morocco, to Barbados, July 1970 (Ra I didn't complete the ocean voyage)

Racer X

Speed Racer's older brother (TV cartoon)

Radio Caroline

Pirate radio station (1964-1967): broadcast pop music from a ship off the east coast of England

Raggedy Andy

Raggedy Ann's boyfriend

Rags the Tiger

Crusader Rabbit's sidekick (TV cartoon series)

Rail Splitter, The

Nickname of Abraham Lincoln

Railroads

In the game of Monopoly: Reading; Pennsylvania; B & O; Short Line

Ralph 124C41+

Hero and title of science fiction novel (1911-1912 in *Modern Electronics* magazine) by Hugo Gernsback, founder of *Amazing Stories* (1926), first science fiction magazine: the + in Ralph's name indicates he is one of the 10 best endowed men in the world

Range Riders, The

Johnny Mack Brown, Raymond Hatton, Tim McCoy (movie series)

Ranger John Reid

Identity of The Lone Ranger, an ex-Texas Ranger

Ranger John Smith

Head of Jellystone Park, Yogi Bear's home (TV cartoon series)

Raven and dove

Two birds that Noah sent out from the Ark: the raven returned, indicating that there was yet no dry land; the dove came back with an olive branch, indicating receding waters

Ray, The

Happy Terrill, a member of the Justice League of America (comics)

Raymond

Host of radio program "Inner Sanctum": played by Raymond Edward Johnson

Read Your Bible

Sign on the wall behind Judge John T. Raulston's bench at the Scopes trial, Dayton, Tennessee, 1925

Reata

Sprawling Texas ranch of the Benedict family (Edna Ferber's *Giant*)

Rebel

Johnny Mack Brown's horse

Reckless
>   Hounddog (TV series "The Waltons")

Records
>   Top Singles: 1949-1973:
>> "Forever and Ever," Russ Morgan Orchestra, 1949
>> "Goodnight, Irene," Gordon Jenkins/Weavers, 1950
>> "Tennessee Waltz," Patti Page, 1951
>> "Cry," Johnny Ray, 1952
>> "Song from *Moulin Rouge*," Percy Faith, 1953
>> "Little Things Mean a Lot," Kitty Kallen, 1954
>> "Rock Around the Clock," Bill Haley and the Comets, 1955
>> "Don't Be Cruel," Elvis Presley, 1956
>> "Tammy," Debbie Reynolds, 1957
>> "Nel Blu di Pinto di Blu (Volare)," Domenico Mudugno, 1958
>> "Mack the Knife," Bobby Darin, 1959
>> "Theme from *A Summer Place*," Percy Faith, 1960
>> "Theme from *Exodus*," Ferrante and Teicher, 1961
>> "The Twist," Chubby Checker, 1962
>> "Limbo Rock," Chubby Checker, 1963
>> "I Want to Hold Your Hand," Beatles, 1964
>> "Back in My Arms Again," Supremes, 1965
>> "Ballad of the Green Berets," S/Sgt Barry Sadler, 1966
>> "The Letter," Boxtops, 1967
>> "Hey Jude," Beatles, 1968
>> "Sugar, Sugar," Archies, 1969
>> "Bridge over Troubled Water," Simon and Garfunkel, 1970
>> "Joy to the World," Three Dog Night, 1971
>> "First Time Ever I Saw Your Face," Roberta Flack, 1972
>> "Tie a Yellow Ribbon Around the Old Oak Tree," Dawn, 1973

Red Baron, The
>   Nickname of Baron Manfred von Richthofen, German aviator, top ace in World War I (80 victories)

Red Bee, The
>   Secret identity of Assistant District Attorney Rick Raleigh (comic book series "The Red Bee")

Red and Blue
>   National Broadcasting Company's two early radio networks: Red network renamed NBC, Blue network American Broadcasting Company

Red Pennington
>   Don Winslow's sidekick

Red River Valley

Theme song of radio series "Our Gal Sunday"

Red Rover, U.S.S.

First United States hospital ship

Red Ryder

"Famous fighting cowboy" hero of comic strip by Fred Harman, later on radio played by Reed Hadley, Carlton KaDell, and Brooke Temple. His sidekick, Little Beaver, said, "You betchum, Red Ryder," and Red said to his horse, "Roll, Thunder, roll"

Red Skull, The

Captain America's foe (comic book)

Red-Haired Alibi, The

Shirley Temple's first movie appearance, 1932, age 3

REDUCE

Jack Lalanne's California automobile license plate

Reep Daggle

Chameleon Boy's real name (comic books)

Reeves, George

American actor, real name: George Besselo; played TV's Superman; committed suicide (1959)

Reform Club

London club to which Phileas Fogg belonged (Jules Verne's *Around the World in 80 Days*)

Reggie

The raccoon you are asked to draw for Art Instruction Schools, Inc. (advertisements in magazines)

Reggie Fortune

Detective created by H. C. Bailey

Reggy

Archie Andrews' antagonist

Regulation Dart Board

British:

Reichenbach Falls

Cascade in Switzerland where Sherlock Holmes and Professor Moriarty grapple and apparently fall to their deaths (Arthur Conan Doyle's "The Final Problem")

Reid

Family name of the Lone Ranger and the Green Hornet

Reluctant, U.S.S.

Ship on which Mr. Roberts was stationed (Thomas Heggen's *Mr. Roberts*)

Remembering You

Closing theme of TV series "All in the Family" (opening theme is "Those Were the Days")

Remo Williams

Real name of the Destroyer (detective novel series by Sapir and Murphy)

Renfield

Count Dracula's henchman

Reno, Nevada

Once the divorce capital of the United States, farther west than Los Angeles

Resolution

Captain James Cook's ship on his second and third voyages

Return to Oz

Walt Disney cartoon feature movie

Voices: Dorothy (Liza Minnelli), Cowardly Lion (Milton Berle), Tin Man (Danny Thomas), Wicked Witch (Ethel Merman)

Reuben James

First American warship (a destroyer) lost in World War II, sunk off Iceland by a German U-boat, October 30, 1941 (prior to Pearl Harbor attack): about 100 lives lost

Revere, Paul

His famous ride took him from Boston to near Lexington, April 18-19, 1775

Reverend Leroy

Preacher at the church of What's Happening Now (Flip Wilson TV show)

Rex

Sergeant Preston's horse (was Blackie)

Rhapsody in Blue

Theme music of Paul Whiteman's orchestra

Rhubarb

Cat who inherits a baseball team (H. Allen Smith's *Rhubarb*)

Richard Henry Benson

Real name of the Avenger (detective novel series by Kenneth Robeson)

Richard Kimble

Physician fleeing from arrest by Inspector Gerard (TV series "The Fugitive"): played by David Janssen

Richard Saunders

Supposed author and compiler of *Poor Richard's Almanacs*, actually written by Benjamin Franklin

Richmond, Va.
Capital of the Confederacy (1861-65) after Montgomery, Ala.

Rick Blaine
Humphrey Bogart's role in 1942 movie *Casablanca*

Rickenbacker, Captain Edward Vernon
America's top World War I ace, 26 victories (22 airplanes, 4 balloons): Medal of Honor winner, race car driver, later president of Eastern Airlines. In 1942 his plane was forced down in the Pacific and he spent 3 weeks on a raft before being rescued

Rick's Café Américain
Cafe owned by Rick Blaine (1942 movie *Casablanca*)

Rico
Caesar Enrico Bandello, gangster in movie *Little Caesar*: played by Edward G. Robinson

Riegels, Roy
Center of the California Golden Bears who ran the "wrong way" in the second quarter of the 1929 Rose Bowl game, 65 yards: teammate Benny Lom stopped him 6 inches from California's own goal line. A punt on the next play was blocked for a safety, and California lost the game 8-7 to Georgia Tech

Righteous Brothers
Singing team: Bobby Hatfield, Bill Medley (replaced by Jimmy Walker)

Rikki-Tikki-Tavi
Mowgli's pet mongoose (Rudyard Kipling's *The Jungle Book*)

Rima
The bird-girl (William Henry Hudson's *Green Mansions*). In the 1959 movie, the part was played by Audrey Hepburn

Ringling Brothers
Founders of the Ringling Brothers Circus: Albert, Otto, Charles, Alfred, John

Rip Kirby
Scientist-detective (comic book series "Rip Kirby")

Rippy, Rodney Allen
Small, joyous boy in the Jack-in-the-Box TV commercial

Ritter, Tex
Singer of the theme song in 1952 movie *High Noon*

Ritz Brothers
Zany comedians: Al, Jimmy, Harry

River City
Iowa town visited by Harold Hill (Meredith Willson's *The Music Man*)

Riverdale High
School attended by Archie Andrews (comic books)

Rivets

The SPCA dog mascot

Road Pictures

Series starring Bob Hope, Bing Crosby, and Dorothy Lamour:
Road to Singapore, 1940
Road to Zanzibar, 1941
Road to Morocco, 1942
Road to Utopia, 1946
Road to Rio, 1948
Road to Bali, 1952
Road to Hong Kong, 1961

Road Runner

Large bird, Geococcyx californianus (in Warner Brothers' cartoons it says "Beep beep")

Robby

Robot (1955 movie *Forbidden Planet*; also in 1957 movie *The Invisible Boy*)

Robert Dietrich

A pen name of E. Howard Hunt

Robin

Secret identity of Dick Grayson (TV series "Batman"): played by Burt Ward

Robin Hood

Hero of English folk ballads and of children's stories. Living in Sherwood Forest with his band of men clad in Lincoln Green, robbing the rich to give to the poor, and waging constant war against the Sheriff of Nottingham or the nobility personified in Guy of Gisbourne, Robin is supposedly Earl of Huntingdon.

At least 5 movie versions of his adventures preceded Douglas Fairbanks, Sr.'s feature of 1922. Errol Flynn played Robin in 1938, Jon Hall in 1948, and many others as well have made it a favorite. Richard Greene was Robin on TV, Richard Todd in a Disney movie in 1952.

In Disney cartoon feature movie, the voices were: Robin Hood (Brian Bedford), Prince John (Peter Ustinov), Little John (Phil Harris), Sir Hiss (Terry-Thomas), Allan a Dale (Roger Miller), Sheriff (Pat Buttram), Trigger (George Lindsey), Friar Tuck (Andy Devine)

Robinson, Jack "Jackie" Roosevelt

First Negro to play in major league baseball, Brooklyn Dodgers, 1947

Robotrix

Female robot in Fritz Lang's *Metropolis* (1926): played by Brigitte Helm

Rochester
>Jack Benny's valet: played by Eddie Anderson

Rocinante
>Don Quixote's horse

Rock, The
>Nickname of Alcatraz Prison, federal jail in San Francisco Bay

Rock Around the Clock
>Theme song of 1955 movie *The Blackboard Jungle* (played by Bill Haley and the Comets)

Rock Men and Shell Men
>Two groups of prehistoric people (1940 movie *One Million B.C.* and 1966 movie *One Million Years B.C.*)

Rock 'n' Roll Groups

Lead	*"And The"*
Archie Bell	Drells
B. Bumble	Stingers
Bill Haley	Comets
Billy J. Kramer	Dakotas
Billy Ward	Dominoes
Bobby Vee	Strangers
Booker T	M. G.'s
Buddy Holly	Crickets
Country Joe	Fish
Danny	Juniors
Diana Ross	Supremes
Dicky Doo	Don'ts
Dion	Belmonts
Dr. Feelgood	Interns
Don Juan	Meadowlarks
Duane Eddy	Rebels
Eric Burdon	Animals/War
Frankie Lymon	Teenagers
Freddy	Dreamers
Gary Lewis	Playboys
Gary Puckett	Union Gap
Gene Vincent	Blue Caps
Gerry	Pacemakers
Gladys Knight	Pips
Hank Ballard	Midnighters
Harvey	Moonglows
Herman	Hermits
Huey "Piano" Smith	Clowns
James Brown	Famous Flames
Jay	Americans

Lead	*"And The"*
Jerry Butler	Impressions
Jimmy Gilmer	Fireballs
Joey Dee	Starlighters
Johnny	Hurricanes
Jr. Walker	All-Stars
King Curtis	Kingpins
Lee Andrews	Hearts
Little Anthony	Imperials
Little Caesar	Romans
Little Joe	Thrillers
Lulu	Luvers
Martha	Vandellas
Mitch Ryder	Detroit Wheels
Paul Revere	Raiders
Rosie	Originals
Ruby	Romantics
Sam the Sham	Pharoahs
Shep	Limelites
Sly	Family Stone
Smokey Robinson	Miracles
Sonny Til	Orioles
Spanky	Our Gang
Tommy James	Shondells

Rocky
> Bullwinkle's sidekick squirrel (cartoon series "Bullwinkle")

Rodan
> Flying monster (1957 Japanese motion picture)

Rodeo Big Three
> Championship rodeos: Cheyenne Frontier Days, Calgary Stampede, Pendleton Roundup

Roderick Anthony
> Captain of the "Ferndale" (Joseph Conrad's *Chance*)

Roger Dorn, Captain
> Companion of detective Peter Quill (radio series "Peter Quill")

Roger Wilco
> Message received, will comply (World War II verbal code)

Rokk Krinn
> Name of Cosmic Boy (comic books)

Rolfe, John
> Virginia colonist (1585-1622) who married Pocahontas in 1614

Rolling Stones
> Original members: Mick Jagger, Brian Jones, Keith Richard, Charlie Watts, Bill Wyman

Rollo

Rich boy ("Nancy" cartoons)

Romance of Helen Trent, The

Radio soap opera about a fashion designer:

"The story of a woman who sets out to prove what so many other women long to prove in their own lives . . . that romance can live on at thirty-five . . . and even beyond"

Romulans

Enemies of the Federation (TV series "Star Trek")

Ronald McDonald

McDonald's Hamburgers' clown

Ronson

Brand name of James Bond's cigarette lighter

Rooms

In the game of "Clue" (detective board game): Ball Room, Billiard Room, Conservatory, Dining Room, Hall, Kitchen, Library, Lounge, Study

Rooney, Mickey

American actor, originally as Mickey McGuire, with Our Gang: real name Joe Yule, Jr.

Married to Ava Gardner, 1942-1943; Betty Rase, 1944-1947; Martha Vickers, 1949-1951; Elaine Mahnken, 1952-1959; Barbara Thomasen, 1959-1966; Margaret Lane, 1966-1967

Roosevelt, (Anna) Eleanor

Maiden name of Eleanor Roosevelt (1884-1962), a niece of President Theodore Roosevelt (daughter of his younger brother, Elliott)

Roosevelt, Franklin Delano

Only United States President to be elected for four terms: 1932, 1936, 1940, 1944 (respectively over Hoover, Alf Landon, Wendell Wilkie, T. E. Dewey)

The distant relative shared by him and Theodore Roosevelt was Nicholas Roosevelt, a New York politician in the early 18th century (about 1700)

Roosevelt, Theodore

Leader (Lieutenant-Colonel) of the Rough Riders, 1st Volunteer Cavalry.

Youngest man to become President of the United States: age 42 years, 10 months, 18 days, when inaugurated Sept. 14, 1901

Roosevelt boys

Sons of Franklin and Eleanor Roosevelt who served during World War II while their father was President of the United States:

James, Marine Corps
Elliot, Air Corps

Franklin, Jr., Navy
John, Navy

Root, Charlie

Chicago Cubs' pitcher who threw the baseball in the 4th inning of the third (Oct. 1) 1932 World Series game in Chicago when Babe Ruth pointed to the centerfield bleachers and, after taking two strikes and then two balls, hit right where he indicated he would (Root denied that Babe Ruth ever pointed, but Ruth said that he did)

Rootie Kazootie

TV puppet show, 1950-1952. Host: Todd Russell. Puppets: Rootie Kazootie, El Squeeko Mouse, Gala Poochie, Polka Dottie

Rorschach Test

Psychological personality test utilizing "inkblots," symmetrical patterns in which the subject of the test constructs mental images

Rosa's Cantina

Saloon in El Paso where Senorita Felina danced (1960 hit song "El Paso" by Marty Robbins)

Roscoe Sweeney

Buz Sawyer's friend (comic strip)

Rosebud

Citizen Kane's last word on his deathbed (1941 movie *Citizen Kane*), Rosebud being a sled that he had as a child and the frame story of the movie consisting of a search for the meaning of the word

Rosehill

Town, location of TV serial "Love of Life"

Rosemary's Baby

Named Andrew John; 1968 movie, directed by Roman Polanski and starring Mia Farrow, John Cassavetes, and Ruth Gordon (who won an Academy Award as best supporting actress for her role as a motherly witch) about witchcraft in an urban setting

Rosenkowitz sextuplets

Born January 11, 1974, in Cape Town, South Africa, in order of their birth: David, Nicolette, Jason, Emma, Grant, Elizabeth

Rosenthal, Joe

Photographer who won Pulitzer Prize for picture of U. S. Marines raising the American flag on Mt. Suribachi, Iwo Jima (March 15, 1945): the event was restaged so Rosenthal could get a good picture

Rosey

Family robot of the Jetsons (TV cartoon series "The Jetsons")

Rosie the Riveter

World War II character created by Willie Gillis

Route 66

U. S. highway from Chicago to Los Angeles

Rover Boys, The

Boys' novels created by Edward Stratemeyer; central characters are Dick, Sam, Tom

Roy Harper

Real identity of Speedy, the Green Arrow's sidekick

Royal Canadians

Guy Lombardo's orchestra, established in 1923

Royal Hawaiians

Harry Owens' 1940's orchestra

Rubbles

Neighbors of the Flintstones: Barney, Betty, Bam-Bam

Ruby

Amos's wife ("Amos 'n' Andy"): on radio played by Elinor Harriot

Ruby, Jack

Dallas night club owner (1911-1967) who killed Lee Harvey Oswald, Nov. 24, 1963. Ruby's two night clubs were the Carousel Club and the Vegas Club

Ruby slippers

The shoes that Glinda, the Good Witch of the North, gave Dorothy after Dorothy's house fell on the Wicked Witch of the East (1939 movie *The Wizard of Oz*)

Ruff

Dennis the Menace's dog (daily comic strip)

Ruff and Reddy

Cat and bulldog (comic book series)

Rugby

School attended by Tom Brown (Thomas Hughes' *Tom Brown's Schooldays*, 1857).

Rum and Coca Cola

Song written about 1944, words by comedian Morey Amsterdam: subject of famous copyright suit on grounds that Lord Invader (Rupert Grant) wrote the words

Rumpelstiltskin

Dwarf who could spin straw into gold (Grimms' fairy tales)

Runnymede

Meadow on Thames River west of London where the Magna Carta was signed, June 15, 1215, by King John (it is also said that nearby Charter Island is the place of signing)

Runt

Boston Blackie's sidekick (movie series): played by George E. Stone. On radio his sidekick was Shorty

Rushville Center

Town, location of radio serial "Ma Perkins"

Russell

Bill Cosby's brother (with whom he slept)

Rusty

Boy in TV series "Rin-Tin-Tin": played by Lee Aaker

Rusty

Bob Steele's horse

Rusty

The Shield's boy sidekick (comic book series "The Shield")

Rutgers

New Jersey college that played, Nov. 6, 1869, the first intercollegiate football game, beating Princeton 6-4 under soccer rules

Ruth

Festus's mule (TV series "Gunsmoke")

Ruth, George Herman "Babe"

Most successful slugger in major league history, one of first 5 elected to Baseball's Hall of Fame: pitcher (1914-1919) with Boston Red Sox, outfielder (1920-1934) with New York Yankees and (1935) Boston Bees. He hit 714 home runs in his career; in the 1921 season, he hit 59, passing the previous record holder, Roger Connor, who played from 1880 to 1896 in the National League and hit 137 home runs. His record fell in 1974, after nearly 40 years, when Henry Aaron of Atlanta hit his 715th home run. Ruth's 60 home runs in 1927 still stands as the 154-game season record, though surpassed by Roger Maris's 1961 "asterisked" total of 61 in 162 games. Ruth led the American League in slugging percentage (lifetime, .690) every season from 1918 to 1931, except for 1925, the year he collapsed physically and Ken Williams led; he was consistently a leader in runs batted in, and led in home runs except for 1922 (Williams with 39 to Ruth's 35) and 1925 (Meusel with 33), though he was tied in 1918 by Tilly Walker of Philadelphia (11) and in 1931 by his teammate Lou Gehrig (46). In 2503 games, Ruth struck out 1330 times and walked 2056 times: no other player has as many bases on balls. Ruth's record as a pitcher, in a short mound career, is also impressive. For years he held the World Series record for consecutive scoreless innings pitched (29⅔), broken by Whitey Ford in the 1960 and 1961 series: his World Series earned run average is 0.87 (Harry Brecheen's 0.83 is the only better mark). Ruth's last home runs (713-714) were hit May 25, 1935, off Guy Bush of Pittsburgh at Forbes Field. His "calling the shot" home run in the third game of the World Series (Oct. 1, 1932) was hit off Charlie Root of Chicago at Wrigley Field; it was Ruth's last series homer (15; record held by Mickey Mantle, 18).

Ruth's salary of $80,000 a year in 1930-1931 was the highest ever for its time.

The answer to the question "Whose record did Ruth break when he hit 60 homers?" is of course "His own," since his 59 home runs in 1921 was then the record

Ryman Auditorium

Nashville, Tennessee, location of Grand Ole Opry from 1942 to 1974: known after 1961 as Grand Ole Opry House

S

6

Sides to a snowflake

6

Players on a hockey team

6

The good reporter's questions: Who, What, When, Where, Why, How

7

Number of voyages of Sinbad the Sailor (*Arabian Nights*)

7 Against Thebes

Argive heroes who fought Thebes (Greek mythology): Adrastus, Polynices, Tydeus, Parthenopaeus, Amphiaraus, Capaneus, Hippomedon

7 Ages of Man

Jaques, philosophizing in William Shakespeare's *As You Like It*, enumerates them as embodied in: Infant, Schoolboy, Lover, Soldier, Justice, Pantaloon (retirement), Second childhood ("sans everything")

7 Deadly Sins

Pride, Avarice, Wrath, Envy, Gluttony, Sloth, Lust

7 Destroyers

Ran aground in the Santa Barbara Channel, Sept. 8, 1923: U.S.S. "Chauncey," U.S.S. "Delphy" (flagship), U.S.S. "Fuller," U.S.S. "S. P. Lee," U.S.S. "Nicholas," U.S.S. "Woodbury," U.S.S. "Young." U.S.S. "Farragut" and U.S.S. "Somers" were damaged: 22 sailors died

7 Dwarfs, The

Snow White's woodland companions (Disney cartoon feature movie): Bashful (voice: Scotty Mattraw); Doc (voice: Roy Atwell);

Dopey ("Never had anything to say"); Grumpy (voice: Pinto Colvig); Happy (voice: Otis Hanlon); Sleepy (voice: Pinto Colvig); Sneezy (voice: Billy Gilbert)

7 Hills of Rome

Aventine, Caelian, Capitoline, Esquiline, Palatine, Quirinal, Viminal

7 Little Foys

Brynie, Charlie, Dick, Eddy, Madeleine, Mary, Irving.
Father: Eddie

7 Mules

Linemen for the Four Horsemen on the 1924 Notre Dame football team: Ed Huntsinger, end; Charles Collins, end; Joe Bach, tackle; Edgar (Rip) Miller, tackle; Noble Kizer, guard; John Weibel, guard; Adam Walsh, center

7 Seas, The

Antarctic; Arctic; North Atlantic; South Atlantic; Indian; North Pacific; South Pacific

7 Sisters

Women's Ivy League colleges:

	Location	Date founded
Barnard	New York, N. Y.	1889
Bryn Mawr	Bryn Mawr, Penna.	1885
Mount Holyoke	So. Hadley, Mass.	1837
Radcliffe	Cambridge, Mass.	1879
Smith	Northampton, Mass.	1871
Vassar*	Poughkeepsie, N. Y.	1861
Wellesley	Wellesley, Mass.	1875

7 Sisters, The

Daughters of Atlas (in the constellation Pleiades): Alcyone, Sterope, Celeno, Electra, Maia, Taygeta, Merope (dimmest star, because she married a mortal)

7 Virtues

Faith, Hope, Charity (Love), Fortitude, Justice, Prudence, Temperance

7 Wonders of the World

Antiquity

  Colossus of Rhodes

  Egyptian Pyramids

  Hanging Gardens of Babylon

  Lighthouse (Pharos) at Alexandria

  Mausoleum at Halicarnassus

  Statue of Zeus by Phidias at Olympia

  Temple of Diana at Ephesus

---

* Now co-ed, no longer a women's college

Middle Ages
> Catacombs of Alexandria
> Coliseum of Rome
> Great Wall of China
> Leaning Tower of Pisa
> Mosque of St. Sophia at Constantinople
> Porcelain Tower of Nanking
> Stonehenge, Salisbury Plain, England

7 Works of Mercy, The

Bury the dead; Clothe the naked; Feed the hungry; Give drink to the thirsty; House the homeless; Tend the sick; Visit the fatherless and afflicted

7th

Cavalry regiment that was George Armstrong Custer's last command

7X

Coca Cola's secret ingredient

16

Number on football jersey worn by Mean Mary Jean, the Plymouth girl (TV commercial); later changed to 1

17 Cherry Tree Lane

London home of the Banks family (1964 movie *Mary Poppins*)

17 South Jackson

Home of the Goldbergs (radio series)

60

Home runs hit by Babe Ruth in a 154-game season, 1927 (540 times at bat)

60

Length in feet of a bowling lane from foul line to head pin

60 Feet 6 Inches

Distance between the pitcher's rubber and home plate in baseball

61

Home runs hit by Roger Maris in a 162-game season, 1961 (590 times at bat); number 61 was hit off of Boston Red Sox pitcher Tracy Stallard

62

Self-portraits painted by Rembrandt van Rijn

63

Length in yards of longest field goal in NFL history: by Tom Dempsey (his right—kicking—foot is deformed) of the New Orleans Saints against the Detroit Lions, Nov. 8, 1970. This was the last play of the game and won for the Saints 19-17

64

Squares on a chess board

$64
>Highest prize in CBS radio show "Take It or Leave It"

65th Precinct
>New York setting of TV series "Naked City"

77
>Red Grange's uniform number

77th
>Infantry division to which belonged the "Lost Battalion" (1st Battalion, 308th Infantry), separated near Binarville, France, in the Meuse-Argonne offensive, Oct. 2-Oct. 7, 1918, in World War I

78 RPM records
>Manufacture discontinued in 1958

79 Wistful Vista
>Home of Fibber McGee and Molly

600
>Number of cavalrymen in the Light Brigade (Alfred, Lord Tennyson's "The Charge of the Light Brigade")

632 A. F.
>Time in which is set Aldous Huxley's novel *Brave New World.* A. F. stands for After Ford (Henry Ford)

714
>Badge number of Sgt. Joe Friday (radio/TV series "Dragnet")

714
>Home runs hit (1915-1935) by Babe Ruth: Ruth's first major league home run was hit off Jack Warhop of Yankees (Ruth was member of Boston Red Sox), May 6, 1915, in New York

714 . . . 715
>Hank Aaron hit his 714th home run in his first time at bat, opening day, April 4, 1974, in Cincinnati Riverfront Stadium, off Cincinnati pitcher Jack Billingham; ball was retrieved by policeman Clarence Williams.
>
>Hank Aaron hit his 715th home run off Dodger pitcher Al Downing at Atlanta Stadium, April 8, 1974. Braves' relief pitcher Tom House retrieved the ball in the Atlanta bullpen. (Pearl Bailey sang the National Anthem before the game.)
>
>Aaron's first major league home run was hit off Vic Raschi of the St. Louis Cardinals April 23, 1954, at St. Louis

776 B. C.
>First Greek Olympic games

1600
>Address on Pennsylvania Avenue in Washington, D. C. of the White House

7190
>Number stamped on the gold bar James Bond uses as bait for Auric Goldfinger (1964 movie *Goldfinger*)

773,692

Number of words in the English Bible (King James version)

17,576,000

Different combinations using 3 numbers and 3 letters (license plates)

S

Middle initial in Harry S. Truman's name: doesn't stand for any name

SAM

Surface-to-Air Missile

SALT

Strategic Arms Limitation Talks: between U. S. and U.S.S.R. at Helsinki (1970) and Geneva (1972)

SHADO

Supreme Headquarters Allied Defense Organization: 1980's setting of TV series "UFO"

SHAPE

Supreme Headquarters, Allied Powers in Europe: military center for NATO command

SIA

Government agency (United States Intelligence Agency) for which Alexander Mundy (played by Robert Wagner) steals: agency head is Noah Bain (TV series "It Takes a Thief")

SOS

· · · – – – · · · (distress signal); before SOS it was CQD

SPQR

Senatus Populusque Romanus ("The Roman Senate and People"): initials on Roman standards and elsewhere, especially during the republic

Sabrina

Teenage witch (cartoon)

Sacred Cow

C-54, first presidential airplane, 1944

Sad Sack, The

The essential GI of World War II, a cartoon character by George Baker featured in *Yank* from its first issue

Sadie

Sad Sack's girlfriend (comic strip series "Sad Sack")

Sadie Hawkins Day

First Saturday after November 11 (in the strip originally November 4, 1939), when girls chase boys to catch a husband: originally adopted by college groups and others from recurrent event in Al Capp comic strip "Li'l Abner"

Safi

Baby monkey that rode with Thor Heyderdahl on Ra I

Sailor

Spin's horse (Spin and Marty, on TV's "Mickey Mouse Club")

Saint, The

Simon Templar, detective/adventurer created by Leslie Charteris

St. Andrew

Patron saint of Scotland

St. Boniface

Patron saint of Germany

St. Denis

Patron saint of France

St. George

Patron saint of England

St. Gregory

Hotel in Arthur Hailey's *Hotel*

St. James (Santiago)

Patron saint of Spain

St. Patrick

Patron saint of Ireland

St. Valentine's Day Massacre

The February 14, 1929, machine-gunning of 7 members of Bugs Moran's (or Dion O'Banion's) gang by 5 members of Al Capone's mob, some dressed like policemen, who arrived in a Cadillac touring car at the S. M. C. Cartage Co. warehouse, 2122 North Clark Street, Chicago. Killed were James Clark, Al Weinshank, Adam Heyer, John May, Reinhardt Schwimmer, Pete Gusenberg, Frank Gusenberg (Highball, John May's dog, was present)

Saki

Pseudonym of Hector Hugh Munro (1870-1916), English author of macabre humorous stories

Salem

Town, locale of daytime serial "Days of Our Lives"

Salem

Cat belonging to Sabrina (the teenage witch in a TV cartoon series

Salomey

Li'l Abner's pig (comic strip)

"Salty" Bill Barnacle

Popeye's sidekick (pre-1929)

Sam

Piano player (1942 movie *Casablanca*): played by Dooley Wilson. Wilson could not play the piano himself and the music was actually played by Elliott Carpenter. Sam sang three songs: "As Time Goes By," "It Had To Be You," and "Knock on Wood"

Rick (Humphrey Bogart) never says, "Play it again, Sam," in the picture

Sam

Richard Diamond's switchboard operator (on TV played by Mary Tyler Moore, but all the viewers ever saw were her legs)

Sam Catchem

Dick Tracy's freckle-faced detective companion

Sam 'n' Henry

Names of Freeman Gosden and Charles Correll in the radio series preceding "Amos 'n' Andy"

Sam Spade

Detective created by Dashiell Hammett in the novel *The Maltese Falcon* (1930)

On radio Spade was played by Howard Duff and Steve Dunne. In the movies he was played by Humphrey Bogart in *The Maltese Falcon* (1941), by Ricardo Cortez (1931 version *Dangerous Female*; also known as *The Maltese Falcon*), and by Warren William (1936 *Satan Met a Lady*, a version of *The Maltese Falcon*)

Samantha

Witch (TV series "Bewitched"): played by Elizabeth Montgomery, daughter of Robert Montgomery

Samantha

Pet goose (1956 movie *Friendly Persuasion*)

Samson

Prince Philip's horse (Walt Disney version of *Sleeping Beauty*)

San Bernardino

California, largest county (20,117 sq. mi.) in the United States (larger than 9 states of the U. S.)

San Clemente

Site of the "Western White House" during the Nixon administration

San Francisco Beat

Title of reruns of the TV show "The Lineup"

San Juan Hill

Place near Santiago, Cuba, where the Rough Riders made their famous charge (on foot), July 1, 1898, under the command of Theodore Roosevelt

San Quentin

California prison in which country and western singer Merle Haggard served 3 years of a 1-to-5-year term

San Tanco

Convent in Puerto Rico to which Sister Bertrille belongs (TV series "The Flying Nun")

Sancho Panza

Don Quixote's squire (in Cervantes' novel)

Sanders, George

British actor, brother of actor Tom Conway.

Academy award (1950) for best supporting role, Addison De Witt in *All About Eve*.

Autobiography (1960): *Memoirs of a Professional Cad*

Sanders, Colonel Harland

Goateed and mustached founder of Kentucky Fried Chicken

Sandwich Islands

Former name of the Hawaiian Islands

Sandy

Orphan Annie's dog (comic strip and radio): "Arf" says Sandy (in the radio voice of Brad Barker)

Sandy

The Sandman's boy sidekick (comic book series "The Sandman")

Santa Claus' reindeer

In Clement Clarke Moore's poem "A Visit from St. Nicholas" (1823): Dasher, Dancer, Prancer, Vixen, Comet, Cupid, Donner, Blitzen

Santa Fe & Disneyland

Railroad running throughout Disneyland

Santa Fe Trail

Kansas City, Missouri, to Santa Fe, New Mexico

Santa Maria

Christopher Columbus's flagship, a carack, in 1492 voyage, accompanied by "Nina" and "Pinta": wrecked off Hispaniola Christmas Day 1492

Santana

Name of boat that Frank McCloud (Humphrey Bogart) takes over from Johnny Rocco (Edward G. Robinson) and his gang (1948 movie *Key Largo*)

Santana

Humphrey Bogart's private boat

Santiago

The old fisherman in Ernest Hemingway's novel *The Old Man and the Sea*

Saperstein, Abe

Founder (1927) of the basketball team the Harlem Globetrotters

Sapphire

Wife of George "Kingfish" Stevens (radio series "Amos 'n' Andy"): played by Ernestine Wade

Saratoga

Jean Harlow's last movie (1937). She died while filming the picture; Mary Dees replaced her in the role of Carol Clayton, with Paula Winslowe dubbing in her voice

Sarek and Amanda

Mr. Spock's father (Vulcan) and mother (human) (TV series "Star Trek")

Sasha

Bear appearing with his bearded owner and trainer, Earl Hammond, in Hamm's Beer TV commercials

Sasha

Bird in "Peter and the Wolf"

Satchmo

Nickname of Louis Armstrong (1900-1971), American musician famed for his New Orleans jazz trumpet style

Satellite

Jules Verne's dog

Satin Doll

Theme song of Duke Ellington's orchestra

Saturday Evening Post

Magazine that claimed to have been founded by Benjamin Franklin though first issue was in August 1821, more than 30 years after Franklin's death

SAYHEY

Willie Mays' California car license plate

Say-Hey Kid

Nickname of baseball player Willie Howard Mays, outfielder with New York and San Francisco Giants and New York Mets, sometimes called the best ballplayer of his time

Scamp

Puppy of The Lady and the Tramp (Disney cartoon-movie)

Scandinavia

Norway, Sweden, Denmark, Iceland, Finland

Scheherazade

Wife of King Shahriar, who told tales for 1001 nights (the so-called "Arabian Nights' Entertainment")

Schlitz

"The beer that made Milwaukee famous" (slogan)

Schmoo

Animal created by Al Capp ("Li'l Abner" comic strip): lays eggs, gives milk, tastes like steak and chicken

Schnozzola

Nickname for Jimmy Durante, because of the size of his nose or "schnozzola"

Schwab
> Drug store in Hollywood where Lana Turner was discovered

Schyler
> Sky King's first name

Scorpion
> U. S. nuclear submarine lost at sea May 21, 1968

Scott Jordon
> Detective in stories by Harold Q. Masur

Scout
> Tonto's horse

Scout Law, The
> A scout is:

Trustworthy	Obedient
Loyal	Cheerful
Helpful	Thrifty
Friendly	Brave
Courteous	Clean
Kind	Reverent

Scout Motto
> "Be Prepared"

Scout Oath
> "On my honor I will do my best: to do my duty to God and my country, and to obey the scout law; to help other people at all times; to keep myself physically strong, mentally awake and morally straight"

Scout Slogan
> "Do a Good Turn Daily"

Scraggs
> Daisy Mae's maiden name (comic strip "Li'l Abner")

Scruffy
> Family dog of the Muirs (TV series "The Ghost and Mrs. Muir")

SCUBA
> Self-Contained Underwater Breathing Apparatus

Scuffy and Little Toot
> Cartoon tugboats

Sea Dart
> Jetmarine (submarine) of Tom Swift, Jr. (novel series)

Sea Hound
> Captain Silver's ship (comic books)

Sea of Tranquility
> Mare where Apollo 11 landed on the moon, July 20, 1969, at 4:17:20 p.m. EDT: "The Eagle has landed"

Seagulls
> Of Red Skelton (comedy routine): Gertrude, Heathcliffe

Second cousins

Presidents James Madison and Zachary Taylor: James Taylor, who died in 1729, was their great-grandfather in common

Secret identities

Pseudonym	"Real" identity
Airboy	Davy Nelson
Atom, The	Al Pratt
Batgirl	Babs Gordon
Batman	Bruce Wayne
Black Bat	Tony Quinn
Black Condor	Senator Tom Wright
Blue Beetle	Dan Garrett
Blue Tracer	Wild Bill Dunn
Bulletgirl	Susan Kent
Bulletman	Jim Barr
Captain America	Steve Rogers
Captain Freedom	Don Wright
Captain Future	Curtis Newton
Captain Marvel	Billy Batson
Captain Marvel, Jr.	Freddie Freeman
Captain Midnight	Captain Albright
Captain Triumph	Lance Gallant
Catwoman	Selina Kyle
Chameleon Boy	Reep Daggle
Chandu the Magician	Frank Chandler
Clock, The	Brian O'Brien
Cosmic Boy	Rokk Krinn
Dr. Fate	Kent Nelson
Doll Girl	Martha Roberts
Doll Man	Darrel Dane
Face, The	Tony Trent
Firebrand	Rod Reilly
Flash (Original)	Jay Garrick
Flash (New Series)	Barry Allen
Golden Arrow	Roger Parsons
Green Arrow	Oliver Queen
Green Hornet	Britt Reid
Green Lantern	Alan Scott
Hawkgirl	Shiera Sanders
Hawkman	Carter Hall
Heap	Baron Von Emmelmann
Hourman	Rex Tyler
Human Bomb	Roy Lincoln

Pseudonym	*"Real" identity*
Human Torch	Jim Hammond
Human Torch, The	Johnny Storm
Kid Flash	Wally West
Lone Ranger	John Reid
Madam Fatal	Richard Stanton
Manhunter	Dan Richards
Mary Marvel	Mary Blomfield
Minute-Man	Jack Weston
Mister Fantastic	Reed Richards
Mr. Scarlet	Brian Butler
Mouthpiece, The	Bill Perkins
Phantom Detective	Richard Curtis Van Loan
Phantom Eagle	Mickey Malone
Phantom Lady	Sandra Knight
Plastic Man	Eel O'Brian
Ray, The	Happy Terrill
Red Bee	Rick Raleigh
Red Torpedo	Jim Lockhard
Robin	Dick Grayson
Robotman	Bob Crane (Paul Dennis)
Sandman	Wesley Dodds
Saturn Girl	Irma Ardeen
Shadow, The	Lamont Cranston
Shield, The	Joe Higgins
Skyman	Allen Turner
Spectre	Jim Corrigan
Speedy	Roy Harper
Spider, The	Richard Wentworth
Spiderman	Peter Parker
Spirit, The	Denny Colt
Spitfire	Tex Adams
Spy Master	Alan Armstrong
Starman	Ted Knight
Sub Mariner	Namor
Supergirl	Linda Lee Danvers
Superman	Clark Kent
Swordfish	Jack Smith
Tarzan	Lord Greystoke
Thing, The	Ben Grimm
Tor, Magic Master	Jim Slade
Wonder Woman	Diana Prince

Selfridge, Lt. Thomas E.

First airplane fatality in the world, September 17, 1908, at Fort Myer, Virginia, in a plane piloted by Orville Wright. Selfridge was in the Army Signal Corps

Selkirk, William

Scottish sailor (1676-1721), the original Robinson Crusoe: put ashore October 1704 on Más a Tierra, one of the Juan Fernandez Islands (uninhabited), off the coast of Chile by Captain Thomas Stradling, rescued in February 1709 by Captain Woodes Rogers after 4 years alone

Sellers, Peter

Roles in 1959 movie *The Mouse that Roared*: Count of Mountjoy (Bobo); Duchess Gloriana XII; Tully Bascomb, head of the army
Roles in 1964 movie *Dr. Strangelove*: Group Captain Lionel Mandrake; President Merkin Muffley; Dr. Strangelove

Semper Fidelis

"Always faithful": motto of United States Marines

Senior Service

British Royal Navy

Sequoia

The presidential yacht

Sequoya

Indian name of George Guess, who created (1809-1821) the Cherokee alphabet

Sergeant Carter

Gomer Pyle's drill instructor and friend (TV series "Gomer Pyle, U.S.M.C."): played by Frank Sutton

Sergeant Cuff

Early detective in English fiction (Wilkie Collins' *The Moonstone*, 1868)

Sergeant Joe Friday

Central character of "Dragnet" (radio & TV): played by Jack Webb. His partners were officers Ben Romero (Barton Yarborough), Frank Smith (Ben Alexander), and Bill Gannon (Harry Morgan). For one season only Friday was a lieutenant and Smith a sergeant, but they soon reverted

Sergeant Preston of the Yukon

"I arrest you in the name of the Crown"

Sergeant Frank Smith

Sgt. Joe Friday's first TV partner ("Dragnet"): played by Ben Alexander

Sergeant (Orville) Snorkel

Beetle Bailey's sergeant (cartoon series)

Sergeant Tibbs

Cat (1961 Disney movie *101 Dalmatians*)

Sergeants 3

1962 movie (*Gunga Din* in the American West) starring, as 3 Army sergeants, Frank Sinatra (Mike Merry), Dean Martin (Chip Deal), Peter Lawford (Larry Barrett)

Service

Rotary Club motto

Sesame Street

Muppets: Grover, Bert, Sherlock Hemlock, Cookie Monster, Ernie, Roosevelt Franklin

Seth

Third child of Adam and Eve, father of Enos

Seward's Folly

U. S. purchase of Alaska from Russia, 1867, for $7,200,000

Shadow, The

Identity secretly assumed by Lamont Cranston: on radio played by Bret Morrison, Bill Johnstone, and Orson Welles (originally by Robert Hardy Andrews). But see *Kent Allard*.

"Who knows what evil lurks in the hearts of men? The Shadow knows"

Shady Rest

Hotel (TV series "Petticoat Junction")

SHAEF

Supreme Headquarters Allied Expeditionary Force

Shamrock

Sir Thomas Lipton's yachts: in his attempts to win the America Cup, all 5 of them had the name Shamrock (I through V) (1899-1930)

Shangri-La

Hidden Tibetan valley paradise (James Hilton's *Lost Horizon*)

Name under which Franklin D. Roosevelt hid the identity of the U.S. aircraft carrier "Hornet," from which Lt. Col. James Doolittle led 16 Army B-25 bombers in his raid (April 18, 1942) against Japan (Tokyo, Yokosuka, Yokohama, Nagoya)

Sharpie

The Gillette Parrot (TV commercial)

SHAZAM

Ancient Egyptian wizard who gave the Marvel family their magic powers: in his underground throne-room (an old subway tunnel) are seven statues, "The Seven Deadly Enemies of Man": Pride, Envy, Greed, Hatred, Selfishness, Laziness, Injustice (Captain Marvel comic books)

SHAZAM

Magic word that changes Billy Batson into Captain Marvel and back again:

S = (Wisdom of) Solomon
H = (Strength of) Hercules
A = (Stamina of) Atlas
Z = (Power of) Zeus
A = (Courage of) Achilles
M = (Speed of) Mercury

SHAZAM

Magic word that changes Mary Batson into Mary Marvel and back again:

S = (Grace of) Selena
H = (Strength of) Hippolyta
A = (Skill of) Ariadne
Z = (Fleetness of) Zephyrus
A = (Beauty of) Aurora
M = (Wisdom of) Minerva

Sheik, The

Rudolph Valentino

Shelby, Montana

Site of the heavyweight championship fight between Jack Dempsey and Tom Gibbons, July 4, 1923: Dempsey won a 15-round decision

Shell Men

One of the 2 groups of prehistoric people in the movies *One Million B.C.* and *One Million Years B.C.*

Shell Scott

Detective in stories of Richard S. Prather

Sheriff of Nottingham

Robin Hood's foe

Sherlock Holmes

Detective created by Sir Arthur Conan Doyle, perhaps the best-known fictional character in the world. Home address: 221B Baker Street, London, England, where he lives with Dr. John Watson (before and between Watson's marriages) and with Mrs. Hudson as landlady.

Movies starring Basil Rathbone as Sherlock Holmes and Nigel Bruce as Dr. Watson:

1939: *The Adventures of Sherlock Holmes*
1942: *Sherlock Holmes and the Voice of Terror*
1942: *Sherlock Holmes and the Secret Weapon*
1943: *Sherlock Holmes in Washington*

1943: *Sherlock Holmes Faces Death*
1944: *Sherlock Holmes and the Spider Woman*
1944: *The Scarlet Claw*
1944: *The Pearl of Death*
1945: *The House of Fear*
1945: *The Woman in Green*
1945: *Pursuit to Algiers*
1946: *Terror By Night*
1946: *Dressed to Kill*

Other actors who played Sherlock Holmes (stage, movies, radio) were: William Gillette, John Barrymore, Raymond Massey, Clive Brook, Peter Cushing, Ed Wynn, Fritz Weaver, Robert Stephens, Richard Gordon, Louis Hector, Tom Conway, Ben Wright, John Stanley

Sherman
Master of Peabody (the genius dog) (cartoon series "Peabody")

Sherwood Forest
Haunt of Robin Hood and his band

Shield, The
Secret identity of Joe Higgins (comic book series "The Shield")

Shields, Arthur
Character actor, especially in movies: brother of Barry Fitzgerald

Shiloh
Wyoming ranch on which the Virginian serves as foreman (TV series "The Virginian")

Ships of U. S. Navy
Naming of ships during World War II:

Battleships	named for	States
Aircraft Carriers		Battles
Cruisers		Cities
Destroyers		Dead war heroes
Submarines		Fish
Ammunition Ships		Gods of mythology
Tugs		Indian tribes

Shipwreck Kelly
Alvin Kelly, America's great flagpole sitter of the 1920's and 1930's

Shire, The
Land where the Hobbits live (J. R. R. Tolkien's *The Hobbit* and other novels)

Shoeless Joe Jackson
Chicago White Sox outfielder involved in 1919 World Series scan-

dal: banned in 1920 from baseball. One of the American League's best players (he batted .408 in 1911, led the league in slugging percentage in 1913, and had a lifetime batting average of .356, behind only Cobb and Hornsby), he was idolized and the principal casualty of the "Black Sox" scandal; one little boy is supposed to have brought him to tears by saying, "Say it ain't so, Joe"

Shorty

Boston Blackie's henchman (radio series): played by Tony Barrett (in movie serials the Runt was Blackie's sidekick)

Shutters and Boards

Country-western song written by Audie Murphy, most decorated World War II hero and postwar movie star

Sic Semper Tyrannis

Cry ("Thus ever to tyranny") by John Wilkes Booth as he leaped to Ford's Theater stage after shooting Abraham Lincoln

Si-Fan

Secret evil organization over which Dr. Fu Manchu presides, its agents in every major city in the world (Sax Rohmer's Fu Manchu novels)

Silly, little ass

Tinker Bell's favorite expression (James M. Barrie's *Peter Pan*)

Silver

The Lone Ranger's horse: "Come on, Silver! Let's go, big fellow! Hi-yo, Silver! Awa-a-ay!"

Silver Albatross

Jack Armstrong's Uncle Jim's airplane

Silver-B

Buck Jones's horse, Silver Buck

Silver Dart

Captain Midnight's airplane

Silver King

Horse of Fred Thomson, 1920's movie cowboy

Silversmith

Occupation of Paul Revere

Silverstone

The Millionaire's estate (TV series "The Millionaire")

Simon

Kangaroo that advertises Quangaroos breakfast cereal

Simon and Garfunkel

Paul and Art, respectively; singing team. Paul Simon's tunes, "Mrs. Robinson" and "The Sounds of Silence," were sung by them as background in 1967 movie *The Graduate*

Simon Legree

Evil overseer and slave-driver (Harriet Beecher Stowe's *Uncle Tom's Cabin*)

Simon Templar

Real name of the Saint

Simpson, Mrs. Wallis Warfield

Baltimore, Md., divorcee for whom King Edward VIII of England abdicated his throne (1936) to marry "the woman I love"

Simpsonville

Town, location of radio serial "Young Widder Brown"

Sinatra, Frank

Popular baritone singer, began his singing career with The Hoboken Four, sang with Harry James and Tommy Dorsey orchestras, then on radio's "Hit Parade." Won an Oscar as best supporting actor (1953 movie *From Here To Eternity*) as Maggio

His nicknames: The Voice, The Swooner, King of the Ratpack, Chairman of the Board, Ole Blue Eyes

His wives: Nancy Sinatra (1939-1951), Ava Gardner (1951-1957), Mia Farrow (1966-1968)

His children (with Nancy): Nancy, Frank, Jr., Christina

Sinbad

Pet duck on the Ra I with Thor Heyerdahl and his crew

Sing-A-Long Gang

Mitch Miller's 25-member singing group

Singers/Bands

Singer	Band
Amy Arnell	Tommy Tucker
Mildred Bailey	Paul Whiteman; Red Norvo
Bonnie Baker	Orrin Tucker
June Christy	Stan Kenton
Rosemary Clooney	Tony Pastor
Perry Como	Ted Weems
Don Cornell	Sammy Kaye
Bing Crosby	Paul Whiteman
Doris Day	Les Brown
Mike Douglas	Kay Kyser
Billy Eckstine	Count Basie
Dale Evans	Anson Weeks
Ella Fitzgerald	Chick Webb
Helen Forrest	Artie Shaw; Benny Goodman; Harry James
Merv Griffin	Freddy Martin
Connie Haines	Tommy Dorsey

Singer	Band
Billy Holiday	Artie Shaw
Marion Hutton	Glenn Miller
Peggy Lee	Benny Goodman
Marilyn Maxwell	Ted Weems; Buddy Rogers
Helen O'Connell	Jimmy Dorsey
Ginny Powell	Boyd Raeburn
Jo Stafford	Tommy Dorsey
Kay Starr	Charlie Barnet; Joe Venuti
Martha Tilton	Benny Goodman
Louise Tobin	Benny Goodman; Will Bradley
Bea Wain	Larry Clinton
Helen Ward	Benny Goodman
Frances Wayne	Woody Herman
Edythe Wright	Tommy Dorsey
Nan Wynn	Hal Kemp

Singing Brakeman, The

Nickname of country singer Jimmie Rodgers

Singing Nun, The

Belgian nun Soeur Sourire: sang the 1963 hit record "Dominique"

Singing Sam

The Barbasol Man, radio singer Harry Frankel

Sir Henry Merrivale

Detective created by John Dickson Carr

Sirius

Orion's dog: the Dog Star

Skate, U.S.S.

First submarine to surface at the North Pole, 1959

Skeeter

Tom Swift, Jr.'s helicopter (novel series)

Skelton, Red

His radio and TV roles: Bolivar Shagnasty, Cauliflower McPugg, Clem Kadiddlehopper, Freddie the Freeloader, George Appleby, J. Newton Numskull, Junior, the Little Kid (mean widdle kid), San Fernando Red, Willie Lump Lump, Sheriff Deadeye

Skipper

Jungle Jim's pet dog (movie series "Jungle Jim")

Skull Cave

Place where the Phantom's large treasure is kept in the Bengali jungle (comic strip/book series "The Phantom")

Skull Island

King Kong's home, from which he was brought to New York aboard the ship "Venture"

Skully Nell
> Dummy of Max Terhune in vaudeville

Sky Hound
> Captain Silver's airplane

Sky King
> Captain Midnight's airplane

Sky Queen
> Tom Swift Jr.'s flying lab (novel series)

Skyrocket
> Marty Marham's horse (Spin and Marty "Mickey Mouse Club")

Skytruck
> Type of airplane from which the "Phoenix" was made (Elleston Trevor's novel *The Flight of the Phoenix*)

Slazenger I
> Golf ball used by Auric Goldfinger when he played against James Bond (1964 movie *Goldfinger*). In Ian Fleming's novel, Goldfinger used a Dunlop 65 Number One

Sleeping Beauty
> Princess Aurora, who had become Briar Rose and then went into a deep sleep until Prince Philip awakened her with a kiss (1959 Walt Disney cartoon movie *The Sleeping Beauty*)

Slue-Foot Sue
> Wife of Pecos Bill (American folklore)

Sluggo
> Nancy's boyfriend (comic strip)

Smallville
> Town in which Superboy was raised by Mr. and Mrs. Kent

Smee
> Captain Hook's companion (James M. Barrie's *Peter Pan*)

Smilin' Ed
> Ed McConnell, children's radio and TV host and singer

Smith, Captain Edward J.
> Captain of the "Titanic" April 14, 1912, when she struck an iceberg and sank on her maiden voyage

Smith, Captain John
> His life, according to legend, was saved by Powhatan's daughter Pocahontas. President (1608-1609) of the Virginia colony, he was largely responsible for its success

Smith Brothers
> Cough drops: William, Andrew (on radio they were called Trade and Mark because the words appeared under their pictures on the box in which the drops were sold)

Smoke Rings
> Theme song of Glen Gray's Casa Loma Orchestra

Smokey
>Drunken horse (Lee Marvin's) (1965 movie *Cat Ballou*)

Smokey the Bear's motto
>"Only you can prevent forest fires"

Smothers Brothers
>Dick and Tom, popular singers and entertainers; their TV show's satire slew so many sacred cows it was canceled in 1969

Snagglepuss
>TV cartoon lion whose favorite phrase is "Exit Stage Left"

Snap, Crackle, and Pop
>Kellogg's Rice Krispies (3 little elf-type men)

Snark
>Yacht built to Jack London's order and on which he lived 1906-1908 sailing the high seas

Snidely Whiplash
>Arch-enemy of Dudley Do-Right (cartoon series)

Sniffles
>Little mouse friend of Mary Jane (comic book series)

Snoop Sisters
>Ernesta (played by Helen Hayes) and Gwen ("G" played by Mildred Natwick) (TV series): the sisters get involved in and solve crimes

Snoopy
>Charlie Brown's pet, a beagle, who pretends to fly a Sopwith Camel against the Red Baron, tries writing novels, etc. (Charles Schulz's comic strip "Peanuts")

Snoopy
>Apollo 10 lunar module: it descended to 9 miles from the lunar surface then docked with its command module

Snow Baby
>Admiral Peary's daughter, Marie, born (1893) in the Arctic Circle at Inglefield Gulf

Snowball
>Albino dolphin: only one known to exist (Miami Seaquarium, 1962)

Snowbirds
>Canadian Air Force's aerobatic team

Snuffleupagus
>Large elephant-like animal seen only by Big Bird (TV series "Sesame Street")

Soccer
>North American Soccer League
>>Western Division
>>>Los Angeles Aztecs
>>>San Jose Earthquakes

> > Seattle Sounders
> > Vancouver White Caps
> > Central Division
> > > Dallas Tornado
> > > Denver Dynamo
> > > St. Louis Stars
> > Eastern Division
> > > Baltimore Comets
> > > Miami Toros
> > > Philadelphia Atoms
> > > Washington Diplomats
> > Northern Division
> > > Boston Minutemen
> > > New York Cosmos
> > > Rochester Lancers
> > > Toronto Metros

> World Cup
> > The Jules Rimet Trophy, first played for in 1930, representing the world's championship, contested every 4 years (even non-Olympics years): candidate teams are grouped in 4 divisions and playoffs are by a complex system controlled by the International Federation of Football Associations (FIFA)

> World Cup Winners
> > 1930 - Uruguay
> > 1934 - Italy
> > 1938 - Italy
> > 1950 - Uruguay
> > 1954 - West Germany
> > 1958 - Brazil
> > 1962 - Brazil
> > 1966 - England
> > 1970 - Brazil
> > 1974 - West Germany

Solar Scouts
> Buck Rogers' listeners' fan club

Soldiers Three
> Story collection (1889) by Rudyard Kipling: the soldiers are Learoyd, Mulvaney, and Ortheris, serving with the British Army in India

Someday I'll Find You
> Theme song of radio series "Mr. Keen, Tracer of Lost Persons"

Something's Got to Give
> Movie on which Marilyn Monroe was working (1962) at the time of her death

Song-writing teams
> Leiber and Stoller
> Lennon and McCartney
> Henderson, De Sylva, and Brown
> Rodgers and Hart
> Schwartz and Dietz
> Gilbert and Sullivan
> McHugh and Fields
> Rodgers and Hammerstein
> Kern and Hammerstein
> Loewe and Lerner
> Ira and George Gershwin
> Burt Bacharach and Hal David
> Dubin and Warren
> Weill and Brecht (Blitzstein)

Songbird
> Sky King's airplane

Songbird of the South
> Nickname of Kate Smith

Sonia
> Duck (Prokofiev's "Peter and the Wolf")

Sonny
> Wild Bill Elliott's horse

Sons of the Desert
> Fraternal organization to which Stan Laurel and Oliver Hardy belonged (movie series)

Sothern, Ann
> Played Susie MacNamara in TV series "Private Secretary"
> The voice (Mrs. Crabtree) of the car (TV series, 1965, "My Mother the Car")

Soupy Sales Show
> Four supporting puppets: Black Tooth, Hippy, Pookie, White Fang

Spacecraft/Ship movements
> Pitch (up-and-down motion of the nose or bow)
> Roll (side-to-side movement around the long axis)
> Yaw (angular motion of the nose or bow away from the line of flight)

Spar
> Female member of the U. S. Coast Guard: from the service's motto, Semper Paratus

Sparkle Plenty
> Daughter of Gravel Gertie and B. O. Plenty (Dick Tracy cartoon series)

Sparkplug

Barney Google's horse, always in a blanket (comic strip by Billy DeBeck)

Sparrow, The

Killed Cock Robin (nursery rhyme)

Sparta, Mississippi

Locale of movie *In the Heat of the Night*

SPECTRE

Special Executive for Counter-Terrorism, Revenge and Extortion (James Bond series)

Spectre, The

Secret identity or ghost of detective Jim Corrigan (comic book series "The Spectre")

Spectrum

The rainbow colors: Violet, Indigo, Blue, Green, Yellow, Orange, Red: mnemonic Roy G. Biv

Speech, parts of

Traditional in English: Noun, Pronoun, Verb, Adverb, Adjective, Preposition, Conjunction, Interjection

Speedwell

Ship that was not seaworthy enough to accompany the "Mayflower" in 1620

Speedwell Boys

Children's novels: Billy, Dan

Speedy

Secret identity of Roy Harper, Green Arrow's boy partner (comic book character)

Speedy

Alka-Seltzer boy (TV commercial)

Speedy Gonzales

Mexican mouse (movie cartoon)

Spider Man

Secret identity of Peter Parker (comic book series "Spider Man")

Spin and Marty

Adventure series on the Mickey Mouse Club (boys stayed on a ranch)

Spindrift

Jack Armstrong's Uncle Jim's yacht

Spindrift

Airship on Flight 703, Los Angeles to London, piloted by Captain Steve Burton, that crashes in the Land of the Giants (TV series "Land of the Giants")

SPIRIT

License plate of the Magician's Corvette

Nickname of the private plane of Anthony Blake, the Magician (TV series "The Magician")

Spirit, The

Super-crimefighter Denny Colt, who was "killed" when Dr. Cobra threw chemicals on him. In a sleep resembling death, he was buried in Wildwood Cemetery, but awoke and broke out as the Spirit (comic book series "The Spirit")

Spirit of America

Racing driver Craig Breedlove's jet-powered car

Spirit of St. Louis

Charles Lindbergh's N-X-211 Ryan monoplane on his Atlantic flight, May 20-21, 1927

Spirit of '76

Air Force One: Presidential airplane

Spitz

Dog that is Buck's deadly rival (Jack London's *The Call of the Wild*)

Spitz, Mark

U. S. swimmer who won 7 gold medals (more than any athlete before him) in the 1972 Munich Olympics. The events: (individual: all world's record performances) 100-meter freestyle, 200-meter freestyle, 100-meter butterfly, 200-meter butterfly; (relay) 400-meter freestyle, 800-meter freestyle, 400-meter medley. Spitz, who won 2 gold medals in the 1968 Olympics, is tied with Paavo Nurmi at 9 for most total gold medals in the Olympics, the latter having won his in the 1920, 1924, 1928 Olympics

Sponsors

Radio programs:

The Aldrich Family: Jell-O

Amos 'n' Andy: Rinso Soap

Jack Armstrong: Wheaties

Jack Benny: Canada Dry, Chevrolet, Jell-O, Lucky Strike

Edgar Bergen and Charlie McCarthy: Chase & Sanborn Coffee

Burns and Allen: Maxwell House Coffee

Jimmy Durante Show: Rexall

The Falcon: Gem Blades

Buck Jones: Grape Nuts Flakes

Spike Jones: Coca-Cola

Little Orphan Annie: Ovaltine

Fibber McGee and Molly: Johnson's Wax

Tom Mix: Ralston

Sergeant Preston: Quaker Puffs

The Shadow: Blue Coal
Superman: Kellogg's
Terry and the Pirates: Quaker Puffs
Your Hit Parade: Lucky Strike

Spot

Dick and Jane's dog (school primary book)

Spot

The household dragon of the Munsters (TV series "The Munsters")

Springfield

Town location of TV serial "The Guiding Light"

Springfield, Mass.

Location of professional basketball's Hall of Fame: basketball invented here 1891 by James Naismith

Spruce Goose, The

Nickname of Howard Hughes' 8-engine flying boat (Hughes HK-1 "Hercules"): flown only once, 1,000 yards, in 1947

Spud

Tim Tyler's sidekick (cartoon series "Tim Tyler's Luck")

Sputnik I

First satellite in orbit, launched by U.S.S.R. October 4, 1957: flight ended January 4, 1958

Squeaky

Smilin' Ed's pet mouse (radio and TV)

Stage Show

TV show, starring the Dorsey brothers, on which Elvis Presley made his TV debut (1956)

Stagg, Amos Alonzo

Football coach, died 1965 aged 103 years: "The Grand Old Man of Football": a Yale All-American, coached for 57 years, especially at Chicago, 1892-1932, and College of the Pacific, 1933-1946, winning 314 games, more than any other coach (Glenn Warner won 313, though there are those who say Warner won 316 and Stagg 311)

Stalactite

Limestone deposit hanging from roof of cave

Stalag 13

German prison camp (TV series "Hogan's Heroes)

Stalagmite

Limestone deposit rising from floor of cave

Stalin, Joseph

Pseudonym of Iosif Dzhugashvili, premier of U.S.S.R.; *Time* magazine's "Man of the Year" for 1939 and 1942

Standish, Miles

Sent John Alden to propose for him to Priscilla Mullins; Priscilla answered, "Why don't you speak for yourself, John?" (H. W. Longfellow's "The Courtship of Miles Standish")

Historically, Standish, one of the "Mayflower" settlers (1620), was captain of the Pilgrims' military forces; a widower, he remarried in 1623, about a year after John Alden and Priscilla married

Stanley Cup

National Hockey League's trophy, won by annual champions since 1911-1912 season: originally (1893) bought for 10 pounds donated by Frederick Arthur Stanley, Baron Stanley of Preston

Stanwood

Town location of radio serial "When a Girl Marries"

Star Spear

Tom Swift, Jr.'s rocket ship (novel series)

Star Trek

Science-fiction TV series created by Gene Roddenberry. Crew members (part of the ship's complement of 430) of the U.S.S. "Enterprise":

Role		Actor
James T. Kirk	Captain	William Shatner
Mr. Spock	First Officer	Leonard Nimoy
Leonard McCoy	Doctor	DeForest Kelley
Montgomery Scott, "Scotty"	Chief Engineer	James Doohan
Sulu	Helmsman	George Takei
Lt. Uhuru	Communications	Nichelle Nichols
Chekov	Ensign	Walter Koenig
Christine Chapel	Nurse	Majel Barrett

Starbuck

First mate of the "Pequod" (Herman Melville's *Moby Dick*)

Stars and Bars

The Confederate flag

Stars and Stripes Forever, The

March composed (1897) by John Philip Sousa

Star-Spangled Banner, The

Words by Francis Scott Key set to tune "To Anacreon in Heav'n"; became U.S. National Anthem in 1931

States

Last three admitted to the Union:

Arizona	48th state	February 1912
Alaska	49th state	January 1959
Hawaii	50th state	August 1959

Steamboat Willie

Mickey Mouse's first sound cartoon film (1928), Mickey does variations on "Turkey in the Straw": preceded by silent Mickey shorts, *Plane Crazy* and *Gallopin' Gaucho*

Stephens, Alexander Hamilton

Southern patriot (1812-1883), vice-president (1861-1865) of the Confederacy

Stepin Fetchit

Stage name of movie actor Lincoln Perry

Steptoe and Son

British TV series on which the American series "Sanford and Son" is based

Sterling Morris

Bill Batson's boss at radio station WHIZ (Captain Marvel comic books)

Stern, Bill

The Colgate Shave Cream man, highly imaginative sports broadcaster

Steve Trevor

Wonder Woman's boyfriend (comic books)

Steve Wilson

Editor of the "Illustrated Press" (radio/TV series "Big Town"): played on radio by Edward G. Robinson, Edward Pawley, and Walter Greaza; on TV by Mark Stevens and Pat McVey. His society editor was Lorelei Kilbourne

Steven Kiley

Colleague of Doctor Welby (TV series "Marcus Welby, M.D.")

Stone Mountain

Granite dome (650 feet above the level around it) near Atlanta, Georgia, on which appear deep-relief sculptures (90 feet high, 190 feet long) of Jefferson Davis, Robert E. Lee, Stonewall Jackson. Begun by Gutzon Borglum, who later did the heads on Mt. Rushmore, the work was taken over by Henry Augustus Lukeman, who destroyed the head of Lee that Borglum had finished; the project, after 47 years of work, was finished by Walker Hancock

Stonewall

Nickname of Confederate General Thomas Jonathan Jackson (1824-1863): called "Stonewall" by Gen. B. E. Bee for the firm stand of his troops at the first battle of Bull Run, July 21, 1861

Stormy

Wild Bill Elliot's horse (movie series)

Straight Arrow
>   Secret identity of Steve Adams (comic books)

Straight Flush
>   B-29 photographic and weather-reporting plane that took pictures of the atomic bomb explosions on Hiroshima and Nagasaki: piloted by Major Claude Eatherly

Straight Shooters
>   Tom Mix's radio fan club (sponsored by Ralston): listening boys and girls were invited to join

Streaky
>   Superman's super cat (comic books)

Stuart, Jeb
>   James *E*well *B*rown Stuart, Confederate cavalry general (1833-1864)

Stuart, Mary
>   Mary, Queen of Scots, rival of Elizabeth I for the throne of England, mother of James I of England

Studs Lonigan
>   Trilogy of novels by James T. Farrell: *Young Lonigan,* 1932; *The Young Manhood of Studs Lonigan,* 1934; *Judgment Day,* 1935

Study in Scarlet, A
>   Novel in which Sherlock Holmes first appeared, 1886, by Sir Arthur Conan Doyle

Submarines
>   Names of submarines in Disneyland underwater adventure: Skip Jack, Sea Wolf, Ethan Allen, George Washington, Nautilus, Skate, Patrick Henry, Triton

Sugar Bear
>   Advertises Post's Super Sugar Crisp cereal (TV cereal box ad)

Sugar Blues
>   Theme song of Clyde McCoy's band

Sugarfoot
>   Tom Brewster (TV series "Sugarfoot"): played by Will Hutchins

Suicide Is Painless
>   Theme song of TV series "M*A*S*H"

Suicides
>   Cleopatra: bitten by an asp
>   Judy Garland: overdose of drugs
>   Hannibal: poison
>   Ernest Hemingway: gunshot
>   Adolf Hitler: gunshot
>   Judas Iscariot: hanged
>   Mark Antony: his own sword

Nero: cut throat

Socrates: drank poison hemlock

Vincent Van Gogh: gunshot

Sullivan, Anne

American teacher (Anne Mansfield Sullivan Macy), chosen (1887) to teach Helen Keller, a child left blind, deaf, and dumb by scarlet fever; they became lifelong friends. In the 1962 movie *The Miracle Worker*, Sullivan was played by Anne Bancroft

Summer of '42

Trio of boys (novel/1971 movie): Benjie, Hermie, Oscy

Sun Bonnets, The

Walt Disney characters (young female bears in Disneyland): Beulah, Bubbles, Bunny

Sun Records

Memphis, Tennessee, recording company: between 1954 and 1957 these stars recorded under the Sun label: Elvis Presley, Johnny Cash, Jerry Lee Lewis, Carl Perkins, Roy Orbison, Charlie Rich

Sunshine State

Nickname of Florida, South Dakota, and New Mexico

Super Bowl

Professional football's championship game; played 1967-1970 between American Football League and National Football League, since 1971 between winners of American and National Conferences in National Football League

	Winner	Loser	Score
1967	Green Bay Packers	Kansas City Chiefs	35-10
1968	Green Bay Packers	Oakland Raiders	33-14
1969	New York Jets	Baltimore Colts	16-7
1970	Kansas City Chiefs	Minnesota Vikings	23-7
1971	Baltimore Colts	Dallas Cowboys	16-13
1972	Dallas Cowboys	Miami Dolphins	24-3
1973	Miami Dolphins	Washington Redskins	14-7
1974	Miami Dolphins	Minnesota Vikings	24-7

Super Circus

TV series:

Ringmaster: Claude Kirschner

Clowns: Cliffy the Tramp, Scampy the box clown, Nick Francis the fat clown

Leader of the Super Circus Band: Mary Hartline

Supercalifragilisticexpialidocious

Magic word in song sung by Julie Andrews (1964 Disney movie *Mary Poppins*)

Supergirl

Secret identity of Linda Lee Danvers, Superman's cousin (comic book series): she was called Kara when she was born on the planet Krypton

Superman

Identity assumed secretly by Clark Kent (comic strip and book/movie series/TV series): played on radio by Clayton "Bud" Collyer and Michael Fitzmaurice; in movies and TV by George Reeves

Debut: *Action Comics* 1938; writer: Jerry Siegel; artist: Joe Shuster

"Faster than a speeding bullet, more powerful than a locomotive, able to leap tall buildings at a single bound, look! Up in the sky! Is it a bird? Is it a plane? It's Superman!!"

Supersnipe

Secret identity of Koppy McFad (comic book character)

Suspects

In the game of "Clue": Colonel Mustard, Miss Scarlett, Mr. Green, Mrs. Peacock, Mrs. White, Professor Plum

Susy

Little blue car (movie cartoon)

Swamp Fox, The

Nickname of General Francis Marion (about 1732-1795), Revolutionary War guerrilla leader in the South

Swedish Nightingale, The

Nickname of Jenny Lind (1820-1887), opera and concert singer; client of P. T. Barnum in her American tour

Swee' Pea

Popeye's adopted son

Sweet Georgia Brown

Theme song of the Harlem Globetrotters basketball team

Sweet Polly Purebred

Underdog's girlfriend (TV cartoon series)

Sweety Face

Wallace Wimple's fat wife (radio's "Fibber McGee and Molly")

Swimming Hall of Fame

Located at Fort Lauderdale, Florida

Sydenstricker

Pearl S. Buck's middle name

Sylvester

Professor Marvel's horse (1939 movie *The Wizard of Oz*)

Sylvester Cat

Cat who tries to catch Tweety Pie (cartoon)

Symbols

Of the Evangelists: St. Matthew, Angel; St. Mark, Lion; St. Luke, Ox; St. John, Eagle

Syndics of the Cloth Hall, The

Rembrandt's painting (1661) embossed in lining of Dutch Masters cigar boxes (the man on the far left of the painting was left out of the Dutch Masters reproduction)

T

2

The only even prime number

2 thieves

Crucified with Jesus: Dismas, Gestas

3 B's

Great composers of classical music:

    Bach (Johann Sebastian, 1685-1750);

    Beethoven (Ludwig van, 1770 or 1772-1827);

    Brahms (Johannes, 1833-1897)

3 Caballeros, The

Panchito, Jose Carioca, Donald Duck (Walt Disney cartoon feature movie, 1944)

3 cardinal virtues

Faith, Hope, Charity. Compare *7 virtues*

3 Fates

Lachesis (who determined the fate)

Clotho (who spun the thread of life)

Atropos (who cut the thread)

3 Furies

Alecto (the unresting), Megaera (the jealous), Tisiphone (the avenger)

3 Good Fairies

Mistress Flora, Mistress Fauna, and Mistress Merryweather, who befriend Sleeping Beauty (Walt Disney cartoon feature movie *Sleeping Beauty*, 1958)

3 Graces

Aglaia, Thalia, Euphrosyne: sisters, daughters of Zeus and Eurynome

3 Little Maids

Yum-Yum, Peep-Bo, Pitti-Sing: three schoolgirl sisters, wards of Ko-Ko (Gilbert and Sullivan's operetta *The Mikado*)

3 men in a tub
> Butcher, Baker, Candlestick Maker (nursery rhyme)

3 Musketeers
> Athos, Porthos, Aramis (Alexander Dumas' novel *The Three Musketeers*): D'Artagnan later becomes a member of the group

3 Musketeers' motto
> "All for one, one for all"

3 R's
> Elements of learning
>> Reading, Writing, 'Rithmetic
> New Deal program
>> Relief, Recovery, Reform

3 Stooges
> Larry Fine and the brothers Moe and Curly Howard.
> Shemp Howard, another brother, replaced Curly Howard in 1947; Joe Besser replaced Shemp Howard in 1955; Joe DeRita (Curly Joe) replaced Joe Besser in 1958

3 Wise Men
> Gaspar, Melchior, Balthasar: the "3 kings of Orient" who came to worship the baby Jesus in Bethlehem

3 wise monkeys
> Japanese Little Apes of Nikko
>> Mizaru: See no evil
>> Mikazaru: Hear no evil
>> Mazaru: Speak no evil

3X2(9YZ)4A
> Formula spoken by Johnny Chambers to change himself into superhero Johnny Quick (comic book series "Johnny Quick")

10
> Height in feet of basket ring in basketball

10
> Number on football jersey worn casually by Mary Tyler Moore (as Mary Richards) (TV series "The Mary Tyler Moore Show")

10-2-4
> Numbers on Dr. Pepper bottle, suggest right time for a Dr. Pepper break

10 plagues of Egypt
> Water becomes blood
> Frogs
> Lice
> Flies (swarms)
> Cattle murrain
> Sores (boils)

Hail and fire
Locusts
Darkness
Slaying of Egyptian first-born (Exodus 7-12)

12

Number of pints of blood in the average human body

12 Apostles

The immediate disciples of Jesus Christ: Peter, James, John, Andrew, Philip, Bartholomew, Matthew, James (son of Alphaeus), Thomas, Simon, Judas Iscariot, Thaddaeus (or Judas [Jude] son of James)

12 astrological houses

The House of Life, The House of Fortune and Riches, The House of Brethren, The House of Parents and Relatives, The House of Children, The House of Health, The House of Marriage, The House of Death, The House of Religion, The House of Dignities, The House of Friends and Benefactors, The House of Enemies

12 Days of Christmas

Carol in which "My true love gave to me: a partridge in a pear tree, two turtle doves, three french hens, four calling birds, five golden rings, six geese a-laying, seven swans a-swimming, eight maids a-milking, nine ladies dancing, ten lords a-leaping, eleven pipers piping, twelve drummers drumming"

12 labors of Hercules

1. The killing of the Nemean lion
2. The killing of the Hydra
3. The killing of the Erymanthian boar
4. The capture of the Cerynean hind (or stag)
5. The killing of the birds of Stymphalus
6. The cleansing of the Augean stables
7. Capturing the Cretan bull
8. Capturing the man-eating horses of Diomedes of Thrace
9. Obtaining the girdle of Hippolyta, Queen of the Amazons
10. Capturing the oxen of Geryon
11. Bringing of Cerberus, the three-headed dog, up from Hades
12. Bringing back the apples of the Hesperides

13

A baker's dozen (many bakers still sell 13 to the dozen)

13

Age of Huckleberry Finn in Mark Twain's novel

20 Questions

Quiz game in which contestants usually began by asking "Is it animal, vegetable, or mineral?"

23

Number of station house (TV series "Firehouse")

23rd

Century in which TV series "Star Trek" is set

24

Estimated dollar value of beads and trinkets paid for Manhattan Island by Peter Minuit to the Indians in 1626

24

Willie Mays' uniform number with the Giants

25th

Century to which Buck Rogers, a 20th century native, is transported

26

Age at which George Armstrong Custer became a general during the Civil War

26

Letters in the English alphabet

26

Number of innings in longest major league baseball game: both starting pitchers, Leon Cadore of the visiting Brooklyn Dodgers and Joe Oeschger of the Boston Braves, pitched all the way (3 hours, 50 minutes) to a 1 to 1 tie, May 1, 1920; Boston tied the score in the sixth inning and then there were 20½ scoreless innings

26 Bar Ranch

John Wayne's ranch in Arizona

26 miles, 385 yards

Distance from Marathon to Athens: length of Olympic marathon race. The first running (1896) of the race was over a 25-mile course

27

Wives married by the Mormon leader Brigham Young

28

Years spent by Frank Faraday (Dan Dailey) in a Caribbean prison before obtaining his freedom (precisely 28 years, 4 months, 13 days) (TV series "Faraday and Company")

30

Pieces of silver Judas Iscariot was paid for betraying Jesus (Matthew 26:15)

30-Foot Bride of Candy Rock, The

Only movie (1959) made by Lou Costello without Bud Abbott

31 Flavors

Baskin-Robbins Ice Cream

33 hours 29 minutes

Charles Lindbergh's New York-to-Paris flight time, May 20-21, 1927

35 Plus

Helen Trent's age (radio serial)

37

Age of Rick Blaine (Humphrey Bogart) in 1942 movie *Casablanca*

39

Age Jack Benny has claimed for years (actually born 1894 in Waukegan, Ill.)

206

Number of bones in the human body

212-A West 87th Street

New York City home address of Ellery Queen, detective

221B Baker Street

London address of Sherlock Holmes, with Dr. Watson at various times his roommate and Mrs. Hudson as the housekeeper

237

Weight in pounds of Brad Runyon, radio's "The Fat Man"

250

Age of the High Lama of Shangri-La (James Hilton's *Lost Horizon*)

263 Princengracht

Address of Amsterdam house in which Anne Frank and 7 others hid from the Nazis for 2 years and a month (1942-1944): *Anne Frank: The Dairy of a Young Girl*

336

Dimples on a golf ball

.367

Ty Cobb's lifetime batting average (highest in history of the major leagues)

1313 Blueview Terrace

Chester A. Riley's address ("Life of Riley")

1313 Mockingbird Lane

Home address of the Munsters (TV series "The Munsters")

2001

Most striking part of musical score was part of Richard Strauss' *Also Sprach Zarathustra*

2,130

Consecutive baseball games played by New York Yankees' Lou Gehrig (began June 1, 1925, until May 2, 1939): he replaced Wally Pipp and was replaced by Babe Dahlgren

2355

Year in which TV series "Tom Corbett, Space Cadet" is set

2430

Year in which Buck Rogers, World War I pilot, awoke after 500 years of suspended animation (comic strip/books, radio series "Buck Rogers in the 25th Century," TV series, 1939 movie serial; all drawn from Philip Nowlan's 1928 novel *Armageddon 2419 A.D.*)

3955

Year the U. S. astronauts return to Earth to find the planet ruled by intelligent apes (Planet of the Apes movie series)

20,000

Number of pounds bet by Phileas Fogg that he could go "Around the World in 80 Days"

29,028

Elevation of Mt. Everest above sea level

$10,000,000

Price United States paid Mexico in the Gadsden Purchase, 45,535 sq. mi. (1853)

$25,000,000

United States paid Denmark for the Danish Virgin Islands, 1917

TBI

Initials on Kodak cameras: T = time; B = bulb; I = instantaneous

T. C.

Top Cat (cartoon character)

T.H.E. Cat

Thomas Hewett Edward Cat (TV series): starred Robert Loggia

T-M Bar Ranch

Tom Mix's ranch, located in Dobie Township (radio series)

TNT

Trinitrotoluene, explosive chemical

TU-144

First supersonic transport (SST) to fly (Russian-built)

Tabard Inn, The

Inn in Geoffrey Chaucer's *Canterbury Tales* where the pilgrims begin and end their journey: Harry Baillie, the host, joins the pilgrims for their good company

Tackhammer

Woody Woodpecker's dog foe (comic books)

Taft, William Howard

First U. S. President to throw out the baseball to open the baseball season (April 14, 1910, Philadelphia at Washington)

Tagg

 Annie Oakley's younger brother (TV series)

Taliaferro

 Booker T. Washington's middle name (pronounced Tolliver)

Talmadge Sisters

 Norma (1897-1957), Constance (born 1898), Natalie (1899-1969)

 Norma was the first actor to leave a mark in the cement outside Grauman's Chinese Theater when, in 1927, she stumbled accidentally onto a freshly laid sidewalk; press-agentry soon made it a distinction and a tradition

Tamba

 Ape in "Jungle Jim" movie series

Tang, U.S.S.

 U. S. submarine that sank itself with its own torpedo, October 1944 (nine crew members survived to tell the tale)

Tank Tinker

 Hop Harrigan's mechanic (radio series)

Tara

 Plantation in Margaret Mitchell's *Gone with the Wind*

Target

 Annie Oakley's horse (TV series)

Tarleton twins

 Stuart and Brent (Margaret Mitchell's *Gone with the Wind*)

Tarots

 22-card deck (larger deck has 56 additional cards in 4 suits):

I	The juggler	XII	The hanging man
II	The high priestess (Popess)	XIII	Death (often unlabeled)
		XIV	Temperance
III	The empress	XV	The devil
IV	The emperor	XVI	Lightning (The tower)
V	The hierophant (Pope)	XVII	The stars
VI	The lovers	XVIII	The moon
VII	The chariot	XIX	The sun
VIII	Justice	XX	Judgment
IX	The hermit	XXI	The world
X	Fortune (the wheel of)	XXII	The fool (often unnumbered)
XI	Strength		

Tarzan

 Fictional jungle hero, created (1914) by Edgar Rice Burroughs in *Tarzan of the Apes*: next to Sherlock Holmes as the most widely known character in fiction in English

 Comic strip by Harold Foster, begun January 7, 1929, and continued by Rex Maxon, Burne Hogarth, and others; one of the first strips to tell a consecutive adventure story and one of the first to appear in modern comic books

Novels: *Tarzan of the Apes*
The Return of Tarzan
The Beasts of Tarzan
The Son of Tarzan
Tarzan and the Jewels of Opar
Jungle Tales of Tarzan
Tarzan the Untamed
Tarzan the Terrible
Tarzan and the Golden Lion
Tarzan and the Ant Men
The Tarzan Twins (juvenile)
Tarzan, Lord of the Jungle
Tarzan and the Lost Empire
Tarzan at the Earth's Core
Tarzan the Invincible
Tarzan Triumphant
Tarzan and the City of Gold
Tarzan and the Lion Man
Tarzan and the Leopard Men
Tarzan's Quest
Tarzan and the Forbidden City
Tarzan the Magnificent
Tarzan and the Foreign Legion
Tarzan and the Tarzan Twins (juvenile)
Tarzan and the Madman
Tarzan and the Castaways

In the movies, played by:
Elmo Lincoln (silents)
Gene Polar (silents)
P. Dempsey Tabler (silents)
James Pierce (silents)
Frank Merrill (silents)
Johnny Weissmuller
Herman Brix (Bruce Bennett)
Buster Crabbe
Glenn Morris
Lex Barker
Gordon Scott
Denny Miller
Jock Mahoney
Mike Henry

Ron Ely (TV)
Charlie Chase (1932 comedy)
Unauthorized:
Peng Fei (Chinese), 1940
Joe Robinson (Italian), 1963
Vladimir Korenev (Russian), 1963
Don Bragg, 1964
Darasingh (India), 1963-1965

Tarzan
Ken Maynard's horse (movies)

Tate
College where events occur in 1947 MGM musical *Good News*

Taxi Boys, The
Ben Blue and Billy Gilbert (comedy team in movie shorts)

Taylor, Elizabeth
English-born American actress in movies: Academy Awards as best actress for Gloria Wandrous in *Butterfield 8* (1960) and Martha in *Who's Afraid of Virginia Woolf?* (1966)

Her husbands: Conrad Hilton, Jr., 1949-1951; Michael Wilding, 1952-1957; Michael Todd, 1957-1958; Eddie Fisher, 1959-1964; Richard Burton, 1964-1974

Teachers
Socrates taught Plato
Plato taught Aristotle
Aristotle taught Alexander the Great

Teapot Dome
Navy oil reserve in Wyoming: Harding's Secretary of the Interior Albert B. Fall was found guilty (1929) of having been bribed to grant oil leases to private individuals

Teddy
Mack Sennett's dog, trained to do tricks in Sennett comedies

Teddy Bear, The
Cuddly toy bear named after President Theodore Roosevelt

Teddy Bear Picnic, The
Theme song of radio series "Big Jon and Sparkle"

Teenie
Paul Bunyan's daughter

Teeth
Human (32 teeth):
Incisors: 8
Cuspids (canines): 4
Bicuspids (premolars): 8
Molars: 12

Telemachus

Son of Odysseus and Penelope (Homer's *Odyssey*): he helped his father kill Penelope's suitors

Television

Top Programs:
1951-1952: Texaco Star Theater
1952-1955: I Love Lucy
1955-1956: $64,000 Question
1956-1957: I Love Lucy
1957-1961: Gunsmoke
1961-1962: Wagon Train
1962-1964: Beverly Hillbillies
1964-1967: Bonanza
1967-1968: Andy Griffith Show
1968-1970: Laugh-In
1970-1971: Marcus Welby, M.D.

Telstar I

First U. S. communications satellite (A. T. & T. Co.) to amplify radio and TV signals (launched July 10, 1962)

Tenafly

Harry Tenafly, black detective (TV series "Tenafly"): played by James McEachin

Tennessee Plowboy, The

Nickname of country singer Eddy Arnold

Tennis Big Four (Grand Slam)

Championship tournaments:
Australian Open
French Open
Wimbledon (English)
Forest Hills (U. S.)

Tennis Hall of Fame

Located at Newport, Rhode Island

Teresa (Tracy) Draco

James Bond's wife for a brief time (Ian Fleming's novel *On Her Majesty's Secret Service*)

Terhune, Max

One of the Three Mesquiteers. His sidekick was the dummy Elmer Sneezewood

Terrified Typist, The Case of the

Only case Perry Mason ever lost in court: after the guilty verdict, Attorney Mason convinced Judge Hartley that a retrial was in order, since there were two Duane Jeffersons, one his client and the other the accused

Terry Lee
> Hero of Milt Caniff's comic strip "Terry and the Pirates": he was the young sidekick of Pat Ryan (name originally suggested for Terry was Tommy Tucker)

Tess Trueheart
> Dick Tracy's wife (comic strip)

Texas, The
> Confederate locomotive that chased the stolen locomotive "The General" in the Great Locomotive Chase of the Civil War (April 12, 1862)

Thanks for the Memory
> Bob Hope's theme song

The Buck Stops Here
> Sign on President Truman's desk

Theodore
> Hamm's Beer's bear (cartoon)

There's One Born Every Minute
> Elizabeth Taylor's first movie appearance, 1942, age 10 years

They Only Kill Their Masters
> Last movie made (1972) on the MGM lot

Thimble Theatre
> Original comic strip (beginning 1919) by Elzie Segar that featured Olive Oyl, Castor Oyl, Popeye, Alice the Goon, Blozo, Eugene the Jeep, Poopdeck Pappy, Sea Hag, Swee' Pea, Toar, Wimpy, George W. Geezil, Pooky Jones, Bluto

Thin Man, The
> Novel (1932) by Dashiell Hammett (the Thin Man was the victim, Clyde Wynant)
> On radio and TV it was the title of a series about the adventures of Nick and Nora Charles, inadvertent mystery-solvers
> On radio Nick Charles was played by Lester Damon, Les Tremayne, Joseph Curtin, and David Gothard; Claudia Morgan was Nora
> In movies Nick and Nora were played by William Powell and Myrna Loy
> On TV they were played by Peter Lawford and Phyllis Kirk

Thing
> Living hand belonging to the Addams family (TV series "The Addams Family")

Thing, The
> Eight-foot carrot-like alien plant played by James Arness in the 1951 movie *The Thing* (from science-fiction story "Who Goes There?" by John W. Campbell, writing as Don A. Stuart)

Think

Motto of IBM

Thinking Machine

Professor S. F. X. Van Dusen, detective created by Jacques Futrelle

Thinking of You

Theme song of Kay Kyser's orchestra

This Could Be the Start of Something Big

Steve Allen's theme song, which he wrote

This Is It

Bugs Bunny's theme song (TV cartoon)

This Old Man

Children's marching song

"This old man he played (----),
He played nick-nack on my (----)":

one . . . drum	six . . . sticks
two . . . shoe	seven . . . oven
three . . . tree	eight . . . gate
four . . . door	nine . . . line
five . . . hive	ten . . . hen

Thomson, Bobby

New York Giants' third baseman, known as the Flying Scot, wearing No. 23, who hit a three-run home run off pitcher Ralph Branca, wearing No. 13, in the last half of the ninth inning of the third playoff game (October 3) at the Polo Grounds to win the 1951 National League pennant

Final score of the game: New York Giants, 5; Brooklyn Dodgers, 4

Branca had just relieved Don Newcombe after Alvin Dark singled and Don Mueller did the same, sending Dark to third, and then Monte Irvin popped out, Whitey Lockman doubled, scoring Dark and sending Mueller to third. Mueller hurt his leg sliding into third and Clint Hartung came in to run for him. Rather than give Thomson an intentional walk (rookie Willie Mays was in the on-deck circle), Manager Charlie Dressen ordered Branca to pitch to Thomson, who hit the second pitch over the left-field fence. Larry Jansen, who had relieved Sal Maglie in the 8th inning, was the winning pitcher

Thor

Pet dog of Manhunter

Thorny

Ozzie and Harriet's neighbor (radio and TV): on radio played by John Brown

Thorpe, Jim (James Francis Thorpe)
American Indian (Sac and Fox) athlete (1888-1953)—Indian name: Bright Path—won both the pentathlon (4 firsts) and the decathlon (8412.96 points out of possible 10,000) in the 1912 Stockholm Olympics. Forced to return prizes in 1913 when his history of having played baseball for money was discovered; Olympic records expunged. The teams were Rocky Mount and Fayetteville of the Eastern Carolina League, where he played in 1909-1910
Voted (1950) greatest athlete and football player of first half of 20th Century
Played football under Glenn "Pop" Warner at Carlisle Indian School, helping beat Harvard and Army
Professional football for Canton Bulldogs and baseball for the New York Giants, Cincinnati Reds, and Boston Braves

Those Were the Days
Opening theme of TV series "All in the Family" (closing theme "Remembering You")

Three Faces of Eve
Three distinct personalities manifested in one person (from true accounts documented by Doctors Thigpen and Cleckley): Eve White, Eve Black, Jane (1957 movie made of this story featured Joanne Woodward as Eve in an Oscar-winning performance)

Three Little Pigs
1932/33 Oscar-winning short cartoon by Walt Disney: the houses of the 3 pigs (huffed and puffed by the Big Bad Wolf) were made of straw, sticks, bricks. The story comes from an English fairy tale traced by Joseph Jacobs to one of the Grimms' tales

Three Little Words
Theme song of radio's "Double or Nothing"

Three Oaks Medical Center
Hospital where Dr. Jerry Malone worked (radio series "Young Dr. Malone")

Three Soldiers
Dan Fuselli, Chrisfield, John Andrews (novel by John Dos Passos, 1921)

Thresher and Scorpion
U. S. nuclear submarines lost at sea:
> Thresher, April 10, 1963
> Scorpion, May 21, 1968

Throckmorton P.
First name and middle initial of The Great Gildersleeve, a character played on radio by Hal Peary and Willard Waterman:

originally on "Fibber McGee and Molly" and then on "The Great Gildersleeve"

THRUSH

The Technological Hierarchy for the Removal of Undesirables and the Subjugation of Humanity (evil society in TV series "The Man from U.N.C.L.E.")

Thumper

Rabbit (1942 Disney feature cartoon morie *Bambi*)

Thunder

Red Ryder's horse (movies, cartoons, and radio): "Roll, Thunder, roll"

Thunder Riders

Evil residents of Murania who sometimes came above ground (Gene Autry serial *The Phantom Empire*)

Thunderbirds

U. S. Air Force's aerobatic team

Thunderbolt

Johnny West's horse (toy doll)

Tibbets, Paul, Jr.

Colonel who piloted the B-29 "Enola Gay" that dropped the atomic bomb on Hiroshima, August 6, 1945

Tige

Buster Brown's bulldog (comic strip and radio)
"I'm Buster Brown and I live in a shoe
This is my dog Tige, and he lives there too"

Tiger Lily

Indian maiden, daughter of the chief of the Piccaninnies, rescued by Peter Pan (James Barrie's *Peter Pan*)

Tiki

Yacht (TV series "Adventures In Paradise")

Tilda

The Gumps' maid (comic strip)

Till Death Do Us Part

BBC TV series on which the American series "All in the Family" is based

Time zones

U. S. and possessions: Atlantic Time, Eastern Time, Central Time, (Rocky) Mountain Time, Pacific Time, Yukon Time, Alaska-Hawaii Time, Bering Time (from 60th to 165th meridians of longitude)

Timmy Tinkle

Robot handyman who works at radio station WHIZ along with Billy Batson (Captain Marvel) (comic books)

Timothy Q. Mouse
> Dumbo's friend (1941 Disney cartoon feature movie)

Tin Goose
> Nickname of Ford trimotor passenger airplane of the 1930's: an adaptation from Tin Lizzie

Tin Lizzie
> Nickname of the Ford Model T automobile

Tinker Bell
> Peter Pan's companion, a fairy for whose fading light Peter always successfully appeals to the audience to believe in fairies

Tinker to Evers to Chance
> Chicago Cubs' famous double-play trio (1903-1910): Joe Tinker, shortstop; Johnny Evers, 2nd baseman; Frank Chance, 1st baseman (the third baseman was Harry Steinfeldt)
>
> F. P. A.'s poem ("Baseball's Sad Lexicon" by Franklin Pierce Adams):
>
> > These are the saddest of possible words:
> > "Tinker to Evers to Chance."
> > Trio of bear cubs and fleeter than birds,
> > Tinker and Evers and Chance.
> > Ruthlessly pricking our gonfalon bubble,
> > Making a Giant hit into a double—
> > Words that are heavy with
> > Nothing but trouble:
> > "Tinker to Evers to Chance."

Tinkerbelle
> Robert Manry's 13½-ft. sailboat: crossed Atlantic Ocean in 78 days (1965)

Tiny Tim
> Bob Cratchit's crippled son (Charles Dickens' *A Christmas Carol*)

Tiny Tim
> Pseudonym of "camp" performer and singer Herbert Buckingham Khaury

Tip
> *T*o *i*nsure *p*romptness: an acronym

Titan
> Largest moon of Saturn, home of Saturn Girl (Imra Ardeen), where all citizens have the power of ESP (comic book series)

Titanic
> A supposedly unsinkable White Star liner, she hit an iceberg and sank April 15, 1912, south of Newfoundland on her maiden voyage: "Carpathia" answered "Titanic's" radio distress call

Titusville, Pa.
>   Site of first oil well (drilled by Edwin Drake) August 27, 1859 (Seneca Oil Company)

To Anacreon in Heav'n
>   Tune used for "The Star-Spangled Banner," words by Francis Scott Key: music by John Stafford Smith

To Hell and Back
>   Autobiography of Audie Murphy, the most decorated United States soldier of World War II

Toast of the Town
>   Ed Sullivan's first TV show. Those appearing June 20, 1948, the opening night:
>   Singing Fireman John Kokoman
>   Pianist Eugene List
>   Comedian Jim Kirkwood
>   Comedians Jerry Lewis and Dean Martin
>   Dancer Kathryn Lee
>   Composers Richard Rodgers and Oscar Hammerstein II
>   Fight Referee Ruby Goldstein
>   Comedian Lee Goodman

Toastettes
>   Dancers on Ed Sullivan's TV program "Toast of the Town"

Tobor
>   "Robot" spelled backwards
>   Captain Video's evil foe (TV series)
>   Space-traveling robot in 1954 science-fiction movie *Tobor the Great*

Toby
>   Dog in the Punch and Judy puppet show

Tod Stiles
>   One of the automobilists in TV's "Route 66": played by Martin Milner

Today's World
>   San Francisco magazine for which Doris works (TV series "The Doris Day Show")

Tokens
>   Used in the game of "Monopoly" (metal): Thimble, Iron, Shoe, Dog, Battleship, Top hat, Cannon, Race car

Tokyo Rose
>   Pseudonym of Iva Ikuko Toguri d' Aquino, World War II propaganda agent on Japanese radio. Broadcasts from Germany and Italy were made by Axis Sally

Tom and Jerry
>   Rock 'n' roll duet, 1950's: name originally used by Simon and Garfunkel

Tom Sawyer's gang

Tom Sawyer, Huckleberry Finn, Joe Harper, Ben Rogers, Tommy Barnes

Tom Swift

and His . . . (boys' novels, created by Edward Stratemeyer, 1862-1930):

Electric Locomotive
Flying Machine
Motor Boat
Air Ship
Photo Telephone
Air Scout
Motorcycle
(list not exhaustive)

Tom Swift, Jr.

and His . . . (boys' novels in the 1950's by Victor Appleton II)

Flying Lab
Jetmarine
Rocket Ship
Giant Robot
Atomic Earth Blaster
Outpost in Space
Diving Seacopter
Ultrasonic Cycloplane
Deep-Sea Hydrodome
Space Solartron
Electronic Retroscope
Spectromarine Selector
Electronic Hydrolung
Triphibian Atomicar

Tom Thumb

First American steam locomotive (Baltimore and Ohio Railroad), built by Peter Cooper in 1830 at Canton Iron Works, Baltimore, Md.

Tom Thumb, "General"

Nickname of Charles Sherwood Stratton (1838-1883), American dwarf, 36 inches tall, married (1863) Lavinia Warren (Mercy Lavinia Bump), who stood 32 inches tall: both worked for P. T. Barnum

Toma, David

Newark, N.J., detective on whose real-life exploits the TV series "Toma" is based. Toma is played by Tony Musante, but the real David Toma makes cameo appearances in many episodes

Tommy Atkins

Nickname for the British soldier

Tommy Hambledon
>Detective created by Manning Coles

Tonight We Love
>Theme song of Freddy Martin's orchestra

Tonto
>The Lone Ranger's sidekick: on radio played by John Todd; on TV played by Jay Silverheels; in movies played by Chief Thundercloud

Tonto's horse
>Scout; earlier, also, White Feller, Paint

Tony
>Tom Mix's horse

Tony Award
>Annual award for theatrical excellence, given in several categories: named for Antoinette Perry, American theater producer who died in 1946

Tony the Tiger
>Advertises Kellogg's Sugar Frosted Flakes

Top
>Cyrus Smith's pet dog that traveled in the balloon with its 5 passengers to Lincoln Island (Jules Verne's *The Mysterious Island*)

Topo Gigio
>Mechanical Italian mouse that spoke with a heavy accent as part of a comedy routine with Ed Sullivan on his TV show

Topper
>Hopalong Cassidy's horse

Topsy
>Young slave girl who jes' grewed (Harriet Beecher Stowe's *Uncle Tom's Cabin*)

Tornado
>Zorro's horse (TV series)

Toro
>The Human Torch's sidekick (comic books)

Torrin, H.M.S.
>Destroyer commanded by Captain Kinross (Noel Coward) (1942 movie *In Which We Serve*)

Toto
>Dorothy's dog (1939 movie *The Wizard of Oz*)

Toucan Sam
>Parrot that advertises Kellogg's Froot Loops breakfast cereal

Touchdown Twins
>Fullback Felix "Doc" Blanchard (Mr. Inside) and halfback Glenn Davis (Mr. Outside): Army Cadets football team, 1944-1946, and both All-Americans for those 3 years

Track 29

On which the "Chattanooga Choo Choo" leaves

Tracy-Hepburn movies

Spencer Tracy and Katharine Hepburn appeared together in:

Woman of the Year (1942)
Keeper of the Flame (1942)
Without Love (1945)
The Sea of Grass (1947)
State of the Union (1948)
Adam's Rib (1949)
Pat and Mike (1952)
The Desk Set (1957)
Guess Who's Coming to Dinner (1967) (for which she got
an Oscar)

Tramp

Family's pet dog (TV series "My Three Sons")

Trans-America

Airline company whose plane (Trans-America 2 flight) is blown
up but lands safely (Arthur Hailey's *Airport*)

Transylvania

Homeland of Count Dracula (Bram Stoker's *Dracula*): actually
an area in Romania

Traveler

Robert E. Lee's horse

Travis McGee

Detective created by John D. MacDonald

Treaty of Versailles

Treaty signed June 28, 1919, at end of World War I (not ratified
by United States), resulting from conference attended by the Big
Four: Woodrow Wilson of the United States, Lloyd George of
the United Kingdom, Georges Clemenceau of France, Vittorio
Orlando of Italy

Trevi Fountain

Fountain in Rome where tourists make wishes after tossing coins
into it: featured in 1954 movie *Three Coins in the Fountain*, from
a novel by John Secondari

Tribbles

Small furry animals that reproduce at a very high rate (episode
"Trouble with Tribbles," TV series "Star Trek")

Trieste

Bathyscaphe, built by Jacques Piccard and his father Auguste,
that descended to 35,800 feet: it explored the lowest part of the
Marianas Trench in the Pacific, January 13, 1960, carrying Don
Walsh and the younger Piccard

Trigger

Roy Rogers' horse

Triple Crown

Baseball: Highest batting average, most home runs, most runs batted in

Won by: Ty Cobb (1909), Heinie Zimmerman (1912), Rogers Hornsby (1922, 1925), Jimmy Foxx (1933), Chuck Klein (1933), Lou Gehrig (1934), Joe Medwick (1937), Ted Williams (1942, 1947), Mickey Mantle (1956), Frank Robinson (1966), Carl Yastrzemski (1967)

Horse racing:

Kentucky Derby (Churchill Downs, Louisville, Kentucky): 1¼ miles; 1½ miles 1875-1895

Preakness (Pimlico, Baltimore, Maryland): 1 3/16 miles

Belmont Stakes (Belmont Park, Elmont, Long Island, New York): 1½ miles

Winner	Jockey	Year
Sir Barton	John Loftus	1919
Gallant Fox	Earle Sande	1930
Omaha	W. Saunders	1935
War Admiral	Charlie Kurtsinger	1937
Whirlaway	Eddie Arcaro	1941
Count Fleet	John Longden	1943
Assault	Willie Mehrtens	1946
Citation	Eddie Arcaro	1948
Secretariat	Ron Turcotte	1973

Triple-R

Ranch at which Spin and Marty stay during the summer

Triskaidekaphobia

Unnatural fear of the number 13

Trixie

Hi and Lois' daughter (comic strip)

Trooper Duffy

Frontier soldier (TV series "F Troop"): played by Bob Steele

Trusty

Old bloodhound (1955 Disney cartoon feature movie *Lady and the Tramp*)

Trylon and Perisphere

Symbol of the 1939-1940 New York World's Fair

Tubby

Little Lulu's boyfriend (comic books): he collected doorknobs

Tubby Watts

Superhero Johnny Quick's assistant

Tuffy

    Jerry's mouse cousin ("Tom and Jerry" cartoon series)

Tukutese quintuplets

    Born Feb. 6, 1966, in Mdantsane, South Africa:

    Tandeka, girl, "well-beloved"

    Zoleka, girl, "serenity"

    Tandekile, boy, "I've got it" (also called Mbambile)

    Tembekile, boy, "trusted"

    Kululekile, boy, "happy"

Turner, Captain William

    Captain of the "Lusitania" when it was sunk by the German submarine U-20, May 7, 1915

Turner, Lana

    Her husbands: Artie Shaw (1940-1941), Stephen Crane (1942-1944), Bob Topping (1948-1952), Lex Barker (1953-1957), Fred May (1960-1962), Robert Eaton (1965)

Turtle

    First submarine: invented by David Bushnell in 1775

Tuskegee Institute

    Founded by Booker T. Washington in 1881

Tuxedo Junction

    Theme song of Erskine Hawkins' orchestra

Twelve Oaks

    The Wilkes family plantation (Margaret Mitchell's *Gone with the Wind*)

Twiggy

    Nickname of model Lesley Hornby

Twin Cessna

    Type of airplane Sky King flies (TV series "Sky King")

Twin Cities

    Minneapolis and St. Paul, Minnesota

Twins

    Syndicated advice columnists Ann Landers (Esther Pauline) and Abigail Van Buren (Pauline Esther): nicknamed Eppie and Popo

Typhoid Mary

    Mary Mallon, carrier of typhoid in New York City in 1906. A cook, she continued to cook for many institutions and households, thus spreading the disease

U

U-2

Reconnaissance plane flown by Francis Gary Powers, departed Peshawar, Pakistan, for Bodo, Norway (shot down over the Soviet Union) May 1, 1960

U-20

German submarine under the command of Kapitan Leutnant Schwieger, that sank the "Lusitania" May 7, 1915

U-58

World War I German submarine: first enemy submarine captured by the United States Navy

U. N. C. L. E.

United Network Command for Law and Enforcement (TV series "The Man From U.N.C.L.E.")

UL

Underwriters Laboratories: seal of approval attached to some electrical apparatus or appliances

Ugly Duckling, The

One nickname of baseball player Lawrence Peter "Yogi" Berra

Ulysses

Freighter in which Jack Lemmon is trapped after collision (1957 movie *Fire Down Below*)

Uncas

Son of Chingachgook; the last of the Mohicans (James Fenimore Cooper's *The Last of the Mohicans*)

Uncle Henry

Dorothy's uncle (1939 movie *The Wizard of Oz*)

Uncle Miltie

Nickname of comedian Milton Berle

Uncle Remus

Negro character who narrates tales in Joel Chandler Harris's stories

Uncle Sam

Member of Justice League of America (comics)

Uncle Wiggily

Central character of children's books by H. R. Garis

Uncola, The

7 Up (soft drink)

Underdog

Secret identity of Shoeshine Boy (TV cartoon series)

Unicorn

Mythological animal resembling a horse with a horn growing from its forehead

Union Jack

    Consists of superimposed
        English flag of St. George
        Scottish flag of St. Andrew
        Irish flag of St. Patrick

Unit 51

    Los Angeles County rescue unit (TV series "Emergency")

United Artists Corporation

    Founded in 1919 by Mary Pickford, Douglas Fairbanks, D. W. Griffith, Charles Chaplin

United Kingdom

    Of Great Britain and Northern Ireland (since 1921)

United Nations

    Security Council (permanent members): United States, Soviet Union, United Kingdom, France, China

United States Coins

    In circulation 1974:

Coin	Portrait (obverse)
Cent	Abraham Lincoln
Nickel	Thomas Jefferson
Dime	Franklin D. Roosevelt
Quarter	George Washington
Half Dollar	John F. Kennedy
Dollar	Dwight D. Eisenhower

United States currency

    Portraits:

$1	George Washington
$2	Thomas Jefferson
$5	Abraham Lincoln
$10	Alexander Hamilton
$20	Andrew Jackson
$50	Ulysses S. Grant
$100	Benjamin Franklin
$500	William McKinley
$1,000	Grover Cleveland
$5,000	James Madison
$10,000	Salmon P. Chase
$100,000	Woodrow Wilson

United States flag

    7 red stripes, 6 white stripes, 50 stars in 9 alternating rows of 6 and 5 stars

United States presidents

    Who died in office (every President elected in a year ending in 0 since 1840):

President	Elected	Died
Harrison	1840	April 4, 1841
Taylor	1848	July 9, 1850
Lincoln	1860	April 15, 1865
Garfield	1880	September 19, 1881
McKinley	1900	September 14, 1901
Harding	1920	August 2, 1923
F. D. Roosevelt	1940	April 12, 1945
Kennedy	1960	November 22, 1963

United States Savings Bonds

Portraits:

$25	George Washington
$50	Thomas Jefferson
$75	John F. Kennedy
$100	Grover Cleveland
$200	Franklin D. Roosevelt
$500	Woodrow Wilson
$1,000	Abraham Lincoln
$10,000	Theodore Roosevelt

Univac I

First commercially sold electronic computer, 1951

Universal Export

Cover organization for the British secret 000 operations of which James Bond is a part (Ian Fleming's James Bond novels)

University of Illinois

School to which Lt. Col. Henry Blake went (TV series "M*A*S*H"): he wears the school jersey whenever possible

Unknown Soldier

Tomb of the Unknown Soldier, Arlington Cemetery, Virginia, in which, since 1921, one unknown serviceman has been buried from each U. S. war

Inscription: "Here rests in honored glory an American soldier known but to God"

Untouchables, The

TV series: Elliot Ness (played by Robert Stack) and the Untouchables: Rico Rosi, Bill Youngblood, Lee Hobson

Upset

Only horse to beat Man O'War: Sanford Memorial Stakes, Saratoga, August 13, 1919

Ural Mountains

Separate Asia from Europe

Utopia

Sir Thomas More's imaginary island in his 1516 work *Utopia*

V

V-E Day

May 8, 1945, end of World War II in Europe

V-J Day

August 15, 1945 (U.K.), September 2, 1945 (U.S.): end of war with Japan

Vagabond Lover

Nickname of Rudy Vallee, from his theme song, "I'm Just a Vagabond Lover"

Valhalla

The great hall where Odin lives and receives heroes fallen in battle (Norse mythology)

Valiant Lady

Radio daytime serial adventures of Joan Hargrave-Scott

Valley Forge

Name of American Airlines space vehicle in which Lowell Freeman (played by Bruce Dern) tries to save the last of the Earth's trees and plants with the aid of 3 drones he names Dewey (#1), Huey (#2), Louie (#3) (1972 movie *Silent Running*)

Vegas Club

One of Jack Ruby's two night clubs

Velda

Secretary to private eye Mike Hammer

Venture

Ship that carries King Kong from Skull Island (movies *King Kong* and *Son of Kong*)

Vera

Captain Herr Thiele's ship (Katherine Anne Porter's *Ship of Fools*)

Veronica and Betty

Archie Andrews' girlfriends (comic books): Veronica is the brunette, Betty is the blonde

Very Thought of You, The

Theme song of Ray Noble's orchestra

Veterans' Day

Name by which Armistice Day has been observed since 1954

Vic

General Custer's horse

Vice-Presidents of the United States

	Under President
John Adams	George Washington
Thomas Jefferson	John Adams

	Under President
Aaron Burr	Thomas Jefferson
George Clinton	Jefferson / James Madison
Elbridge Gerry	Madison
Daniel D. Tompkins	James Monroe
John Caldwell Calhoun	J. Q. Adams / Andrew Jackson
Martin Van Buren	Jackson
Richard Mentor Johnson	Martin Van Buren
John Tyler	W. H. Harrison
George Mifflin Dallas	James K. Polk
Millard Fillmore	Zachary Taylor
William Rufus Devane King	Franklin Pierce
John Cabell Breckinridge	James Buchanan
Hannibal Hamlin	Abraham Lincoln
Andrew Johnson	Lincoln
Schuyler Colfax	U. S. Grant
Henry Wilson	Grant
William Almon Wheeler	Rutherford Hayes
Chester Alan Arthur	James Garfield
Thomas Andrews Hendricks	Grover Cleveland
Levi Parsons Morton	Benjamin Harrison
Adlai Ewing Stevenson	Cleveland
Garret Augustus Hobart	William McKinley
Theodore Roosevelt	McKinley
Charles Warren Fairbanks	Theodore Roosevelt
James Schoolcraft Sherman	W. H. Taft
Thomas Riley Marshall	Wilson
Calvin Coolidge	W. G. Harding
Charles Gates Dawes	Coolidge
Charles Curtis	Herbert Hoover
John Nance Garner	F. D. Roosevelt
Henry Agard Wallace	F. D. Roosevelt
Harry S. Truman	F. D. Roosevelt
Alben William Barkley	Truman
Richard Milhous Nixon	Dwight Eisenhower
Lyndon Baines Johnson	J. F. Kennedy
Hubert Horatio Humphrey, Jr.	Johnson
Spiro Theodore Agnew	Nixon
Gerald Rudolph Ford	Nixon
	Ford

Vicki, Miss

Victoria May Budinger, wife of Tiny Tim (Herbert Khaury), married on TV's "Tonight" show, Dec. 17, 1969

Vicky

Richard Nixon's French poodle

Victor

Dan Reid's horse, a descendant of the Lone Ranger's horse Silver

Victoria

Balloon in Jules Verne's novel *Five Weeks in a Balloon*

Victoria

Ship in Ferdinand Magellan's fleet of 5: first ship to circumnavigate (1519-1522) the world (piloted by Juan Sebastian del Cano)

Victory

Admiral Nelson's flagship at the Battle of Trafalgar, Oct. 21, 1805, in which he was killed

Victory at Sea

TV documentary series covering World War II: scored by Richard Rodgers, narrated by Leonard Graves

Virgil Tibbs

Pasadena, California, police officer who travels to Wells, a city in one of the Carolinas, and solves a murder there for police chief Bill Gillespie (John Ball's novel *In the Heat of the Night*)

Philadelphia detective (played by Sidney Poitier) who travels to a small Mississippi town, Sparta (Rod Steiger as Chief Gillespie) (1967 movie)

Virginia

The Old Dominion state is also called the Mother of Presidents; 8 United States Presidents were born there: Washington, Jefferson, Madison, Monroe, W. H. Harrison, Tyler, Taylor, Wilson

Virginia

Virginia O'Hanlon, 8-year-old girl who wrote a letter to the *New York Sun*, 1897, asking if there was a Santa Claus; she received the answer (published Sept. 21, 1897): "Yes, Virginia, there is a Santa Claus . . ." from Francis Pharcellus Church

Virginian, The

Hero, known only by that name, of Western novel (1902) by Owen Wister; his reply to Trampas: "When you call me that, *smile!*"

Played in movies by Dustin Farnum (1914), Gary Cooper (1929), Joel McCrea (1945)

Played in TV series "The Virginian" by James Drury: the first Western series to run 90 minutes

Vivian

The Coca-Cola girl (radio series "The Musical Comedy Hour")

Voodoo

McDonnell F-101 jet fighter

Vulcan
  Jean Laffite's pirate ship in movie *The Buccaneer*

Vulture, The
  British ship upon which Benedict Arnold made his escape from
  West Point to New York City (1780)

W

WASP
  White Anglo Saxon Protestant

WGBS-TV
  Television station in Metropolis where Clark Kent (Superman)
  works as a reporter (after quitting his newspaper job at the *Daily
  Planet*)

WHIZ
  Radio station for which Billy Batson (Captain Marvel) worked
  (comic book series)

WJM
  Fictional TV station, channel 12, Minneapolis, for which Mary
  Richards (Mary Tyler Moore) works (TV's "Mary Tyler Moore
  Show")

WSM
  Nashville radio station that broadcasts Grand Ole Opry

WWJ
  First commercial radio station (Detroit, August 20, 1920);
  KDKA, Pittsburgh, Pa., began broadcasting August 31, 1920,
  and made the first regular scheduled broadcasts beginning Nov.
  2, 1920

WXYZ
  Radio station for which Alan Scott (The Green Lantern) is program director (comic books). Actually WXYZ is a Detroit radio
  station

W. C. Fields
  William Claude Dukinfield

W. C. joke
  Four-minute toilet (w.c.) story cut by NBC from Jack Paar's
  "Tonight" show of February 10; he walked off the show at 11:41
  P.M. Eastern Standard Time, February 11, 1960, as a result. He
  returned to the show on March 7, after a trip to Hong Kong

Wa saba ani mako, o Tar Vey, Rama Kong
  Chant of the witch doctor on Skull Island when Ann is tied to

two pillars and offered to King Kong as a bride (1933 movie *King Kong*): translation "Thy bride is here, O mighty one, great Kong"

Walden Pond
Small lake near Concord, Mass., where Henry David Thoreau lived from July 1845 to September 1847 in a small cabin

Waldo
Dog in TV series "Nanny and the Professor"

Wallace, De Witt
American publisher, founder of the *Reader's Digest*

Wally
Beaver's older brother (TV series "Leave It to Beaver")

Walrus
Captain Flint's ship (Robert Louis Stevenson's *Treasure Island*)

Walt Whitman High
High school on TV series "Room 222"

Waltz King, The
Nickname of Wayne King

Waltz You Saved For Me, The
Theme song of Wayne King's orchestra

Waltzing Matilda
Australia's national song, first published 1903: words by A. B. Paterson (1864-1941), music by James Barr (1779-1860)

Walz, Jacob
Prospector (died 1891) who discovered (1870) the "Lost Dutchman" mine in Arizona, perhaps in the Superstition Mountains, only to have its location become lost

Wanderer
Ship that brought King Kong from Skull Island to New York (novelization). In the movies the ship is "Venture"

Waner
Last name of brothers who played in Pittsburgh Pirates' outfield from late 1920's to 1940's: Paul, known as Big Poison, led the National League in batting 3 times; Lloyd, known as Little Poison, also has a lifetime batting average of over .300

Wanted—Dead or Alive
TV Western series starring Steve McQueen, first shown 1958

War Paint
Kansas City Chiefs' football team mascot (a horse)

Ward, U.S.S.
Destroyer; first American ship to fire at Japanese at Pearl Harbor (Dec. 7, 1941); sunk in December 1944 during Philippines invasion (Ormoc Bay, Leyte) acting as transport

Warner Brothers

Motion picture studio founded 1923 by the brothers Albert, Harry, Jack, and Samuel

Warp factor

Indicator of the speed of Star Ship "Enterprise" (TV series "Star Trek"):

Warp Factor One $=$ the speed of light

Warp Factor Two $=$ 24 times the speed of light

Warp Factor Six $=$ 216 times the speed of light*

Warp Factor Eight $=$ 512 times the speed of light

Wash

Washington Jefferson Lincoln Lee, Tom Mix's Negro cook (radio series)

Water

The one word that Helen Keller (played by Patty Duke) attempts to say in the 1962 movie *The Miracle Worker*

Watergate Seven

James W. McCord, E. Howard Hunt, G. Gordon Liddy, Jr., Bernard L. Barker, Eugenio R. Martinez, Frank A. Sturgis, Virgilio R. Gonzalez: arrested June 17, 1972, breaking into the Democratic Campaign Headquarters at Watergate building, Washington, D. C. The resulting cover-up and crisis led eventually to the resignation of President R. M. Nixon, August 9, 1974

Way You Look Tonight, The

Theme song of radio series "Mr. and Mrs. North"

We

First word of the United States Constitution

We

Title of Charles A. Lindbergh's autobiographical account (1936) of his flight across the Atlantic: "We" are Lindbergh and his plane, "The Spirit of St. Louis"

We belong dead

Last words of the monster before he blows up the laboratory destroying himself and his intended mate (1935 movie *The Bride of Frankenstein*)

We Learn to Do by Doing

Motto of the 4H Club

Weapons

Used in the game of Clue: knife, revolver, wrench, lead pipe, rope, candlestick

---

* Maximum safe cruising speed of "Enterprise"

Weary Willie

Sad-faced clown portrayed by Emmett Kelly

Wedding Anniversaries

1	paper	11	steel
2	cotton	12	silk
3	leather		linen
4	fruit	13	lace
	flowers	14	ivory
5	wood	15	crystal
6	sugar	20	china
	candy	25	silver
7	wool	30	pearl
	copper	35	coral
8	bronze	40	ruby
	pottery	45	sapphire
9	pottery	50	golden
	willow	55	emerald
10	tin	75	diamond

Weight limits

Professional boxer can weigh no more:

Flyweight	112 lbs.
Bantamweight	118 lbs.
Featherweight	126 lbs.
Lightweight	135 lbs.
Welterweight	148 lbs.
Middleweight	160 lbs.
Light Heavyweight	175 lbs.
Heavyweight	Over 175 lbs.

Weissmuller, Johnny

American swimmer and actor (born 1904)

He was the sixth actor to play Tarzan, the first in talkies, the role he is best known for and which he played 12 times

At the 1924 Paris Olympics, he won gold medals in the 100-meter and 400-meter freestyle races

In 1922, he became the first man to break 1 minute in the 100 meters (58.6 seconds)

In 1923, he became the first to break 5 minutes for the 400 meters (4:57)

Weller, Charles E.

Originated "Now is the time for all good men to come to the aid of the party" as a typing exercise

Wells, H. G.

Herbert George Wells (1886-1946), English novelist

Wendy
> The older Darling girl (Sir James Barrie's *Peter Pan*)

Wendy
> "The Good Little Witch" (comic book series)

We're Here
> Schooner in Rudyard Kipling's *Captains Courageous*, commanded by Disko Troop

Wessex
> Thomas Hardy's dog

West 35th Street
> New York location of Nero Wolfe's old brownstone house

Western outlaws, fraternal section
> *Younger brothers*: Cole, Bob, Jim, John
> *Dalton brothers* (cousins to James brothers and Younger brothers and related to Johnny Ringo): Bob, Grant, Emmett, Bill
> *Reno brothers*: John, Clinton (not in the gang), Frank, Simon, William
> *Harpe brothers*: Micajah ("Big Harpe"), Wiley ("Little Harpe")
> *James brothers*: Jesse, Frank

Westerns on TV

Series	Central role	Actor
Adventures of Jim Bowie	Jim Bowie	Scott Forbes
Adventures of Kit Carson	Kit Carson	Bill Williams
Annie Oakley	Annie Oakley	Gail Davis
Bat Masterson	Bat Masterson	Gene Barry
Bonanza	Ben Cartwright	Lorne Greene
Broken Arrow	Tom Jeffords	John Lupton
Bronco	Bronco Lane	Ty Hardin
Cheyenne	Cheyenne Bodie	Clint Walker
Cimarron City	Matt Rockford	George Montgomery
Cisco Kid, The	Cisco Kid	Duncan Renaldo
Colt .45	Natty Christopher	Wayde Preston
Custer	George A. Custer	Wayne Maunder
Daniel Boone	Daniel Boone	Fess Parker
Deputy, The	Simon Fry	Henry Fonda
Gunslinger	Cord	Tony Young
Gunsmoke	Matt Dillon	James Arness
Have Gun, Will Travel	Paladin	Richard Boone
Hotel de Paree	Sundance	Earl Holliman
Judge Roy Bean	Roy Bean	Edgar Buchanan

Series	Central role	Actor
Kung Fu	Caine	David Carradine
Laramie	Jess Harper	Robert Fuller
Lawman, The	Dan Troop	John Russell
Life and Legend of Wyatt Earp	Wyatt Earp	Hugh O'Brien
A Man Called Shenandoah	Shenandoah	Robert Horton
Maverick	Bret Maverick	James Garner
Overland Trail	Kelly	William Bendix
Rawhide	Rowdy Yates	Clint Eastwood
Rebel, The	Johnny Yuma	Nick Adams
Restless Gun, The	Vint Bonner	John Payne
Rifleman, The	Lucas McCain	Chuck Connors
Shotgun Slade	Slade	Scott Brady
Stoney Burke	Stoney Burke	Jack Lord
Sugarfoot	Tom Brewster	Will Hutchins
Tall Man, The	Billy	Clu Gulager
Tate	Tate	David McLean
Tombstone Territory	Clay Hollister	Pat Conway
Trackdown	Hoby Gilman	Robert Culp
Virginian, The	Owen Wister	James Drury
Wagon Train	Major Seth Adams	Ward Bond
Wanted, Dead or Alive	Josh Randall	Steve McQueen
Wells Fargo	Jim Hardy	Dale Robertson
Wichita Town	Mike Dunbar	Joel McCrea
Wild Bill Hickok	Bill Hickok	Guy Madison
Wild Wild West	Jim West	Robert Conrad
Yancy Derringer	Yancy Derringer	Jock Mahoney

Westminster Abbey

London church, parts of which date to the 13th century: coronation place of the kings of England; burial place of the notables of England

What's My Line

TV game show:

M.C.: John Charles Daly

Panel (1951 to 1965): Dorothy Kilgallen, Arlene Francis, Bennett Cerf, and guest (such as Hal Block or Fred or Steve Allen)

When

First word of the Declaration of Independence

When It's Round-Up Time in Texas
  Tom Mix's theme song
When you call me that, <u>smile</u>!
  The Virginian to Trampas (Owen Wister's *The Virginian*)
Where the Blue of the Night Meets the Gold of the Day
  Bing Crosby's theme song
Whisky A Go Go
  Los Angeles nightclub at which singer Johnny Rivers appeared
  and recorded a number of albums (1960's)
Whistler, The
  Radio program: introduction, "I am the Whistler, and I know
  many things, for I walk by night. I know many strange tales hid-
  den in the hearts of men and women who have stepped into the
  shadows. Yes, I know the nameless terrors of which they dare not
  speak"
Whistler's Mother
  Popular title of James McNeill Whistler's painting "Arrange-
  ment in Grey and Black"
White Flash
  Tex Ritter's horse
Whitewind
  Golden Arrow's horse (comic book series "The Golden Arrow")
Whitey
  Hoot Gibson's horse (movies)
Whitey
  White Owl Cigars' owl
Who's on First?
  Well-polished Abbott and Costello comedy routine used by them
  in 1945 movie *The Naughty Nineties*

First base	Who
Second base	What
Third base	I Don't Know
Shortstop	I Don't Give a Darn (I Don't Care)
Catcher	Today
Pitcher	Tomorrow
Left Field	Why
Center Field	Because

  (No right fielder is mentioned in the routine)
Wicked Witch of the East
  Witch killed when Dorothy's house fell on her; Dorothy got the
  magical red shoes from her (1939 movie *The Wizard of Oz*)
Wicket Gate, The
  Entrance to the road which leads to the Celestial City; over the

door is written: "Knock, and it shall be opened unto you" (John Bunyan's *The Pilgrim's Progress*)

Widow Maker

Pecos Bill's horse (American folklore)

Wiere Brothers

Comedy team: Harry, Herbert, Sylvester

Wilbur

The Wright brother who first flew at Kitty Hawk, N.C., December 17, 1903

Wilbur

Fern's small pig, saved by Charlotte A. Cavatica, a large grey spider (E. B. White's *Charlotte's Web*)

Wild Bill Hickok

James Butler Hickok (1837-1876), Western gunfighter and lawman; killed by Jack McCall August 2, 1876, while holding the famous "dead man's hand" of aces and 8's

Wildcat

Secret identity of Ted Grant, motorcycle-riding crime fighter (comic book series)

Wile E. Coyote

Pursuer of the Roadrunner (Warner Brothers cartoon)

William Tell Overture

Theme song of the Lone Ranger (composed by Gioacchino Rossini). Also known as "The Mickey Mouse Overture," Mickey having conducted it in a Disney short cartoon

Willie and Joe

Bill Mauldin's World War II GI cartoon characters

Willie Loman

Salesman in Arthur Miller's play *Death of a Salesman*

Willis Brothers

Country and western group: Guy, Skeeter, Vic

Wills, Chill

Voice of Francis, the talking mule

Wills, Frank

Janitor who discovered the break-in at the offices of the Democrats in the Watergate building, June 17, 1972

Wilma Deering

Buck Rogers' girlfriend

Wilson, Samuel

The original Uncle Sam, a meatpacker during the War of 1812 who stamped his kegs "U. S."

Wimpy (J. Wellington Wimpy)

Popeye's hungry friend always munching on a hamburger

Winchell, Paul

His dummies: Jerry Mahoney, Knucklehead Smiff, Irving the Mouse

Winchell, Walter

New York newspaperman (1897-1972), noted for his Broadway column in which he invented words widely adopted

Radio's "The Jergens' Journal" reporter: "Good evening, Mr. and Mrs. North and South America and all the ships and clippers at sea." Another version: "Good evening, Mr. and Mrs. America and all the ships at sea, let's go to press"

Narrator of TV series "The Untouchables"

Winchester House

Rambling "mystery" house in San Jose, California, built by Sarah L. Winchester, heir to the Winchester Arms fortune. She believed that as long as she kept building onto the house she would keep living. The house has 160 rooms, 200 doors, 10,000 windowpanes, 47 fireplaces

Windy Wales

Bobby Benson's sidekick

Wingfoot Express

Walt Arfons' J-46 jet-powered car: driven (1965) by Tom Green

Wings

First movie to win an Academy Award (1928): starred Charles "Buddy" Rogers and Clara Bow (Gary Cooper appeared in the movie)

Winky Dink

TV cartoon boy; the show "Winky Dink and You" was narrated by Jack Barry

Winnie

Woody Woodpecker's girlfriend (comic books)

Winnie Mae

Lockheed Vega, piloted by Wiley Post (using a Sperry automatic pilot), first world solo flight, July 1933: 15,596 miles in 7 days, 18 hours, 49 minutes

Winnie the Pooh

Teddy bear of Christopher Robin's: central character of A. A. Milne's *Winnie-the-Pooh* (1926) and *The House at Pooh Corner* (1928)

Winston

Hector Heathcoat's dog (cartoon)

Wise Guys (Little Wise Guys)

Comic book series featured with "Daredevil": Jock C. H. Herendeen, Meatball (later Curley), Pee Wee (later Slugger), Scarecrow

Wives of Henry VIII

> Catherine of Aragon (married 1509; divorced 1533; mother of Mary Tudor)
>
> Anne Boleyn (married 1533; beheaded 1536; mother of Elizabeth I, born 1533)
>
> Jane Seymour (married 1536; died in childbirth 1537; mother of Edward VI, born 1537)
>
> Anne of Cleves (married and divorced 1540)
>
> Catherine Howard (married 1540, beheaded 1542)
>
> Catherine Parr (married 1543, survived him)

Wizard of Menlo Park

> Nickname of Thomas A. Edison, whose laboratory was at Menlo Park, New Jersey

Wizard of Oz, The

> Novel (*The Wonderful Wizard of Oz*, 1900) by Lyman Frank Baum (1856-1919)
>
> It was staged as early as 1901, and was made into silent movies in 1910 and 1924 (with Larry Semon)
>
> In 1939 it became a musical film with Judy Garland as Dorothy, Jack Haley as the Tin Woodsman (Hickory), Ray Bolger as the Scarecrow (Hunk), Bert Lahr as the Cowardly Lion (Zeke), Margaret Hamilton as the Wicked Witch (Miss Gulch), Frank Morgan as the Wizard (Professor Marvel), and Billie Burke as the Good Witch, Glinda

Wodehouse, P. G.

> Pelham Grenville Wodehouse (born 1881), English author, notably of the "Jeeves" novels and of plays and musicals

Wohelo

> Watchword of the Campfire Girls, made up of the first letters of *Wo*rk, *He*alth, *Lo*ve

WOL

> Winnie the Pooh's friend the Owl spells his name this way

Wolf

> Rip Van Winkle's dog

Wolf Larsen

> The "Sea Wolf," captain of the schooner "Ghost" (Jack London's *The Sea Wolf*)

Wolf Man

> Lawrence (Larry) Talbot (played by Lon Chaney, Jr.) in 1941 movie *The Wolf Man*: a werewolf (makeup by Jack Pierce). The character of the Wolf Man appeared in later pictures. In the earlier *The Werewolf of London* (1935) Henry Hull had played Wilfred Glendon, who changes to a werewolf at the full moon

Wolfman Jack
>   Pseudonym of disc jockey Robert Smith, whose program is syndicated to 1,453 radio stations

Wonder Woman
>   Secret identity of Diana Prince

Woodbridge
>   Town location of TV serial "The Secret Storm"

Woodstock
>   New York State rock 'n' roll festival, weekend of August 15-17, 1969, on a Bethel, N. Y., dairy farm: filmed and made into a movie

Woodstock
>   Snoopy's bird friend/secretary (Charles Schulz's "Peanuts" cartoon strip)

Woodsy Owl
>   Symbol of the anti-pollution movement: "Give a hoot; don't pollute"

Woody Woodpecker
>   Slightly mad bird character in Walter Lantz cartoon shorts and comic books: niece, Knothead; nephew, Splinter

Woofer
>   Winky Dink's dog (TV cartoon series "Winky Dink and You")

Wooley, Sheb
>   Entertainer who recorded one of 1958's big hits "The Purple People Eater"
>   Recorded comedy albums under pseudonym Ben Colder
>   Played on TV in series "Rawhide"

Woolworth, F. W.
>   Frank Winfield Woolworth (1852-1919), five-and-dime store magnate

Woozy Winks
>   Plastic Man's partner (comic books)

World Football League
>   *Western Division*
>   Honolulu Hawaiians
>   Southern California Sun
>   Portland Storm
>   Houston Texans
>   *Central Division*
>   Chicago Fire
>   Birmingham Americans
>   Memphis Southmen
>   Detroit Wheels

Eastern Division
  Philadelphia Bell
  Florida Blazers
  New York Stars
  Jacksonville Sharks

World Tennis teams
  Pacific Division
    Golden Gaters
    Los Angeles Strings
    Hawaii Leis
    Denver Racquets
  Gulf Plains Division
    Minnesota Buckskins
    Houston E. Z. Riders
    Florida Flamingos
    Chicago Aces
  Central Division
    Cleveland Nets
    Detroit Loves
    Pittsburgh Triangles
    Toronto Royals
  Atlantic Division
    Philadelphia Freedoms
    Boston Lobsters
    Baltimore Banners
    New York Sets

World Turned Upside Down, The
  Tune played as Cornwallis surrendered at Yorktown, October 19, 1781

World's Wonder Horse
  Title given to Gene Autry's horse, Champion

Worthless
  Mule belonging to Dirty Sally (Jeanette Nolan) (TV series "Dirty Sally")

Worth's Law
  "When something fails to work and you demonstrate it for a repairman, it works better than ever, as if it never failed to work at all": first appearance of this law in print

Wright Whirlwind
  Type of engine on Charles Lindbergh's "Spirit of St. Louis" when he solo-hopped the Atlantic Ocean, May 20-21, 1927

Wrightsville
  Town invaded by two rival motorcycle gangs, one led by Johnny

(played by Marlon Brando), leader of the Black Rebels, and the other led by Chino (Lee Marvin) (1954 movie *The Wild One*, based on the actual takeover of the California town of Hollister by a motorcycle gang in 1947)

Wrigley Field
National League ball park in Chicago, only major league baseball stadium not equipped with lights for night baseball

Wynken, Blynken, and Nod
Sailed in a wooden shoe (from Eugene Field poem)

X

XP-59
First United States jet-propelled airplane (1942)

Xanadu
Citizen Kane's mansion, on a 55,000-acre estate (1941 movie)

Xantippe
Socrates' shrewish wife

Y

Yahoos
Human-like dumb animals in the land of Houyhnhnms (intelligent, rational horses) (Jonathan Swift's *Gulliver's Travels*)

Yakky Doodle
Bird friend of the bulldog Chopper (TV cartoon)

Yale
University attended by Flash Gordon, where he played polo. It was also the school of Frank Merriwell

Yamato and Musashi
Two largest battleships ever built, Japanese, World War II

Yankee Clipper
Apollo 12 command module; landing module was "Intrepid"

Yankee Clipper
Nickname of baseball player Joe DiMaggio

Yankee Doodle Dandy
Biographical film (1942) about George M. Cohan: James Cagney played, sang, and danced the title role

Yankee Stadium
"The House that Ruth built": New York Yankees' home ball park at River Ave. and 161 St. in the Bronx: opened in 1923.

Memorial plaques in centerfield to Miller Huggins, Lou Gehrig, and Babe Ruth

Yellow

Color that takes away Green Lantern's power (All-Star comics)

Yellow Kid, The

First comic strip type cartoon, created (Feb. 16, 1896) by Richard Outcault for New York *World*

Yojo

Queequeg's wooden god that he carries with him (Herman Melville's *Moby Dick*)

Yokum

Family name of Li'l Abner

Yorktown, U.S.S.

Aircraft carrier sunk by the Japanese, June 4, 1942, in the Battle of Midway

You Are My Sunshine

Written by two-time governor of Louisiana Jimmie Davis

Young Allies

Comic book characters: Henry "Tubb" Tinkle, Toro, Bucky, Knuckles, Jefferson Worthington, Whitewash Jones

Young Defenders

Crimefighters (comic book series): Joanie, Lefty, Slim, Whitey (replaced later by Beanie).

Captain Freedom watches over them

Your Hit Parade

On radio from 1935 with many soloists and orchestras: sponsored by Lucky Strike cigarettes

On TV: 1950—Raymond Scott's Orchestra, Eileen Wilson, Snooky Lanson, Russell Arms, June Valli; Dorothy Collins replaced Wilson, and Gisele MacKenzie replaced Valli. 1957—Original group replaced by Tommy Leonetti, Jill Corey, Alan Copeland, Virginia Gibson. Show went off air in 1958. 1959—Dorothy Collins, Johnny Desmond. 1974—Kelly Garrett, Sheralee, Chuck Woolery

Your Show of Shows

TV variety program starring Sid Caesar and Imogene Coca

Yukon King

Sgt. Preston's dog (radio)

Z

Zaharias, Mildred Babe Didrikson
Best-known woman athlete of 20th century, who concentrated on golf but competed in track and field (4 world's records broken in 1932 Olympics), swimming, diving, baseball, boxing, basketball, and many other sports
Babe was a given name, not a nickname

Zapruder, Abraham
Bystander who filmed the assassination of President John F. Kennedy, November 22, 1963, in Dallas

Zarkov, Dr.
Flash Gordon's companion: played by Frank Shannon in movies

Zebra
A white animal with black stripes

Zeke
Li'l Bad Wolf's father (comic book)

Zenith
Town in Sinclair Lewis' *Babbitt*

Zero
Annie Rooney's dog (comic strip series "Annie Rooney")

Ziggy
The 6¼-ton elephant that had been chained indoors for over 30 years in the Brookfield, Ill., Zoo and was unchained July 4, 1973

Zip
Zoning Improvement Plan (post office system)

Zippie
Roller-skating chimpanzee (TV in 1950's)

Zodiac

	Sun enters
Aries, The Ram	March 21
Taurus, The Bull	April 20
Gemini, The Twins	May 21
Cancer, The Crab	June 21
Leo, The Lion	July 23
Virgo, The Virgin	August 23
Libra, The Balance	Sept. 23
Scorpio, The Scorpion	Oct. 23
Sagittarius, The Archer	Nov. 22
Capricorn, The Goat	Dec. 22
Aquarius, The Water Carrier	Jan. 20
Pisces, The Fish	Feb. 19

Zorba, Dr.
Superior of Dr. Ben Casey (TV series)

Zorro

Don Diego de Vega, a California Robin Hood type (a milksop until he dons his mask), created by Johnston McCulley in the story "The Curse of Capistrano"

In movies played by Douglas Fairbanks, Sr., who played both Zorro and Don Q., the son of Zorro; Robert Livingston; John Carrol, who played the great-grandson of the original Zorro; Tyrone Power; Reed Hadley; George Turner; Clayton Moore; Gordon Scott

On TV played by Guy Williams

The name means "fox" in Spanish

Zwolfte Stunde, Die

Re-release (1930), with sound, of *Nosferatu*, 1922 German film version of *Dracula*: in English, probably, *The Last Moment*, but not released in English

Index

310

313

323

341

347

353

372

Bestsellers you've been hearing about—and want to read

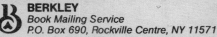